Soup
of the
Day

Soup

of the Day

150 DELICIOUS AND COMFORTING RECIPES FROM OUR FAVORITE RESTAURANTS

ELLEN BROWN

PHOTOGRAPHY BY

FELLECIA PERRETTI

Running Press
PHILADELPHIA · LONDON

ISBN 978-0-7624-4327-7
Library of Congress Control Number: 2014936542

E-book ISBN 978-0-7624-5542-3

9   8   7   6   5   4   3   2   1
Digit on the right indicates the number of this printing

Design by Joshua McDonnell
Edited by Zachary Leibman
Typography: Avenir and Wisdom Script
Food Styist: Brian Croney
Prop Stylist: Lisa Russell

Running Press Book Publishers
2300 Chestnut Street
Philadelphia, PA 19103-4371

Visit us on the web!
www.runningpresscooks.com

Table of Contents

Lifelong friendship is even more
comforting than a bowl of soup,
and this book is dedicated to my
lifelong friend, Nancy Gray.

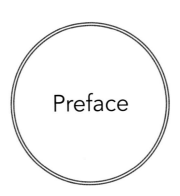

Preface

"Soup puts the heart at ease, calms down the violence of hunger, eliminates the tension of the day, and awakens and refines the appetite," is the way Auguste Escoffier, the preeminent French chef of the early twentieth century, saw the role of soup at meals. Later in the century, legendary food writer M.F.K. Fisher asserted that "it is impossible to think of any good meal, no matter how plain or elegant, without soup or bread in it."

Perhaps this is why soups play such an important role on restaurant menus as well as in home kitchens. Chefs create "signature soups" as a reflection of their philosophy of cuisine. And then there are those wonderful surprises—the "soup of the day"—added to the menu to reflect seasonal ingredients and the climate at that precise time of year.

For most months of the year, the soup put before you is hot, and the fragrance of the long-simmered ingredients waft upward in the steam to your nose. But then there are times when soups are served chilled, and these comfort you by naturally reducing your temperature on the hottest of summer days.

Soups are the epitome of "comfort food," a term that only entered the dictionary in the mid-1970s but has been around since cooking began. Neuroscientists define comfort as the opposite of stress, and humans are constantly finding ways to relieve themselves of stress. While pharmaceuticals can play a role, even faster and easier is finding this restorative state through food.

Comfort foods bring us a sense a security, a reward, and a feeling of connectedness to a larger community. This is why we crave different comfort foods when we're in different moods. If you're feeling isolated and lonely, you might want a comfort food linked to a sense of community in your brain; at other times, when facing daunting physical or metal tasks, the need is for food that signifies a reward.

Soup can be any and all of these. It harkens back to our earliest memories, before food had to be chewed or we had teeth with which to chew it. Our muscles prefer foods that don't make them work very hard, and a bowl of soup certainly fits that category, even if topped by crunchy croutons. As poet Maya Angelou writes, "Whenever something went wrong when I was young—If I had a pimple or if my hair broke—my mom would say, 'Sister mine, I'm going to make you some soup.' And I really thought the soup would make my pimple go away or my hair stronger."

Foods create both chemical and emotional responses. Sugar and starch produce serotonin, a neurotransmitter that increases one's sense of happiness. Antidepressants like Prozac replicate how serotonin works in the brain. Salty foods like potato chips make the brain release oxytocin, a hormone also triggered by sexual satisfaction.

While these are physiological responses to food, the brain also generates our concomitant emotional responses. Certain foods, especially those eaten in childhood, have specific memories associated with them. And all around the world people eat soup. My childhood memories are not of a homemade soup, although we ate many of them. Back in the 1950s, Campbell's had a line of frozen soup concentrates, and it was from them that I discovered the magical flavors of New England clam chowder and lobster bisque.

There is not a cuisine or culture that doesn't have a cherished category for this food, and many cuisines have similar soups. The wonton soup of classic Cantonese cooking is very similar to Italian tortellini al brodo and the meat-filled kreplach found floating in the soups of Eastern European Jews. The starch in the pasta creates serotonin, while the salt in the broth triggers production of oxytocin.

Another way in which soups are comforting is that they're so easy to make. Truly, if you can boil water, you can make a delicious soup. There are no spun-sugar swans lurking around.

Soups, of all categories of food, carry the lowest fear of failure. Perhaps that's why soups are stalwarts of home cooking as well as restaurant menus.

For generations, people have been called to the table when they hear "soup's on." It means that the meal is set to begin, and the first thing to be consumed will be a bowl of soup. That's why the soupspoon is set farthest out on the right side of the charger plate in a place setting. It will be the first eating implement used.

I hope you find comfort, as well as delicious flavors, when cooking—and eating—the soups found in this book. They run the gamut from traditional to innovative, and they are drawn from a veritable United Nations of cuisines as well as all regions of American cooking. While some are specifically small soups to start a meal, others are hearty enough to be the full meal if accompanied by a loaf of crusty bread and a crunchy tossed salad.

Food—especially a food like soup—is more than the fuel to power our bodies with the nutrients necessary to live. It's also our emotional ally. As the late food writer Laurie Colwin wrote, "To feel safe and warm on a cold wet night, all you really need is soup." And that's what comfort foods are all about.

Happy cooking!
Ellen Brown
Providence, Rhode Island

Introduction

Writing as her proper Victorian persona, Miss Manners, author Judith Martin wrote, "Do you have a kinder, more adaptable friend in the food world than soup? Who soothes you when you are ill? Who refuses to leave you when you are impoverished and stretches its resources to give you hearty sustenance and cheer? Who warms you in winter and cools you in summer? Yet who is also capable of doing honor to your richest table and impressing your most demanding guests? . . . Soup does its loyal best, no matter what undignified conditions are imposed upon it. You don't catch steak hanging around when you're poor or sick, do you?"

And it's true. Soup is a category of food that transcends classes, cuisines, and eating occasions. While certain soups may be more appealing than others, there's no one who can say, "I don't like soup." That's probably why it's been around for many thousands of years.

Soup is as old as the history of cooking, and there is evidence of soup dating from 20,000 BCE. While turning a hunk of animal over a fire on a spit is likely older, combining various ingredients in a large vat to create a dish that's filling, nutritious, and easily digested was probably right behind it. Before the development of waterproof clay containers, boiling took place in animal hides or watertight baskets of reeds, with hot rocks added to make the water boil.

Like other categories of food, soups evolved over the centuries according to what ingredients were local.

Physicians in many cultures have prescribed soups to counteract illness since ancient times. Soups simmered with medicinal herbs have been part of Chinese medicine for centuries, and are based on the concept of yin and yang. Yin foods are cooling and yang foods are heating, and all foods are categorized by their yin and yang properties. Foods like oranges, pork, and dried figs all are yin foods that reduce fevers and inflammation, while ginseng, quail, and azuki beans are yang foods that promote circulation and vitality.

Our modern English word "soup" comes from the French word *sope* and the Middle Ages English word *soupe*. Back then, however, what they really meant was not a soup as we know it today but a "*sop*," which was a thick piece of bread that became soaked in a liquid as it was used as a combination plate and spoon. The most common eating implement at the time was the knife, which was much more like a dagger than the place knife of today. Forks and spoons did not become commonplace for another few centuries.

Soups were important in the medieval diet, as was the bread by which they were sopped up, and they usually were served at the end of the day as the lesser of the day's two meals. From this custom of including a sop as part of the end of the day meal is where we get our word *supper*. The same root word accounts for the Italian *zuppa* (soup), which comes from the Greek *suppa* (or "slice of bread, soaking").

Street vendors in sixteenth-century Paris sold concentrated soups as a pick-me-up for physical exhaustion and they were referred to as *restaurants*, meaning something that was restoring. In 1765 a shop specializing in such soups opened, and thus the word *restaurant* entered our vocabulary. And soups have played a role on restaurant menus ever since.

Soups started to gain their position as sophisticated foods in the late-eighteenth and early-nineteenth centuries. In 1790, Francesco Leonardi, who was chef to King Louis XV of France and later to the Russian Queen, Catherine II, published *L'Apicio moderno*, a six-volume cookbook. The first volume was *Zuppa e Minestre*, which he described as "dishes fit for princes."

In Auguste Escoffier's *Le Guide Culinaire*, first published in 1903, he credits the development of classic French soups to famed French chef Marie-Antonin Carême, who was chef to Napoleon and Tsar Alexander I before serving as chef to the Rothschild family in Paris. Escoffier wrote that "the culinary preparations of current-day France date only from the early part of the nineteenth century, and on this point as on many others, the culinary arts owes much to Carême."

Escoffier did not take soups for granted, however. In the same book he wrote that "of all the items on the menu, soup is that which exacts the most delicate perfection and the strictest attention."

While fancy consommé and delicate creamed soups were becoming the fare of the elegant table, the soups that were being cooked in America came along with the settlers and waves of immigration beginning with the English, French, and Spanish in the seventeenth century.

The first colonial cookbook was published by William Parks in Williamsburg, Virginia, in 1742; it was based on Eliza Smith's *The Compleat Housewife; or Accomplished Gentlewoman's Companion*, a London best seller published in 1727. Parks did make some attempts to Americanize it, deleting certain recipes "the ingredients or material for which are not to be had in this country," but for the most part it remained loyal to Mrs. Smith. Included were both soup and bisque recipes. The first truly American cookbook, and one that contained a chapter on soups, is Amelia Simmons's *American Cookery*, published in 1796. It was the first book to use corn, pumpkin and other squash, cranberries, and other foodstuffs native to this continent.

Another landmark book for American soup cookery is Lydia Maria Child's *The American Frugal Housewife: Dedicated to Those Who Are Not Ashamed of Economy*, published in 1828. This first culinary Mrs. Child was an abolitionist, women's rights activist, novelist, and poet who is perhaps best remembered for her Thanksgiving poem "Over the River and Through the Wood." Part of frugality is stretching meals by making soups, and she has many recipes included, along with listings on such topics as "the cheapest cuts of meat," all of which are appropriate for soup making.

As successive waves of immigrants from around the world arrived on American soil, they brought their soups with them. In fact, the melting pot metaphor was in use as early as the 1780s. The German immigrants in Pennsylvania were known for their potato soups, while their brethren arriving later and settling down the Ohio River in Cincinnati had a special sauerkraut soup. While Italian Wedding Soup is really Italian-American, the abundance of Italian restaurants in this country today has added immeasurably to the repertoire of authentic soups served.

But American menus in the twenty-first century include a cornucopia of innovative soups as well as authentic ones, and many of the country's wonderful chefs have shared their soup recipes with me. In some cases you'll find related recipes juxtaposed that demonstrate the approach taken to the same ingredients by two different chefs.

Many of these recipes are for small soups—both hot and cold—to serve in the time-honored place of the first food of a meal. "From soup to nuts" means from the beginning to the end, and soup is doing its part to remain loyal to the definition.

But then there are some heartier soups that could really be the meal itself, including ones made with all sorts of animal protein and others made with beans and legumes. These are the soups referenced by Judith Martin as Miss Manners, and they come from around the world.

Making Great Soups

1

Each chapter in this book is introduced with some instructions pertinent to the soup recipes it contains. What you'll find here are some general pointers to increase your level of "soup savvy."

This chapter begins with recipes for the essential building block of a great soup—the stock to which you add the flavoring ingredients. You'll also learn how to make a foolproof béchamel sauce, which is the key to the whole world of cream soups. And then there are some general pointers on fun ways to garnish soups and how to cook them in your slow cooker.

The Importance of Long-Simmered Stocks

Perhaps you never equated buying commercial stocks—many of which are loaded with sodium—with "convenience food." But that's what they are, and starting soups with homemade stock is what makes them great from the get-go.

It's the long-simmered homemade stocks that add the depth of flavor to the soups and sauces enjoyed at fine restaurants. Classically trained chefs have known for centuries what you're about to learn in this chapter—making stocks is as hard as boiling water and, if you're judicious and save bits and pieces destined for the garbage when prepping foods to be cooked, they're almost free.

Those onion and carrot peels, the bottom of celery ribs, the stems from which you've stripped the leaves of fresh parsley are all used to flavor stocks. If you take the time to bone your own chicken breasts or cut up your own beef stew meat from a roast, then you have everything you need to make stock.

But there are times that you'll spend money at the supermarket specifically to make stocks. I do it all the time and it's still less expensive than buying cartons of tasteless salted water.

On the subject of salt, please note that I do not add any to these stocks, which gives you the greatest degree of versatility when using them. While you will add salt to soups, there are times when you want to drastically reduce a stock to form a sauce. That's almost impossible with a salted stock, because as the water evaporates during reduction the salinity rises.

Chicken Stock

This is the most important stock, because it's used for pork and vegetable soups (assuming you're not a strict vegetarian) as well as with poultry. The good thing about this stock is that you actually get more flavor from the inexpensive parts of the bird, like the leg quarters and backs.

Makes 4 quarts

5 pounds chicken bones, skin, and trimmings (including giblets)

4 celery ribs, cut into thick slices

2 onions, trimmed and quartered

2 carrots, trimmed, scrubbed, and cut into thick slices

2 tablespoons whole black peppercorns

6 garlic cloves, peeled

4 sprigs fresh parsley

3 sprigs fresh thyme

2 bay leaves

Place 6 quarts of water and the chicken in a large stockpot, and bring to a boil over high heat. Reduce the heat to low, and skim off any foam that rises during the first 10 to 15 minutes of simmering. Simmer the stock, uncovered, for 1 hour, and then add the celery, onions, carrots, peppercorns, garlic, parsley, thyme, and bay leaves. Simmer for 2½ hours.

Strain the stock through a fine-mesh sieve, pushing with the back of a spoon to extract as much liquid as possible. Discard the solids, spoon the stock into smaller containers, and refrigerate when the stock reaches room temperature. Remove and discard the fat layer from the surface of the stock once chilled.

NOTE: The stock can be refrigerated and used within 3 days, or it can be frozen for up to 6 months.

Variation:

For turkey stock, substitute the same amount of turkey giblets and necks as chicken pieces.

....

The giblets—the neck, heart, and gizzard—are what's in that little bag from inside a whole chicken that you probably toss. Save them all for stock. But freeze the liver separately. Livers cannot be used in stock, but once you've got enough of them, you can make a pâté or sauté them for dinner. If you live near an Asian market, you might also be able to buy chicken feet. They make wonderful stock.

Beef Stock

While beef stock is not specified in recipes as often as chicken stock, it is the backbone of certain soups, the recipes for which are in Chapter 8. Beef shank is about the least expensive cut of beef that makes good stock, but it is even better to get a chuck roast and then cut the meat off it yourself to make beef stew and then use the bones to make stock.

Makes 2 quarts

2 pounds beef trimmings (bones and fat) or inexpensive beef shank

1 carrot, trimmed, scrubbed, and cut into thick slices

1 medium onion, trimmed and sliced

1 celery rib, trimmed and sliced

1 tablespoon whole black peppercorns

3 sprigs fresh parsley

2 sprigs fresh thyme

2 garlic cloves, peeled

2 bay leaves

Preheat the oven broiler, and line a broiler pan with heavy-duty aluminum foil. Broil the beef bones or the shank 3 minutes per side, or until browned. Transfer the beef to a large stockpot, and add 3 quarts of water. Bring to a boil over high heat. Reduce the heat to low, and skim off any foam that rises during the first 10 to 15 minutes of simmering. Simmer for 1 hour, uncovered, and then add the carrot, onion, celery, peppercorns, parsley, thyme, garlic, and bay leaves. Simmer the stock for 3 hours.

Strain the stock through a fine-mesh sieve, pushing with the back of a spoon to extract as much liquid as possible. Discard the solids, spoon the stock into smaller containers, and refrigerate once the stock reaches room temperature. Remove and discard the layer of fat from the surface of the stock.

NOTE: The stock can be refrigerated and used within 3 days, or it can be frozen for up to 6 months.

....

Most really good restaurants make veal stock instead of beef stock, but they have access to veal bones and we would have to spend a fortune for them. The least expensive cut of veal is the shank cooked for osso buco. Another option is breast of veal, which is difficult to find, too.

Vegetable Stock

You may think it unnecessary to use vegetable stock if making a vegetarian dish that includes the same vegetables, but that's not the case. Using stock creates a richly flavored soup that can't be replicated by increasing the quantity of vegetables cooked in the soup.

Makes 2 quarts

2 carrots, scrubbed, trimmed, and thinly sliced

2 celery ribs, sliced

2 leeks, white and pale green parts only, thinly sliced and rinsed well

1 small onion, thinly sliced

1 tablespoon whole black peppercorns

4 sprigs fresh parsley

3 sprigs fresh thyme

2 sprigs fresh rosemary

2 garlic cloves, peeled

1 bay leaf

Pour 3 quarts of water into a stockpot, and add the carrots, celery, leeks, onion, peppercorns, parsley, thyme, rosemary garlic, and bay leaf. Bring to a boil over high heat, then reduce the heat to low and simmer the stock, uncovered, for 1 hour.

Strain the stock through a fine-mesh sieve, pushing with the back of a spoon to extract as much liquid as possible. Discard the solids, and spoon the stock into smaller containers. Refrigerate once the stock reaches room temperature.

NOTE: The stock can be refrigerated and used within 3 days, or it can be frozen for up to 6 months.

Variation

Substitute tarragon for the thyme, or substitute scallion tops for the leeks.

....

While it's fine to save the peels from carrots or parsley stems to use in stocks, unfortunately stock is not a place for the dark green tops of leeks that are always discarded. They will make stocks bitter and taste somewhat grassy, which is why they're discarded. They're good for the compost, however.

Lobster or Shrimp Stock

Lobster stock is a great reason to make friends with the head of the fish department of your supermarket. You can arrange in advance to have them save you bodies if the store cooks lobster meat and purchase them at minimal cost; the same is true with fish bones, if a store actually fillets the fish on site. For shrimp stock, always buy your shrimp with shells and then rinse the shells and freeze them for when you want to make stock.

Makes 2 quarts

3 lobster bodies (whole lobsters from which the tail and claw meat has been removed) or the shells from 3 pounds raw shrimp

1 cup dry white wine

1 carrot, scrubbed, trimmed, and cut into 1-inch chunks

1 medium onion, sliced

1 celery rib, sliced

1 tablespoon whole black peppercorns

3 sprigs fresh parsley

2 sprigs fresh thyme

2 sprigs fresh tarragon

2 garlic cloves, peeled

1 bay leaf

If using lobster shells, pull the top shell off the first lobster body. Scrape off and discard the feathery gills, and then break the body into small pieces, including the swimmerets. Place the pieces into the stockpot, and repeat with remaining lobster bodies. If using shrimp shells, rinse and place in the stockpot.

Add 3 quarts of water, along with the wine, carrot, onion, celery, peppercorns, parsley, thyme, tarragon, garlic, and bay leaf. Bring to a boil over high heat, then reduce the heat to low and simmer the stock, uncovered, for 1½ hours.

Strain the stock through a fine-mesh sieve, pushing with the back of a spoon to extract as much liquid as possible. Discard the solids, and spoon the stock into smaller containers. Refrigerate the stock once it reaches room temperature.

NOTE: The stock can be refrigerated and used within 3 days, or it can be frozen for up to 6 months.

....

Seafood stock is perhaps the hardest to make if you don't live near the coast or a supermarket with a good seafood department. Prepared seafood stock can now be purchased at many places, and another good substitute is bottled clam juice. Use it in place of the water, and simmer it with vegetables and wine to intensify its flavor.

Fish Stock

The key to the success of many of the soups in Chapter 6 is a fish stock enriched with vegetables and herbs and also simmered with a bit of lemon zest. On the other hand, if you're making a fish soup for people who don't really like that "fishy taste," you can substitute vegetable stock.

Makes 2 quarts

2 pounds bones and skin from a firm-fleshed white fish such as halibut, cod, or sole

1 cup dry white wine

1 carrot, scrubbed, trimmed, and cut into 1-inch chunks

1 medium onion, sliced

1 celery rib, sliced

1 tablespoon whole black peppercorns

5 sprigs fresh parsley

2 sprigs fresh thyme

2 garlic cloves, peeled

2 (3-inch) strips lemon zest

1 bay leaf

Rinse the fish bones and skin and place them in a stockpot. Add 3 quarts of water, along with the wine, carrot, onion, celery, peppercorns, parsley, thyme, garlic, lemon zest, and bay leaf. Bring to a boil over high heat, and then reduce the heat to low and simmer the stock, uncovered, for 1½ hours.

Strain the stock through a fine-mesh sieve, pushing with the back of a spoon to extract as much liquid as possible. Discard the solids, and spoon the stock into smaller containers. Refrigerate the stock once it reaches room temperature.

NOTE: The stock can be refrigerated and used within 3 days, or it can be frozen for up to 6 months.

....

You really have to make sure that the skin and bones you're using for fish stock don't come from oily fish like bluefish, mackerel, or salmon. Those fish will give your stock too strong a flavor.

Corn Stock

This is a relatively new addition to the list of stocks I make on a regular basis, but I was convinced it was worth the trouble after a side-by-side comparison of two corn soups, one made with chicken stock and the other made with corn stock. There's lots of sweet corn flavor in those cobs we toss, and they really add to corn soups.

Makes 2 quarts

10 fresh corncobs (kernels removed)

2½ quarts Vegetable Stock (page 16) or Chicken Stock (page 14)

Use a knife and scrape as much milky liquid as possible from the corncobs right into a stockpot. Then cut the cobs into 2-inch pieces with a sharp serrated knife.

Add the stock to the pot and bring to a boil over high heat. Reduce the heat to low, and simmer the stock, uncovered, for 1 hour.

Strain the stock through a fine-mesh sieve, pushing with the back of a spoon to extract as much liquid as possible. Discard the solids, and spoon the stock into smaller containers. Refrigerate the stock once it reaches room temperature.

NOTE: The stock can be refrigerated and used within 3 days, or it can be frozen for up to 6 months.

....

If you don't have time to make the stock the day you buy the corn, it's better to freeze the cobs than to refrigerate them. Like the corn itself, the sugars in corncobs start to convert to starch as soon as the ears are picked. Freezing the cobs stops that process and produces a better product.

Ham Stock

For bean soups and some sausage soups, nothing compares with the smoky richness ham stock brings to the foundation of the dishes. And you can nibble on the meat from the ham bones, too.

Makes 2 quarts

2 ham hocks or 1 ham bone from a baked ham

1 quart Chicken Stock (page 14)

1 carrot, trimmed, scrubbed, and cut into thick slices

1 medium onion, trimmed and sliced

1 celery rib, trimmed and sliced

1 tablespoon whole black peppercorns

3 sprigs fresh parsley

2 sprigs fresh sage

2 garlic cloves, peeled

2 bay leaves

Combine the ham hocks, stock, and 2 quarts of water in a large stockpot. Bring to a boil over high heat. Reduce the heat to low, and skim off any foam that rises during the first 10 to 15 minutes of simmering. Simmer for 1 hour, uncovered, and then add the carrot, onion, celery, peppercorns, parsley, sage, garlic, and bay leaves. Simmer the stock for 3 hours. Strain the stock through a fine-mesh sieve, pushing with the back of a spoon to extract as much liquid as possible. Set aside the ham hocks, and when cool enough to handle, pick off the meat and save it to add to soups later, if desired, discarding the skin and bones.

Discard the solids, spoon the stock into smaller containers, and refrigerate once the stock reaches room temperature. Remove and discard the layer of fat from the surface of the stock.

NOTE: The stock can be refrigerated and used within 3 days, or it can be frozen for up to 6 months.

....

There won't be very much fat solidified on the top of ham stock; it's not like chicken stock or beef stock in that regard. But there is some, and it doesn't add any flavor to the soups you'll make from it.

Making a Superior Béchamel Sauce

It's called béchamel in classic French cooking and white sauce in America. It's a dairy sauce thickened with flour, and it's the key to silky smooth cream soups, as well as to the cheese sauce (Mornay in French) that naps the noodles for mac and cheese.

There are set steps to making the sauce, although variations within each allow you to adjust how thick you want the sauce to be.

THE CRUCIAL COOKING OF THE ROUX

The first step is melting butter, although occasionally you come across a sauce that calls for a mixture of butter and oil or oil alone. Into the butter goes flour, and the mixture of these two simple ingredients gets the fancy name *roux*. Making the roux, pronounced *ROO* as in kangaroo, is the only crucial step to a good sauce. The purpose of stirring the butter and the flour is to coat the protein molecules in the flour with fat. This creates a finished sauce that is silky in texture and does not taste of raw flour, which has an unattractive mouthfeel that I equate to library paste.

It's important that the roux be stirred constantly over low heat. As it cooks, you'll see tiny bubbles foaming, and the mixture will appear to have increased in volume. This usually only takes one minute, but depending on the stove's temperature and the thickness of the pan, it can take longer.

The classic proportion of butter and flour is in equal amounts; however, this ratio is hardly cast in stone, or even Jell-O. More flour creates a thicker sauce, and this is sometimes advantageous if using milk rather than cream.

DAIRY PRODUCT ADDITION

All of the béchamel sauce recipes in this book instruct you to heat the dairy product before it is whisked into the roux.

Heating milk and cream requires constant vigilance to avoid the dairy product reaching a boil and spilling over onto your stove in what seems to be a second. As a dairy product heats, water begins to evaporate from its surface, thus concentrating the fats and proteins in a thick layer at the top. As this layer increases in thickness, the water vapor below it can't escape, so it eventually pushes up the whole top layer—and you have a real mess to clean up as soon as the stove cools down. To prevent this, you've got to watch that pot and stir it on a regular basis. I tested an old wives' tale about leaving a wooden spoon in the pot to provide a conduit for the water vapor to escape. It worked about half the time; the other half, I went through a wad of paper towels dabbing up hot milk.

One suggestion is to heat dairy products in a tall pan rather than one with sides barely higher than the level of the liquid it holds. That way you have a few more seconds to stir it or remove it from the heat before Mount Vesuvius erupts on your stove.

The hot milk or cream should be whisked into the roux slowly. If lumps appear, it means the liquid was added too quickly or the flame was too high under the pan, but whisking will remove the lumps.

Some recipes call for stock to be whisked into the roux, and in that case, it's not necessary to heat it beforehand. Stock is not as problematic as milk and cream in that regard and you can whisk it in over higher heat because there's no fear of scorching.

ADDING CHEESE

Once the sauce has simmered for a few minutes, it becomes thicker, and it's easier to incorporate any cheese specified in a recipe. The cheese should be added gradually while the sauce is being stirred. If too much cheese is added at a time, the temperature of the sauce will drop below a simmer, and the cheese may form a giant lump. Don't worry if your sauce gets cheese lumps: a vigorous whisking will ameliorate this problem, but whisking also changes the texture of the sauce slightly, so it should be avoided if possible.

GLUTEN-FREE BÉCHAMEL SAUCE

There are millions of people who now follow a gluten-free diet. Gluten is a protein found in wheat, barley, and rye, so it's obviously part of traditional breads and pastas. People with celiac disease, an autoimmune disorder, or other related conditions have to avoid this protein, and one of the culprits is the flour used to create the roux for a creamed soup. I've written three cookbooks on gluten-free cooking, and after much experimentation I've devised a formulation that solves this problem: for every two tablespoons of all-purpose flour specified in a recipe use two tablespoons of rice flour and two teaspoons of cornstarch.

Sauces are part of what defined classic French cooking of the nineteenth and most of the twentieth centuries. In the early-nineteenth century, chef Marie-Antonin Carême published an extensive list of sauces, which Auguste Escoffier then consolidated to five "mother sauces." They are sauce béchamel, the cream sauce that serves as the basis for most creamed soups; sauce espagnole, which is a brown sauce made from veal stock; sauce velouté, a roux-thickened, stock-based sauce used in some soups; sauce hollandaise, an emulsion of egg yolks, butter, and lemon juice; and sauce tomate, the basic tomato sauce.

Making Soups in Your Slow Cooker

While the recipes in this book are not devised for the slow cooker, many of the soups, especially the bean and meat soups, could be cooked in that popular appliance. Not all dishes can be easily converted to slow-cooked dishes. If a soup is supposed to cook uncovered or partially covered, chances are it will not be successfully transformed to a slow cooker recipe, because the liquid will not evaporate.

But if a soup is simmered covered over low heat on top of the stove, it can be cooked in a slow cooker—as long as the quantity of the recipe is appropriate.

A huge batch that will fill the insert more than two-thirds full is not a good candidate. If this is the case, fiddle with the batch size to make it appropriate for the slow cooker.

Here are some general guidelines to converting a recipe for the slow cooker:

- Quadruple the time from conventional cooking to cooking on Low, and at least double it for cooking on High.

- Almost any meat or poultry soup takes 7 to 10 hours on Low and 3½ to 5 hours on High.

- Cut back on the liquid by 25 percent. Even when covered, more liquid evaporates from a soup that is simmering on the stove than from one cooked in the slow cooker.

- Add tender vegetables, like tomatoes, for only the last 45 minutes of cooking time.

Crunchy Garnishes

The visual aspects of serving soup can be challenging. There's nothing inherently dramatic about a bowl of liquid. That's where garnishing comes into play. Many of the soup recipes in this book list specific foods with which to garnish them; sometimes it's a chopped herb used in the soup that enhances flavor; other times it's something diverse in terms of color and flavor, such as the julienne of smoked salmon served on Spring Asparagus Bisque (page 48).

Other recipes don't specify any garnishes, and that's where this section is intended to be helpful. Regardless of the nature of a soup, it can always be garnished with some type of bread crouton. Croutons are easy to bake in the oven, and you can personalize them in myriad ways—from the type of bread that's used to the addition of herbs, garlic, or cheese on them.

I keep various types of croutons in heavy resealable plastic bags in my freezer. They thaw in a matter of minutes and they always taste as if they were just baked.

Croutons add a crunchy accent to a soft food, which is why they're so popular as soup garnishes. The same crunchiness can be achieved by sprinkling the soup with freshly popped popcorn or bits of fried corn or flour tortillas or pita bread.

Croutons

While some people fry croutons in a skillet, I think you get better and more uniform results by tossing the bread with fat and then slowly baking the cubes in the oven. Following this master recipe are many variations.

Serves 6 to 8

3 slices (1 inch thick) white country bread

2 tablespoons unsalted butter

2 tablespoons olive oil

Salt and freshly ground black pepper to taste

....

The nature of the bread you use changes the nature of the croutons. Try making them with herb bread, olive bread, cornbread, rye bread, or pumpernickel.

Preheat the oven to 350°F and line a rimmed baking sheet with heavy-duty aluminum foil.

Remove the crusts from the bread and cut the bread into ¾-inch cubes; you should have 4 cups.

Heat the butter and oil in a skillet over medium heat. Add the bread cubes and toss to coat them evenly. Spread the bread cubes out on the prepared baking sheet in an even layer, and sprinkle them with salt and pepper. Bake the croutons in the center of the oven for 15 to 20 minutes, or until brown and crispy. Cool to room temperature and then store in an airtight container or in a heavy resealable plastic bag.

NOTE: The croutons can be kept at room temperature for up to 1 day or they can be frozen for up to 3 months. Allow them to thaw before adding to a soup.

Variations

- Add 4 garlic cloves, 2 teaspoons of fresh thyme leaves, and 2 teaspoons of chopped fresh rosemary to the oil and butter mixture and cook it for 2 minutes over low heat before adding the bread cubes.

- Instead of mixing butter and oil, use 5 tablespoons of unsalted butter and cook it over medium heat, stirring often, for 3 minutes, or until browned and aromatic.

- Toss the cubes with ¼ cup freshly grated Parmesan cheese in addition to the butter and oil mix.

- For peppery croutons, toss the cubes with 2 teaspoons coarsely ground black pepper.

Polenta Croutons

There are a lot of Italian soups in this book, reflecting the popularity of that healthful cuisine in this country. A few times I've had leftover polenta around and fried up some small bits to use as croutons in soups. I liked the results so much that I now make polenta just to fry into these croutons.

Serves 6 to 8

1 cup polenta

1 tablespoon kosher salt

4 tablespoons (½ stick) unsalted butter, cut into thin slices

⅓ cup olive oil

....

The squares are really best right after they are fried, but as with potato pancakes or fritters, you can place them on a baking sheet lined with paper towels and keep them hot in a 150°F oven for up to 30 minutes.

Bring 3 cups of water to a boil in a saucepan placed over high heat. Whisk in the polenta slowly, and then whisk in the salt. Reduce the heat to low, and simmer the mixture, covered, stirring occasionally, for 20 to 25 minutes, or until the polenta is very thick.

Remove the pan from the stove and stir in the butter.

Spray a rimmed baking sheet with nonstick cooking spray. Scrape the polenta onto the sheet and smooth it into an even layer about ¾ inch thick. Cover the polenta with plastic wrap and refrigerate for at least 4 hours, but preferably overnight.

Run a spatula around the edges of the baking sheet and turn the polenta out onto a cutting board. Cut into 1-inch squares, and refrigerate the squares, separating layers with sheets of waxed paper.

To cook, heat 3 tablespoons of the oil in a large skillet over medium-high heat. Add some polenta squares, being careful not to crowd the pan. Cook for 3 minutes per side, or until crisp and brown. Turn the squares with a slotted spatula and brown the other side. Drain on paper towels and fry the remaining polenta in additional oil. Serve immediately.

NOTE: The polenta can be cooked and cut into pieces up to 3 days in advance and kept refrigerated. Do not fry it until just prior to serving.

Variation

Add 2 tablespoons of any chopped fresh herb to the polenta as it cooks.

Useful Equipment

If you already have an efficient kitchen, there's nothing you have to buy to cook any recipe in this book. But here are some things that are called for on a regular basis:

An immersion blender, also called a "stick blender." It saves all sorts of time when you can just purée a soup mixture right in the pot in which it was cooked, and the only messy thing to clean after accomplishing that task is one implement. Most immersion blenders also become electric whisks by changing the attachment, which I find really useful for whipped cream and egg whites.

A food processor. My food processor has a dedicated corner in the dishwasher because I use it every day. In addition to the steel blade for chopping and puréeing, make sure you have a good shredding disk for cheeses and a slicing disk.

A 4-quart soup pot. If a recipe doesn't make more than a few quarts, this size pot is useful.

An ovenproof 10- or 12-inch skillet. There are many tasks like caramelizing onions that are better done in a skillet than a pan with high sides. Plus you can bake Skillet Cornbread (page 223) in it.

A selection of whisks. Whisks are an essential tool to make a smooth béchamel sauce (see page 21) and they're also useful for stirring soups as they simmer. If you use nonstick cookware, your whisks should be made from silicone to avoid scratching the surface of the pans. Regardless of the material, it's good to have one or two that are 9 or 10-inches to operate in small saucepans and then a few 12 or 13-inch balloon whisks that can be used for large quantities and work well to whip cream or egg whites.

A potato masher. There are many recipes that specify mashing up some, but not all, of the solids in a soup as a way to achieve a thicker texture. A potato masher is the ideal tool for the job.

A large fine-mesh sieve. You really need a sturdy one so you can strain your stocks and then press on the solids to get out all the richly flavored liquid. The mesh must be small enough that a peppercorn can't get through, which is why colanders don't work.

2 Small Soups as Starters

Soups have a cherished place in the world of appetizers. Every chef lists a few on their menus, and small soups are without question my favorite way to start a dinner party at home. Leading off with a small bowl of soup immediately calms any hunger pangs guests may be bringing to the table, and there's nothing intimidating about serving it and eating it.

Many of the soup recipes in this chapter are cream soups, based on making a béchamel sauce (see page 21). While there is some flour in these soups, most of them are thickened with the vegetables cooked in stock before the dairy product is added. These soups come from the repertoire of classic French food, and they were popularized in this country via the countless "Continental restaurants" that dominated the scene in the first half of the twentieth century.

Cream was first used by the Italians in the ninth century, but its popularity is most often credited to the Austrians in general and the pastry chefs of Vienna in particular. Topping everything with whipped cream has been a practice in the Austrian cuisine for more than 300 years.

Cutting the Calories

Many of these recipes are written for heavy cream, which has a hefty 50 calories per tablespoon. In contrast, whole milk comes in at 150 calories for a whole cup (9 calories per tablespoon), and half-and-half is 18 calories per tablespoon.

While there's nothing like the luxurious mouthfeel of a soup made with heavy cream, there's also no reason to not make cream soups because of the fat content. You can cut down to half-and-half and not really tell the difference, or you can go to whole milk. If using milk instead of cream, increase the amount of flour in the béchamel sauce by half. If a recipe calls for two tablespoons, use three. If a recipe calls for heavy cream that's not part of a roux, then mix a tablespoon of cornstarch with a little cold water and thicken the soup with the slurry.

But please don't use any reduced-fat milk products, like 2% or 1%. The resulting soups will taste thin and just plain watery.

Beer and Cheese Soup

ADAPTED FROM GELLA'S DINER, HAYS, KANSAS

Gella's Diner is joined in business with the Lb. Brewing Company, and chef Manuel Hernandez uses one of its beers as the base for this soup, which tastes very much like Welsh rarebit. Cheddar Beer Bread (page 226) is a natural companion.

Serves 8 to 10

4 tablespoons (½ stick) unsalted butter

1 medium onion, diced

1 carrot, sliced

1 celery rib, sliced

3 garlic cloves, minced

1 tablespoon fresh thyme leaves

3 tablespoons all-purpose flour

2 cups Chicken Stock (page 14) or purchased stock, heated

2 cups heavy cream

1 (12-ounce) bottle pale ale or beer of your choice

1 bay leaf

1 pound sharp cheddar, grated

Salt and freshly ground white pepper to taste

Heat the butter in a 4-quart soup pot over medium-high heat. Add the onion, carrot, celery, garlic, and thyme. Cook, stirring frequently, for 3 minutes, or until the onion is translucent. Stir in the flour and cook, stirring constantly, for 1 minute, or until the mixture turns slightly beige, is bubbly, and appears to have grown in volume. Increase the heat to medium, and slowly whisk in the stock, and then the cream and beer. Add the bay leaf. Bring to a boil, whisking frequently. Reduce the heat to low, and simmer for 10 minutes, or until the vegetables are almost tender. Add the cheese to the soup by ½-cup measures, stirring until the cheese melts before making another addition. Remove and discard the bay leaf. Allow the soup to cool for 10 minutes.

Purée the soup with an immersion blender, or in a food processor fitted with the steel blade. If using a food processor, you may need to work in batches. Season to taste with salt and pepper and serve immediately.

NOTE: The soup can be prepared up to 2 days in advance and refrigerated, tightly covered. Reheat over low heat, stirring occasionally. Add milk or cream if the soup needs thinning after reheating.

....

Changing the nature of the beer you include will fundamentally change the flavor of this soup. For a more intense flavor, substitute a dark stout for the pale ale. You can also substitute a hard apple cider with good results.

Cream of Celery Soup

ADAPTED FROM BAYONA, NEW ORLEANS, LOUISIANA

Famed chef Susan Spicer has been a culinary force in New Orleans for more than thirty years, and her cozy bistro, Bayona, is housed in a 200-year-old French Quarter cottage. This is one of her signature soups. It's thickened with both potato and a bit of flour, and it really showcases the delicacy of celery. Serve it with Popovers (page 230).

Serves 6 to 8

3 tablespoons unsalted butter

2 medium onions, chopped

10 celery ribs, chopped

1 small russet potato, peeled and diced

2 tablespoons all-purpose flour

1 quart Chicken Stock (page 14), Vegetable Stock (page 16), or purchased stock

1 cup heavy cream

Salt and freshly ground white pepper to taste

Snipped fresh chives, for garnish

Sourdough croutons (page 24), for garnish

Heat the butter in a 4-quart soup pot over low heat. Add the onions, celery, and potato, and cook the vegetables, covered, for 10 minutes, stirring the mixture after 5 minutes. Stir in the flour and cook for 2 minutes, stirring constantly.

Gradually whisk in the stock, and bring to a boil over medium heat. Reduce the heat to low, and simmer the soup for 15 minutes, or until the vegetables are very tender.

Allow the soup to cool for 10 minutes. Purée with an immersion blender, or in a food processor fitted with the steel blade. If using a food processor, you may need to work in batches.

Stir the cream into the soup, and bring it back to a boil. Season to taste with salt and pepper, and serve immediately, garnished with chives and croutons, if desired.

NOTE: The soup can be prepared up to 2 days in advance and refrigerated, tightly covered. Reheat it over low heat, stirring occasionally. Add milk or cream if the soup needs thinning after reheating.

I'm always puzzled by the ribs that are trimmed off of fennel bulbs before they're sliced to eat raw or braised. I experimented and discovered that they were a wonderful substitute for celery in this soup, adding just a hint of anise flavor while remaining subtle.

Cream of Spinach and Mushroom Soup

ADAPTED FROM CIRO, SUN VALLEY, IDAHO

My old friend Mark Caraluzzi joined two perennial small soup favorites, cream of spinach soup and cream of mushroom soup. The resulting soup is more delicious than either alone. Serve it with Pretzel Rolls (page 219) or Focaccia (page 214).

Serves 8 to 10

6 tablespoons (¾ stick) unsalted butter, divided

2 leeks, white and light green parts only, halved, thinly sliced, and rinsed well

1 celery rib, diced

2 garlic cloves, minced

¾ pound fresh spinach, stemmed and rinsed

½ pound fresh mushrooms, wiped with a damp paper towel and diced

¼ cup all-purpose flour

1 quart Chicken Stock (page 14) or purchased stock, divided

1½ cups half-and-half

Salt and freshly ground black pepper to taste

Heat 2 tablespoons of the butter in a 4-quart soup pot over medium-high heat. Add the leeks, celery, and garlic. Cook, stirring frequently, for 3 minutes, or until the leeks are translucent. Add the spinach and mushrooms, and cook, stirring frequently, for 5 minutes, or until the spinach wilts and the mushrooms soften.

While the vegetables cook, heat the remaining butter in a small saucepan over medium-low heat. Stir in the flour and cook, stirring constantly, for 1 minute, or until the mixture turns slightly beige, is bubbly, and appears to have grown in volume. Increase the heat to medium, and slowly whisk in 1 cup of the stock. Bring to a boil, and simmer for 1 minute.

Add the thickened stock, the remaining stock, and the half-and-half to the pot with the vegetables and bring to a boil over medium heat, stirring occasionally. Reduce the heat to low, and simmer the soup for 10 to 15 minutes, or until the vegetables are tender. Season to taste with salt and pepper, and serve immediately.

NOTE: The soup can be prepared up to 2 days in advance and refrigerated, tightly covered. Reheat over low heat, stirring occasionally.

. . . .

I'm all for taking some shortcuts if it doesn't endanger the quality of a dish, and one of my go-to foods is frozen leaf spinach. You have to be diligent about thawing it and pressing it hard in a colander to get the liquid drained, but for something like this soup, a 10-ounce box is the perfect amount.

Cream of Cilantro Soup

Chef Manuel Hernandez is a native of Mexico, and this soup with a crunchy garnish blends cilantro with other vegetables to add a depth of flavor. Serve it with warm flour tortillas.

Serves 8

5 tablespoons unsalted butter

1 medium onion, diced

1 carrot, sliced

1 celery rib, sliced

3 garlic cloves, minced

¼ cup all-purpose flour

2 cups Chicken Stock (page 14) or purchased stock

1 quart heavy cream

2 bunches fresh cilantro, chopped

½ cup pine nuts, for garnish

Salt and freshly ground black pepper to taste

1 cup small croutons (page 24), for garnish

Heat the butter in a 4-quart soup pot over medium-high heat. Add the onion, carrot, celery, and garlic. Cook, stirring frequently, for 3 minutes, or until the onion is translucent. Stir in the flour and cook, stirring constantly, for 1 minute, or until the mixture turns slightly beige, is bubbly, and appears to have grown in volume. Increase the heat to medium, and slowly whisk in the stock and then the cream. Bring to a boil, whisking frequently. Reduce the heat to low, and simmer the soup for 10 minutes, or until the vegetables are almost tender. Add the cilantro and simmer for another 5 minutes.

While the soup simmers, toast the pine nuts in a small dry skillet over low heat, shaking the pan frequently, for 2 to 3 minutes or until brown. Set aside.

Allow the soup to cool for 10 minutes. Purée with an immersion blender, or in a food processor fitted with the steel blade. If using a food processor, you may need to work in batches. Season to taste with salt and pepper and serve immediately, garnishing each serving with toasted pine nuts and croutons.

NOTE: The soup can be prepared up to 2 days in advance and refrigerated, tightly covered. Reheat over low heat, stirring occasionally. Add milk or cream if the soup needs thinning after reheating.

....

Besides anchovies, few foods divide people as violently as aromatic fresh cilantro. If you're in the group that hates fresh cilantro (which is so large it has its own Facebook page and website, www.IHateCilantro.com) and thinks it makes everything taste like soap or hairspray, you can substitute parsley or any other fresh herb.

Cream of Poblano Soup *(Crema de Poblano)*

ADAPTED FROM KOMALI, DALLAS, TEXAS

Chef Abraham Salum has been a culinary force in Texas for many years, and he now runs Komali, an authentic Mexican restaurant, very close to his flagship Salum. Poblano chiles are very mild, and they make a wonderful soup topped with crispy fried tortilla strips, corn kernels, and creamy queso fresco.

Serves 6 to 8

1 cup vegetable oil, divided

4 poblano chiles, seeds and ribs removed, diced

1 large onion, diced

4 garlic cloves, minced

1 quart Chicken Stock (page 14) or purchased stock

2 cups heavy cream

Salt and freshly ground black pepper to taste

4 (6-inch) corn tortillas, cut into thin strips

1½ cups cooked or roasted corn kernels

¾ cup grated queso fresco (substitute mild goat cheese or paneer)

Heat 3 tablespoons of the oil in a 4-quart soup pot over medium-high heat. Add the chiles, onion, and garlic. Cook, stirring frequently, for 3 minutes, or until the onion is translucent. Add the stock and bring to a boil over high heat. Reduce the heat to low and simmer, partially covered, for 15 to 20 minutes, or until the vegetables are tender.

Allow the soup to cool for 10 minutes. Purée with an immersion blender, or in a food processor fitted with the steel blade. If using a food processor, you may have to work in batches. Stir the cream into the soup, season to taste with salt and pepper, and reheat to a simmer.

While the soup cools, heat the remaining oil in a medium skillet over medium-high heat. Add the tortilla strips and fry them for 2 to 3 minutes, or until crispy. Remove the strips from the pan with tongs, and drain well on paper towels.

To serve, ladle the hot soup into bowls and top each serving with tortilla strips, corn kernels, and queso fresco.

NOTE: The soup can be prepared up to 2 days in advance and refrigerated, tightly covered. Reheat over low heat, stirring occasionally. Do not prepare the tortilla strips until just prior to serving.

....

As you'll notice in many of these recipes, the cream enriching a soup is frequently added after the base mixture has been puréed. Then the soup is seasoned and simmered once again before it is served. The reason is that cream has a tendency to scorch if cooked for a long period of time.

Poblano Asiago Soup with Golden Tomato Foam

ADAPTED FROM STEPHAN PYLES, DALLAS, TEXAS

This bright green soup is stunning to serve, and the yellow tomato cream foam on the top adds flavor as well as contrasting color. Serve it with Skillet Cornbread (page 223).

Serves 6

FOAM

1 teaspoon unflavored gelatin

1 large yellow tomato, cored and diced

1 cup heavy cream

Salt to taste

SOUP

2 poblano chiles

4 tablespoons (½ stick) unsalted butter, divided

1 medium onion, chopped

¾ pound tomatillos, husked, rinsed, and chopped

3 garlic cloves, minced

1½ cups Chicken Stock (page 14), Vegetable Stock (page 16), or purchased stock

3 tablespoons all-purpose flour

2 cups whole milk, heated

½ cup heavy cream, heated

1 cup firmly packed fresh cilantro leaves

1 cup firmly packed baby spinach leaves

10 ounces Asiago cheese, grated

Salt and freshly ground black pepper to taste

For the foam, sprinkle the gelatin over 3 tablespoons of cold water to soften. Set aside.

Combine the tomato and cream in a blender and purée until smooth. Place the mixture in a small saucepan and bring to a boil over medium heat, stirring occasionally. Simmer over low heat for 1 minute. Stir in the softened gelatin, and stir until dissolved. Season to taste with salt. Pass the mixture though a fine-mesh sieve, and allow it to cool to room temperature. Transfer to a 1-pint cream whipper fitted with a nitrous oxide canister. Set aside.

For the soup, cut a small slit in the stem end of each of the chiles. Roast the peppers over a gas flame or under the oven broiler. Keep turning the peppers so that the skin chars evenly. Transfer them to a heavy resealable plastic bag and allow them to steam for 10 to 15 minutes. When the peppers are cool enough to handle, pull off the charred skin by hand and dip them in water to remove any blackened bits. Once peeled, discard the stems, seeds, and veins. Dice and set aside.

Heat 2 tablespoons of the butter in a 4-quart soup pot over medium-high heat. Add the onion, tomatillos, and garlic. Cook, stirring frequently, for 3 minutes, or until the onion is translucent. Add the stock and diced chiles, and bring to a boil. Reduce the heat to low and simmer, uncovered, for 15 minutes.

While the vegetables simmer, melt the remaining butter in a saucepan over low heat. Stir in the flour and cook, stirring constantly, for 1 minute, or until the mixture turns slightly beige, is bubbly, and appears to have grown in volume. Increase the heat to medium, and slowly whisk in 1 cup of the milk. Bring to a boil, stirring frequently, and simmer for 1 minute, or until the mixture thickens.

Add the thickened milk to the soup along with the remaining milk and cream. Bring to a boil and

simmer for 3 minutes. Add the cilantro, spinach, and cheese, and cook for 1 minute, or until the spinach wilts and the cheese melts.

Allow the soup to cool for 10 minutes. Purée with an immersion blender, or in a food processor fitted with the steel blade. If using a food processor, you may need to work in batches. Season the soup to taste with salt and pepper.

To serve, ladle the soup into low bowls and create a foam with the yellow tomato mixture around the edge of each bowl.

NOTE: The soup can be prepared up to 2 days in advance and refrigerated, tightly covered. Reheat over low heat, stirring occasionally. Add milk or cream if the soup needs thinning after reheating.

....

Cream whippers are now the darling of professional kitchens for all sorts of foams, and the most common one is manufactured by iSi. It is carried in numerous gourmet shops or can be purchased online. The whipping action is due to aeration provided by a nitrous oxide canister.

Grilled Corn Soup

I love this soup so much that I grill dozens of ears of corn when it's in season and then freeze the kernels. Grilling adds a smoky undertaste to this thick soup, and the corn flavor is reinforced by cornmeal. Serve it with Cheddar Beer Bread (page 226) or Gougères (page 231).

Serves 6 to 8

1 cup mesquite chips

4 large garlic cloves, unpeeled

10 medium ears of corn, unshucked

2 tablespoons unsalted butter

¼ cup yellow cornmeal

1 (4-ounce) can mild green chiles, drained

2 cups Corn Stock (page 19), Vegetable Stock (page 16), or purchased stock

2 cups light cream

Salt and freshly ground black pepper to taste

....

Until the last few decades, grilling was synonymous with charcoal. It was in the early 1950s that George Stephen invented the covered grill, now generically dubbed the Weber kettle. The introduction of the cover represented the first real advance in grilling since cavemen turned the first hunks of meat over smoldering embers. Gas grills arrived on the scene thirty years ago, but have been slow to catch on. In 1989, only 41 percent of households used gas grills; that number in 2010 had grown to 58 percent.

Light a charcoal or gas grill, and soak the mesquite chips in cold water to cover for 30 minutes.

Preheat the oven to 350°F. Wrap the garlic cloves in heavy-duty aluminum foil and bake them for 15 to 20 minutes, or until soft. When cool enough to handle, pop them out of their skins and set aside.

Remove all but one layer of the husks from the corn, and pull out the corn silks. Soak the corn in cold water to cover for 10 minutes.

Drain the mesquite chips and place them on the fire. Grill the corn for 10 to 15 minutes, turning the ears with tongs occasionally. When cool enough to handle, discard the husks, and cut the kernels off the cobs using a sharp serrated knife.

Melt the butter in a 4-quart soup pot over low heat. Add the corn kernels and cook, stirring frequently, for 5 minutes. Remove 1 cup of kernels, and set aside. Purée the remaining corn, roasted garlic, cornmeal, chiles, and stock in a food processor fitted with the steel blade or in a blender. This will probably have to be done in a few batches. Combine the purée with the cream, and heat to a boil over medium heat. Add the reserved corn kernels, and season the soup to taste with salt and pepper. Simmer for 5 minutes over low heat, stirring occasionally.

NOTE: The soup can be prepared up to 2 days in advance and refrigerated, tightly covered. Reheat over low heat, stirring occasionally. Add milk or cream if the soup needs thinning after reheating.

Curried Pear Soup

Many Indian curries call for fruit chutney as a condiment because the sweetness of the fruit tends to balance the spices in the dish. In this easy cream soup, luscious fresh pears are the star. Naan or pita bread goes well with this soup.

Serves 6 to 8

3 tablespoons unsalted butter

1 leek, white part only, thinly sliced and rinsed well

3 tablespoons all-purpose flour

2 to 3 tablespoons curry powder, or to taste

1 cup dry white wine

6 cups Vegetable Stock (page 16) or purchased stock

6 cups diced ripe pears

2 cups heavy cream

Salt and freshly ground white pepper to taste

Melt the butter in a 4-quart soup pot over medium heat. Add the leek and cook, stirring frequently, for 3 minutes, or until the leek is translucent. Stir in the flour and curry powder and cook, stirring constantly, for 1 minute, or until the mixture turns slightly beige, is bubbly, and appears to have grown in volume. Increase the heat to medium, and slowly whisk in the wine. Bring to a boil, whisking frequently. Cook until the wine is reduced by half, and then whisk in the stock. Bring the soup back to a boil and then stir in the pears. Simmer, uncovered, for 20 minutes, or until reduced by one-fourth.

Allow the soup to cool for 10 minutes. Purée with an immersion blender, or in a food processor fitted with the steel blade. If using a food processor, you may have to work in batches.

Stir the cream into the soup and bring it back to a simmer. Simmer for 5 minutes. Season to taste with salt and pepper and serve immediately.

NOTE: The soup can be prepared up to 2 days in advance and refrigerated, tightly covered. Reheat over low heat, stirring occasionally. Add milk or cream if the soup needs thinning after reheating.

....

Commercial curry powder can include upwards of fifteen different spices. But if you want to make it yourself, here's a good basic formulation:

½ cup of curry powder = 3 tablespoons ground coriander; 2 tablespoons each of crushed red pepper flakes, ground cumin, and ground fenugreek seeds; 1 tablespoon each of ground ginger, turmeric, and ground mustard seeds; and 1 teaspoon each of freshly ground black pepper and ground cinnamon.

Roasted Tomato and Basil Cream Soup

ADAPTED FROM SOUTH CITY KITCHEN, ATLANTA, GEORGIA

Cream of tomato soup is an American classic but chef Chip Ulbrich intensifies the flavor of the tomatoes in his version by roasting the vegetables. Aromatic fresh basil gives the soup a Mediterranean inspiration, but I like to serve it with Skillet Cornbread (page 223). After all, the restaurant is in Atlanta.

Serves 6 to 8

2 pounds ripe plum tomatoes, cored and diced

1 large sweet onion, such as Vidalia or Bermuda, diced

3 garlic cloves

3 tablespoons olive oil

4 tablespoons (½ stick) unsalted butter

¼ cup all-purpose flour

2 cups Chicken Stock (page 14) or purchased sock

½ cup firmly packed sliced fresh basil leaves, divided

2 cups heavy cream

Salt and freshly ground black pepper to taste

Preheat the oven to 450°F. Combine the tomatoes, onion, and garlic in a shallow roasting pan, and toss the vegetables with the olive oil. Roast the vegetables for 20 minutes, or until softened, stirring after 10 minutes.

While the vegetables roast, melt the butter in a 4-quart soup pot over low heat. Stir in the flour and cook, stirring constantly, for 1 minute, or until the mixture turns slightly beige, is bubbly, and appears to have grown in volume. Increase the heat to medium, and slowly whisk in the stock. Bring to a boil, whisking frequently. Add the roasted vegetables and ⅓ cup of the basil leaves, and bring to a boil over medium heat. Reduce the heat to low and simmer the soup for 10 minutes.

Allow the soup to cool for 10 minutes. Purée with an immersion blender, or in a food processor fitted with the steel blade. If using a food processor, you may have to work in batches.

Stir the cream into the soup, and bring it back to a boil. Season the soup to taste with salt and pepper, and serve immediately, garnishing each serving with some of the remaining basil.

NOTE: The soup can be prepared up to 2 days in advance and refrigerated, tightly covered. Reheat over low heat, stirring occasionally. Add milk or cream if the soup needs thinning after reheating.

....

If you know you're going to refrigerate a soup and reheat it to serve the next day, only cut up the amount of fresh herb that is cooked in the soup and not any that will be used as a garnish, like the remaining basil in this recipe. Herbs go limp and lose flavor and aroma almost immediately after they're sliced.

Tomato Soup with Mint and Ginger

ADAPTED FROM NEW RIVERS, PROVIDENCE, RHODE ISLAND

Canned tomatoes are a convenience food no cook can live without, especially during the winter, when the tomatoes in most parts of the country are not local. This soup, developed by former New Rivers owner Bruce Tillinghast, proves tomato soup can be a year-round treat. The nuances of fresh mint and sharp ginger add a complexity to the eating experience. Serve it with Popovers (page 23).

Serves 6 to 8

2 tablespoons olive oil

1 large sweet onion, such as Vidalia or Bermuda, diced

1 celery rib, sliced

1 parsnip, diced

2 garlic cloves, minced

Pinch of crushed red pepper flakes

1 bay leaf

2 teaspoons fresh thyme leaves

5 sprigs fresh mint, leaves removed from stems and both reserved

2 cups Vegetable Stock (page 16) or purchased stock

4 cups canned tomatoes packed in tomato purée, chopped, undrained

3 tablespoons minced fresh ginger

2 tablespoons firmly packed dark brown sugar

Salt and freshly ground black pepper to taste

Heat the oil in a 4-quart soup pot over medium-high heat. Add the onion, celery, parsnip, and garlic and cook, stirring frequently, for 3 minutes, or until the onion is translucent. Add the crushed red pepper, bay leaf, thyme, mint stems, stock, and tomatoes. Bring to a boil over medium heat, reduce the heat to low, and simmer, uncovered, for 20 minutes.

Remove and discard the bay leaf, and stir in the ginger and brown sugar. Allow the soup to cool for 10 minutes. Purée with an immersion blender, or in a food processor fitted with the steel blade. If using a food processor, you may have to work in batches. Cut the mint leaves into a chiffonade, reserving a few whole leaves for garnish, and stir them into the soup. Season to taste with salt and pepper, and serve immediately, garnishing each serving with whole mint leaves.

NOTE: The soup can be prepared up to 2 days in advance and refrigerated, tightly covered. Reheat over low heat, stirring occasionally. Do not stir in the chiffonade of mint until just prior to serving.

....

Chiffonade is a way of cutting herb leaves and vegetables like spinach that gives you really thin and long slices. Start by stacking the leaves, then roll your stack tightly, and cut the rolled stack into very thin slices.

Fire-Roasted Red Pepper Soup

ADAPTED FROM ROW 14 BISTRO & WINE BAR, DENVER, COLORADO

There's a wealth of flavors in this vegetarian soup. Roasting intensifies the sweetness of the red bell peppers, and the tomatoes and herbs add complexity. You can sprinkle some croutons or freshly popped popcorn on top to add textural interest.

Serves 6 to 8

4 red bell peppers

3 tablespoons olive oil

1 large sweet onion, such as Vidalia or Bermuda, diced

4 garlic cloves

12 ripe plum tomatoes, cored and diced

¾ cup dry red wine

1 quart Vegetable Stock (page 16) or purchased stock

¾ cup firmly packed fresh basil leaves

¼ cup firmly packed fresh parsley leaves

1 tablespoon fresh thyme leaves

Salt and freshly ground black pepper to taste

....

It always seems like a waste of time to me to grill only the number of peppers needed for a specific recipe. You can roast a bunch and store them for up to a week in a tightly covered glass jar. Cover them with olive oil, either with or without a few peeled garlic cloves and some chopped fresh basil or oregano. Roasted peppers also freeze well in heavy resealable plastic bags for up to three months.

Light a gas or charcoal grill or preheat the oven broiler. Cut a small slit in each pepper at the stem end to prevent them from exploding. Grill or broil the peppers 6 inches from the heat element, turning gently with tongs until they are charred all over. Transfer the peppers to a platter and place an overturned mixing bowl over them. Allow the peppers to steam for 10 to 15 minutes. When the peppers are cool enough to handle, discard the stems, seeds, and ribs; pull off the charred skin. Dice and set aside.

Heat the oil in a 4-quart soup pot over medium-high heat. Add the onion and garlic and cook, stirring frequently, for 3 minutes, or until the onion is translucent. Add the tomatoes and wine. Bring to a boil over high heat, reduce the heat to medium, and cook for 3 to 4 minutes, or until the wine is reduced by half. Add the diced peppers, stock, basil, parsley, and thyme. Bring to a boil over medium-high heat, then reduce the heat to low and simmer the soup, uncovered, for 20 minutes.

Allow the soup to cool for 10 minutes. Purée with an immersion blender, or in a food processor fitted with the steel blade. If using a food processor, you may have to work in batches. Season to taste with salt and pepper, and serve immediately.

NOTE: The soup can be prepared up to 2 days in advance and refrigerated, tightly covered. Reheat over low heat, stirring occasionally.

Red Pepper and Fennel Bisque

This recipe is inspired by a soup I ate many years ago at Patrick O'Connell's famed Inn at Little Washington in the Shenandoah Mountains. There's pungency from the herbs and peppers, and the subtle flavor of anise ties it all together.

Serves 6 to 8

3 tablespoons unsalted butter

1 medium onion, diced

½ medium fennel bulb, cored and diced

4 red bell peppers, seeds and ribs removed, diced

3 garlic cloves, minced

1 jalapeño or serrano chile, seeds and ribs removed, diced

1 tablespoon fennel seeds, crushed

¼ cup all-purpose flour

4 cups Chicken Stock (page 14), Vegetable Stock (page 16), or purchased stock

1 tablespoon tomato paste

2 tablespoons chopped fresh basil

1 tablespoon fresh thyme leaves

1 bay leaf

1 cup heavy cream

Salt and freshly ground black pepper to taste

⅓ cup mascarpone

⅓ cup sambuca liqueur

....

It's now relatively easy to find mascarpone, a fresh Italian cheese that originated in the region around Milan, in most supermarkets. But it is pricey. My substitute for it is to mix equal parts of softened cream cheese and softened butter, and then add a few tablespoons of sour cream to replicate the soft texture of mascarpone.

Melt the butter in a 4-quart soup pot over medium heat. Add the onion, fennel, red peppers, garlic, jalapeño, and fennel seeds. Cook, stirring frequently, for 3 minutes, or until the onion is translucent.

Reduce the heat to low, stir in the flour, and cook, stirring constantly, for 2 minutes. Raise the heat to medium, and whisk in the stock and tomato paste. Bring to a boil, add the basil, thyme, and bay leaf, reduce the heat to low, and simmer the soup, partially covered, for 30 minutes.

Remove and discard the bay leaf. Allow the soup to cool for 10 minutes. Purée with an immersion blender, or in a food processor fitted with the steel blade. If using a food processor, you may have to work in batches. Return the soup to the saucepan, and add the cream. Bring to a boil over medium heat, reduce the heat to low, and simmer for 3 minutes. Season to taste with salt and pepper.

To serve, combine the mascarpone and sambuca in a small bowl and whisk well. Place a dollop on the top of each bowl of soup.

NOTE: The soup can be prepared up to 2 days in advance and refrigerated, tightly covered. Reheat over low heat.

Variation

Orange or yellow peppers can be substituted for the red peppers in this recipe, but don't try it with green peppers. Green peppers are immature red peppers, and the flavor will be too bitter.

Coconut Carrot Soup

ADAPTED FROM BINKLEY'S, CAVE CREEK, ARIZONA

Chef-owner Kevin Binkley, who worked in the legendary kitchens of the Inn at Little Washington and The French Laundry, has been referred to as the "Gary Danko of the desert." The menu at his elegant restaurant located in a town of pseudo-Western honky-tonks changes almost nightly. The sophisticated dishes always include a soup or two, and this one pairs the tropical flavor of coconut with the innate sweetness of carrots.

Serves 8 to 10

4 tablespoons (½ stick) unsalted butter

1½ pounds carrots, sliced

2 celery ribs, sliced

1 small onion, diced

2 tablespoons grated fresh ginger

½ cup dry white wine

5 cups Vegetable Stock (page 16) or purchased
    stock

¾ cup coconut milk

½ cup grated unsweetened coconut

3 tablespoons pure maple syrup

1 cup heavy cream

Salt and freshly ground black pepper to taste

Heat the butter in a 4-quart soup pot over medium heat. Add the carrots, celery, onion, and ginger. Reduce the heat to low, cover the pot, and cook the mixture, stirring occasionally, for 5 to 7 minutes, or until the vegetables are soft.

Stir in the wine, raise the heat to medium-high, and cook uncovered for 3 minutes, or until the liquid is reduced by half.

Add the stock, coconut milk, coconut, and maple syrup. Bring to a boil over medium-high heat, then reduce the heat to low and simmer, partially covered, for 35 to 40 minutes, or until the vegetables are very tender.

Allow the soup to cool for 10 minutes. Purée with an immersion blender, or in a food processor fitted with the steel blade. If using a food processor, you may have to work in batches.

Return the soup to the pot, and stir in the cream. Bring back to a simmer. Season the soup to taste with salt and pepper, and serve immediately.

NOTE: The soup can be prepared up to 2 days in advance and refrigerated, tightly covered. Reheat over low heat, stirring occasionally.

Always buy carrots with the green tops attached. That way you can see how fresh they are. But cut off the green tops when you get home or they will rob the carrots of moisture and hasten their decline.

Asparagus Soup with Coconut Foam, Avocado, and Sea Scallop

ADAPTED FROM EUCLID HALL BAR & KITCHEN, DENVER, COLORADO

Jorel Pierce is chef de cuisine at this restaurant—one of three in Denver run by famed *Top Chef Masters* contestant Jennifer Jasinski and her partner Beth Gruitch. This soup is ethereal; the bright green base is ladled over a complex pastiche of sea scallops and sliced avocado, and then topped with a creamy foam.

Serves 6 to 8

SOUP

3 tablespoons unsalted butter

1 medium onion, diced

2 garlic cloves, minced

½ fresh fennel bulb, cored and chopped

2 celery ribs, chopped

2 bay leaves

1 teaspoon fresh thyme leaves

6 cups Vegetable Stock (page 16) or purchased stock

½ teaspoon granulated sugar

Salt to taste

1 pound fresh asparagus, cut into 2-inch lengths

GARNISH

1 (14-ounce) can full-fat coconut milk

¼ teaspoon salt

½ teaspoon granulated sugar

3 tablespoons heavy cream

2 tablespoons olive oil

6 to 8 sea scallops

1 ripe avocado, peeled and thinly sliced

3 tablespoons finely chopped cilantro

Freshly ground black pepper to taste

Heat the butter in a 4-quart soup pot over medium heat. Add the onion, garlic, fennel, and celery. Cook, stirring frequently, for 3 minutes, or until the onion is translucent. Add the bay leaves, thyme, stock, and sugar, and season the soup to taste with salt. Bring to a boil over high heat, then reduce the heat to low, and simmer, partially covered, for 1 hour. Cool the soup for 30 to 45 minutes, or until less than 100°F. Remove and discard the bay leaves.

Bring a large pot of water to a boil over high heat and have a bowl of ice water handy. Add the asparagus, and cook for 3 to 5 minutes, or until the asparagus is crisp-tender. Drain the asparagus, and immediately plunge it into the ice water to stop the cooking action. Once chilled, drain the asparagus.

Combine the asparagus and cooled soup in a blender, and purée until smooth. Pass the mixture through a sieve, if desired. Chill immediately.

For the coconut foam, combine the coconut milk, salt, sugar, and cream in a small saucepan. Bring to a boil over medium heat, stirring frequently. Reduce the mixture by one-third, and transfer the mixture to a 1-pint cream whipper fitted with a nitrous oxide canister. Set aside.

Heat the oil in a sauté pan or skillet over high heat. Rinse the scallops and pat dry with paper towels. Sear the scallops for 1 minute per side, or until browned but still translucent in the center. Dice the scallops, and set aside.

To serve, reheat the soup to a boil over medium heat, stirring frequently. Arrange the avocado slices and scallops in the bottom of warmed soup bowls, and top with the soup. Place a layer of coconut foam over the soup, and then sprinkle the foam with cilantro and pepper. Serve immediately.

NOTE: The soup can be prepared up to 2 days in advance and refrigerated, tightly covered. Reheat over low heat, stirring occasionally. Do not prepare the garnish until just prior to serving.

....

Foams made with whipped cream canisters are all the rage now, but you can replicate the concept without one. Instead of using a canister to create your volume, whip the heavy cream. Fold in the ancillary ingredients and then spoon some of the mixture on top of your soup.

Spring Asparagus Bisque

ADAPTED FROM WILLOW RESTAURANT, ARLINGTON, VIRGINIA

Chef Tracy O'Grady was the executive chef at Bob Kinkead's legendary Kinkead's in Washington, D.C. and then represented the United States at the international Bocuse d'Or competition in Lyon in 2001. In 2005 she teamed up with my old friend pastry chef Kate Jansen to open Willow. There's a hint of smokiness in this luscious green broth from the ham cooked in the base, and an elegant garnish of smoked salmon reinforces the flavor. Serve this soup with Popovers (page 230).

Serves 6 to 8

1½ pounds fresh asparagus

6 sprigs fresh parsley

1 bunch fresh chervil sprigs

2 tablespoons olive oil

1 leek, white part only, thinly sliced and rinsed well

¼ pound smoked ham, diced

2 quarts Chicken Stock (page 14) or purchased stock

6 sprigs fresh thyme, tied with kitchen string or a reusable silicone band

2 cups heavy cream

½ cup crème fraîche

Salt and freshly ground black pepper to taste

6 ounces smoked salmon, julienned, for garnish

3 tablespoons snipped fresh chives, for garnish

....

Silicone has revolutionized the world of kitchen gadgets. I haven't bought a roll of parchment paper since discovering the wonders of silicone baking mats a few years ago, and I've now given up kitchen string because of reusable silicone "rubber" bands. The ones I use are manufactured by Architec and come in a small packet. You can use them for holding herbs together in a *bouquet garni* or at any time you might need to hold foods together instead of using twine.

Bring a large pot of salted water to a boil over high heat, and have a bowl of ice water handy.

Cut the top 2 inches off the asparagus spears. Set them aside, and slice the remaining stems. Lower the asparagus tips into the boiling water and blanch them for 4 to 5 minutes, or until tender. Remove the tips from the water with a wire mesh spoon and plunge them into the ice water to stop the cooking action.

Add the asparagus stem slices to the boiling water and blanch for 4 to 5 minutes, or until tender. Add the parsley and chervil to the water for the last 30 seconds of the cooking time. Remove the stem pieces and herbs from the water with a wire mesh spoon and plunge them into the ice water to stop the cooking action.

Combine the asparagus stem pieces, parsley, and chervil with 2 tablespoons ice water in a blender and purée until smooth. Set aside.

Heat the oil in a 4-quart soup pot over medium heat. Add the leek and ham and cook, stirring frequently, for 3 minutes, or until the leek is translucent. Add the stock and thyme to the pot, and bring to a boil over high heat. Reduce the heat to medium-high and cook for 15 to 20 minutes, or until the stock is reduced by half. Add the cream and simmer over low heat for 10 minutes. Strain the soup base, pressing with the back of a spoon to extract as much liquid as possible. Discard the solids, rinse out the soup pot, and return the soup to the pot.

Whisk in the crème fraîche and bring the soup back to a simmer. Whisk in the asparagus purée, and season the soup to taste with salt and pepper. Serve immediately, garnishing each serving with asparagus tips, smoked salmon, and chives.

NOTE: The soup can be prepared up to 2 days in advance and refrigerated, tightly covered. Reheat it over low heat, stirring occasionally. Add milk or cream if the soup needs thinning after reheating.

Savory Chestnut Soup

ADAPTED FROM RIOJA, DENVER, COLORADO

Chef Jennifer Jasinski thinks of this soup as a perfect way to start Thanksgiving dinner, and I agree. What has revolutionized Thanksgiving for me is the availability of pre-roasted peeled chestnuts. You can find them in just about every supermarket during the months of November and December. Serve this soup with Limpa (page 218) or Popovers (page 230).

Serves 8

¼ cup rendered duck fat, chicken fat, or olive oil

1 large onion, sliced

5 garlic cloves, peeled

½ pound mushrooms, wiped with a damp paper towel and sliced

10 fresh sage leaves

1 bay leaf

¾ pound peeled roasted chestnuts

1¼ cups dry white wine

6 cups Chicken Stock (page 14) or purchased stock

1 (2-inch) cinnamon stick

½ teaspoon ground cardamom

1¼ cups heavy cream

1 tablespoon granulated sugar

Salt and freshly ground black pepper to taste

Heat the duck fat, chicken fat, or olive oil in a 4-quart soup pot over medium-high heat. Add the onion and garlic and cook, stirring frequently, for 3 minutes, or until the onion is translucent. Add the mushrooms, sage leaves, and bay leaf, and cook for 5 minutes, or until the mushrooms soften.

Add the chestnuts and wine to the pan. Raise the heat to high, and cook, stirring frequently, for 5 to 7 minutes, or until the wine has almost evaporated. Add the chicken stock and bring to a boil. Reduce the heat to low and simmer the soup, uncovered, for 40 minutes. Add the cinnamon stick, cardamom, and cream to the pan and simmer for an additional 15 minutes.

Remove and discard the bay leaf and cinnamon stick. Allow the soup to cool for 10 minutes. Purée with an immersion blender, or in a food processor fitted with the steel blade. If using a food processor, you may have to work in batches. Stir in the sugar and season to taste with salt and pepper. Serve immediately.

NOTE: The soup can be prepared up to 2 days in advance and refrigerated, tightly covered. Reheat over low heat, stirring occasionally. Add milk or cream if the soup needs thinning after reheating.

....

It's now possible to buy rendered duck fat in many markets or online. Duck fat adds a wonderful richness to dishes. If you cook ducks at all, you'll always have some around. Freeze it in small amounts for up to 1 year.

Smoked Sweet Potato Soup

ADAPTED FROM TRINA'S STARLITE LOUNGE, SOMERVILLE, MASSACHUSETTS

Chef Suzi Maitland is known for her roster of soups at this casual spot near Boston decorated with photos of old cars and pin-up girls. This is a simple recipe with a tantalizing flavor that's a perfect start to many fall and winter meals.

Serves 6 to 8

3 tablespoons unsalted butter, diced

1 large sweet onion, such as Vidalia or Bermuda, diced

2 leeks, white parts only, sliced and rinsed well

⅓ cup firmly packed dark brown sugar

2 tablespoons sherry vinegar

3 pounds sweet potatoes, peeled and diced

1½ quarts Vegetable Stock (page 16) or purchased stock

½ to 1 teaspoon liquid smoke

1 cup heavy cream

Salt and freshly ground black pepper to taste

Heat the butter in a 4-quart soup pot over medium heat. Add the onion and leeks and cook, stirring frequently, for 5 minutes, or until the vegetables soften. Add the brown sugar, and cook until bubbly. Stir in the vinegar and cook for 2 minutes.

Add the sweet potatoes, stock, and liquid smoke. Bring to a boil over medium heat, reduce the heat to low, and simmer the soup, uncovered, for 30 minutes. Add the cream, and simmer for an additional 10 minutes, or until the potato cubes are very tender.

Allow the soup to cool for 10 minutes. Purée with an immersion blender, or in a food processor fitted with the steel blade. If using a food processor, you may need to work in batches.

Season the soup to taste with salt and pepper, and serve immediately.

NOTE: The soup can be prepared up to 2 days in advance and refrigerated, tightly covered. Reheat over low heat, stirring occasionally. Add milk or cream if the soup needs thinning after reheating.

....

Liquid smoke, produced by a few manufacturers, is not some chemical created by a mad scientist in a test tube. It's a natural product produced by a safe, water-based process when wood chips like hickory and mesquite are burned and the condensed smoke is formed into a liquid. The liquid is filtered to remove impurities before bottling. Use it sparingly; a little goes a long way. But it does add a tantalizing flavor to foods like barbecue sauces, dips, and soups like this.

Hubbard Squash Soup with Shrimp Toast

ADAPTED FROM SWEET LIFE CAFÉ, OAK BLUFFS, MASSACHUSETTS

Browning the butter gives this rich, thick, and colorful squash soup a nutty undertone, and using apple cider plays up the inherent sweetness of the squash. While the shrimp toast croutons are an elegant garnish, the soup really stands on its own. Serve it with squares of Skillet Cornbread (page 223).

Serves 6 to 8

SOUP

1 (3-pound) hubbard or butternut squash

2 tablespoons vegetable oil

2 tablespoons honey

¼ teaspoon cayenne

1 teaspoon ground coriander

½ cup (1 stick) unsalted butter

1½ cups apple cider

1½ to 2 cups Vegetable Stock (page 16) or water, divided

Salt and freshly ground black pepper to taste

GARNISH

2 slices white sandwich bread

¼ pound raw shrimp, peeled and deveined

2 tablespoons unsalted butter, at room temperature

Salt and freshly ground black pepper to taste

2 tablespoons snipped fresh chives

Preheat the oven to 375°F.

Cut the squash in half and discard the seeds and strings. Rub the cut sides with the oil and honey and then sprinkle them with the cayenne and coriander. Place the squash halves in a baking dish and add 1 cup water to the bottom. Wrap the dish in foil and bake the squash for 1 hour, then remove the foil and cook for an additional 30 minutes, or until the squash is very tender. Add more water to the dish if all the water evaporates. When the squash is cool enough to handle, scoop out the pulp.

Melt the butter in a 4-quart soup pot over medium heat. Cook the butter, swirling the pot by its handle, until the milky solids turn brown. Watch the butter carefully to ensure that it does not burn. Add the squash pulp, cider, and 1½ cups of stock or water, smashing the squash with a potato masher. Bring to a boil over medium-high heat, then reduce the heat to low and simmer the soup, uncovered, for 20 minutes.

Allow the soup to cool for 10 minutes. Purée with an immersion blender, or in a food processor fitted with the steel blade. If using a food processor, you may have to work in batches. Add the remaining stock if the soup consistency is too thick. Season to taste with salt and pepper.

While the soup simmers, prepare the garnish. Preheat the oven broiler and cover a baking sheet with heavy-duty aluminum foil. Toast 1 side of each bread slice. Combine the shrimp, butter, salt, and pepper in a blender and purée until smooth. Spread the mixture on the untoasted side of the bread slices. Broil the bread 8 inches from the broiler element for 2 to 3 minutes, or until golden brown. Cut each slice into 9 squares.

To serve, ladle the soup into bowls and top each serving with some of the shrimp croutons and a sprinkling of chives. Serve immediately.

NOTE: The soup can be prepared up to 2 days in advance and refrigerated, tightly covered. Reheat over low heat, stirring occasionally. Add stock or water if the soup needs thinning after reheating. Do not prepare the garnish until just prior to serving.

....

When puréeing a hot mixture in a blender or food processor, it's always important to allow the steam a way to escape. In a food processor this can be done by removing the plunger from the feed tube. The best thing to do when using a blender is to hold a dish towel over the top of the pitcher instead of using the cover.

Butternut Squash and Apple Soup

ADAPTED FROM NEW RIVERS, PROVIDENCE, RHODE ISLAND

Sweet winter squash and apples are a natural pairing, and adding reduced cider to this herbed squash soup reinforces its flavor. Serve this soup with Skillet Cornbread (page 223) or Irish Soda Bread (page 225).

Serves 6 to 8

1 (1½ pound) butternut or acorn squash

½ gallon fresh apple cider

2 tablespoons vegetable oil

2 medium onions, diced

1 celery rib, diced

1 parsnip, diced

1 large carrot, diced

4 sprigs fresh parsley

2 sprigs fresh thyme

2 (4-inch) sprigs fresh rosemary, leaves removed and stems reserved

1 bay leaf

3 Granny Smith apples, divided

4 cups Vegetable Stock (page 16) or purchased stock

Salt and freshly ground black pepper to taste

6 to 8 (1-inch) tops of rosemary sprigs, for garnish

. . . .

Infusing flavor into soups, stews, and sauces with herbs is a fundamental of French cooking, and the packet they are wrapped in is referred to as a *bouquet garni*. While bay leaves are always fished out of foods before serving, when using a *bouquet garni* the whole packet is discarded. By the end of cooking, the herbs have lent their flavor and aroma to the dish and their physical presence is no longer wanted.

NOTE: The soup can be prepared up to 2 days in advance and refrigerated, tightly covered. Reheat over low heat, stirring occasionally. Do not prepare the garnish until just prior to serving.

Preheat the oven to 400°F and line a roasting pan with heavy-duty aluminum foil. Cut the squash in half, and discard the seeds and strings. Pour ½ inch of water into the pan and place the squash in the pan, cut sides down. Roast the squash for 45 minutes to 1 hour, or until it is tender when poked with the tip of a paring knife. Remove the squash from the pan, and when cool enough to handle, scrape the pulp out of the skin. Set aside.

While the squash bakes, bring the cider to a boil over high heat. Reduce the heat to medium-high and reduce until only 2 cups remain. Set aside.

Heat the oil in a 4-quart soup pot over medium-high heat. Add the onions, celery, parsnip, and carrot. Cook, stirring frequently, for 3 minutes, or until the onions are translucent.

Stuff the parsley, thyme, rosemary stems, and bay leaf into a tea infuser or tie them together in a square of cheesecloth. Peel, core, and thinly slice 2 apples.

Add the herb packet, sliced apples, stock, and 1 cup of the reduced cider to the pot. Bring to a boil over medium-high heat, stirring occasionally. Reduce the heat to low and simmer the soup, uncovered, for 15 minutes, or until the vegetables are soft. Add the cooked squash and boil for an additional 3 minutes.

Remove and discard the herb packet, and stir in the reserved rosemary leaves. Allow the soup to cool for 10 minutes. Purée with an immersion blender, or in a food processor fitted with the steel blade. If using a food processor, you may have to work in batches. Season the soup to taste with salt and pepper and stir in additional reduced cider if the soup needs to be a bit sweeter to suit your taste.

To serve, peel, core, and thinly slice the remaining apple. Garnish each serving with some apple slices and a rosemary sprig top, and serve immediately.

3 Chilled Soups

Giving Soups the "Quick Chill"

In their own way, chilled soups in the summer also fulfill the definition of comfort food. They make you feel cooler and happier as you eat them, especially if you've got a glass of iced tea or chilled rosé nearby.

While gazpacho began as an uncooked vegetable soup in Andalucía, its definition has now grown to include just about every purée one can combine in a food processor. One of the trends has been the mixing of melon and some berries and vegetables in these soups. But in addition to these soups of puréed raw ingredients there is a whole category of wonderful soups that are cooked and then chilled and served cold. Most of these come from classic French cuisine or were influenced by it, and some can trace their history back more than a century.

Time in the refrigerator is really all you need to chill a soup, regardless if it starts out hot or at room temperature. If it's the latter, a few hours is all the time needed, and if it starts hot, then allow it to cool for an hour or so on the counter and then transfer it to the refrigerator. But if you are in a hurry to get the soup chilled there is a rather labor-intensive but efficient way to do it.

While the soup is cooking, chill a metal mixing bowl in the freezer, and have a larger mixing bowl, into which the chilled one will fit, chilling too. Then you're going to replicate the environment of an old-fashioned cranked ice cream maker by placing 2 trays of ice cubes and 1 cup rock salt in the larger bowl, and stirring the soup in the smaller bowl until it has chilled. You must be careful, however, as the ice melts that you do not inadvertently get salty ice water into your soup.

If you have an electric ice cream maker with a metal insert that you keep in the freezer, you can also use the insert to help chill soups. It's far less messy than the ice cube method, but you still have to do quite a bit of stirring to keep the liquid moving.

Gazpacho Verde

ADAPTED FROM STEPHAN PYLES, DALLAS, TEXAS

Here is another great marriage of vegetables and fruits playing off of each other in the same soup. On the fruit side there is creamy avocado and aromatic honeydew melon, and they are balanced by tart green tomatoes, tomatillos, and a few species of chile. It's incredibly refreshing with a complex flavor profile.

Serves 4 to 6

1 poblano chile

2 (3-inch) green tomatoes, cored and diced

2 large tomatillos, husked, rinsed, cored, and diced

1 serrano chile, seeds and ribs removed, diced

1 ripe avocado, peeled, seeded, and diced

1½ cups diced honeydew melon

1 cucumber, peeled, seeded, and diced

¼ cup chopped fresh cilantro

¼ cup chopped fresh parsley

2 to 3 tablespoons freshly squeezed lime juice

Salt and freshly ground black pepper to taste

Light a gas or charcoal grill or preheat the oven broiler. Cut a small slit in the poblano at the stem end to prevent it from exploding. Grill or broil the pepper 6 inches from the heat, turning gently with tongs until it is charred all over. Transfer the pepper to a platter and place an over turned mixing bowl over it. Allow the pepper to steam for 10 to 15 minutes. When the pepper is cool enough to handle, discard the stem, seeds, and ribs and pull off the charred skin. Dice the pepper.

Combine the roasted pepper, green tomatoes, tomatillos, serrano chile, avocado, honeydew melon, cucumber, cilantro, and parsley in a blender or food processor fitted with the steel blade. Purée until smooth; this will have to be done in batches. Stir in the lime juice and season the soup to taste with salt and pepper.

Refrigerate the soup until cold, at least 4 hours but preferably overnight. Adjust the seasoning, if necessary. To serve, ladle into chilled bowls.

NOTE: The soup can be prepared up to 2 days in advance and refrigerated, tightly covered. Stir well before serving.

....

It's now fairly easy to find fresh tomatillos in the produce section. If you must substitute for them, use green tomatoes with 1 tablespoon of freshly squeezed lemon juice per large tomato. Tomatillos have a distinctive citrus note in their tart flavor.

Gazpacho

ADAPTED FROM RESTAURANT NORA, WASHINGTON, DC

When Nora Pouillon arrived in Washington, DC, from her native Austria in the late 1960s, she was horrified by the chemical additives that were part of American foods. Nora was decades ahead of her time in her insistence on organic ingredients, and she created a personal network of farm-to-table sources that has kept her restaurant at the top of the dining hierarchy in the nation's capital since 1979. Her version of gazpacho is thick from its huge ratio of fresh vegetables to tomato juice, and its flavors are bright and sparkling.

Serves 6 to 8

2½ pounds ripe plum tomatoes, peeled, cored, and roughly chopped

¾ cup tomato juice

1 English cucumber, diced

1 large red bell pepper, seeds and ribs removed, chopped

1 large green bell pepper, seeds and ribs removed, chopped

1 medium onion, diced

4 garlic cloves, minced

1 large jalapeño or serrano chile, seeds and ribs removed, chopped

3 tablespoons balsamic vinegar

Salt and freshly ground black pepper to taste

6 to 8 tablespoons extra-virgin olive oil

4 scallions, white parts and 4 inches of green tops, chopped

⅓ cup chopped fresh cilantro

Combine the tomatoes, tomato juice, cucumber, red bell pepper, green bell pepper, onion, garlic, and chile in a food processor fitted with the steel blade or in a blender. Purée until the mixture is very finely chopped and has a coarse texture. This may have to be done in batches. Scrape the mixture into a large mixing bowl, and stir in the balsamic vinegar. Season the soup to taste with salt and pepper.

Refrigerate the soup until cold, at least 4 hours but preferably overnight. Adjust the seasoning if necessary. To serve, ladle into bowls, topping each serving with 1 tablespoon olive oil, scallions, and cilantro.

NOTE: The soup can be prepared up to 2 days in advance and refrigerated, tightly covered. Stir well before serving.

Variation

For a thicker soup, add 1 firmly packed cup of ¾-inch bread cubes to the food processor or blender.

....

A way to preserve the freshness of herbs is to treat them like a bunch of flowers. Give the stems a fresh cut and then stand the bunch upright in a glass of water. You'll find they stay fresh and aromatic days longer, even if kept at room temperature.

White Gazpacho with Smoked Paprika Oil

ADAPTED FROM SWEET LIFE CAFÉ, OAK BLUFFS, MASSACHUSETTS

There are many soups on the menu at this popular Martha's Vineyard restaurant housed in a Victorian mansion, and most of them are chilled because it's only open during the spring and summer. This one is ethereal, with nuances of fruit from the grapes, and a drizzle of bright red oil adds some visual punch.

Serves 6 to 8

6 slices white bread, crusts removed, cubed

2 English cucumbers, peeled, seeded, and diced

2 cups seedless green grapes

2 garlic cloves, sliced

2 tablespoons slivered almonds

1 cup low-fat Greek-style plain yogurt

½ cup sour cream or crème fraîche

2 tablespoons freshly squeezed lemon juice

1 tablespoon granulated sugar

1 teaspoon white wine vinegar

Salt and freshly ground black pepper to taste

Hot red pepper sauce to taste

2 tablespoons smoked Spanish paprika

⅓ cup olive oil

Place the bread cubes in a bowl and toss them with ½ cup water to soften. Set aside.

Purée the cucumbers with ¼ cup of water in a blender or a food processor fitted with the steel blade. Add the soaked bread, grapes, garlic, almonds, yogurt, sour cream, lemon juice, sugar, and vinegar. Purée until smooth and then season to taste with salt, pepper, and hot red pepper sauce. Refrigerate the soup until cold, at least 4 hours but preferably overnight. Adjust the seasoning if necessary.

While the soup chills, prepare the paprika oil. Combine the smoked paprika and oil in a small saucepan and warm it over medium heat until the paprika starts to color. Allow the oil to cool to room temperature and then pour it through a strainer lined with a double layer of cheesecloth.

To serve, ladle the soup into bowls, drizzling each serving with some of the paprika oil.

NOTE: The soup can be prepared up to 2 days in advance and refrigerated, tightly covered. Stir well before serving.

....

Flavored oil in a contrasting color to the soup is a way to dress up any very thick soup, hot or cold. An easy way to use an oil as a soup garnish is to pour it into a squeeze bottle like the kind used for ketchup and mustard. You can then drizzle the surface of the soup with lines or dots.

Sesame Gazpacho

The atmosphere of this restaurant is intentionally that of a dive from the '50s, with pictures of pin-ups covering the walls. But the food at this casual spot is inventive and deftly prepared, including a wide range of soups. This is a cooked version of gazpacho made with a large quantity of aromatic sesame oil.

Serves 6 to 8

⅓ cup olive oil

½ cup Asian sesame oil, divided

1 celery rib, chopped

6 garlic cloves, minced

2 jalapeño or serrano chiles, seeds and ribs removed, chopped

3 tablespoons minced fresh ginger

1 large sweet onion, such as Vidalia or Bermuda, chopped

½ red bell pepper, seeds and ribs removed, chopped

2 pounds ripe plum tomatoes, cored and diced

3 scallions, white parts and 4 inches of green tops, sliced

¾ cup firmly packed fresh cilantro leaves

¼ cup firmly packed fresh parsley leaves

1 (46-ounce) can tomato juice

1 stalk lemongrass, trimmed

Salt and freshly ground black pepper to taste

Heat the olive oil and ¼ cup of the sesame oil in a 4-quart soup pot over medium-high heat. Add the celery, garlic, chiles, and ginger. Cook, stirring frequently, for 3 minutes. Add the onion and red bell pepper, and cook, stirring frequently, for 3 minutes, or until the onion is translucent.

Add the tomatoes, scallions, cilantro, parsley, tomato juice, and lemongrass stalk to the pot. Bring to a boil over high heat, stirring occasionally. Reduce the heat to low, and simmer the soup, uncovered, for 20 minutes. Remove and discard the lemongrass.

Allow the soup to cool for 10 minutes. Purée with an immersion blender, or in a food processor fitted with the steel blade. If using a food processor, you may have to work in batches. Add the remaining sesame oil, and season the soup to taste with salt and pepper. Refrigerate the soup until cold, at least 4 hours but preferably overnight. Adjust the seasoning if necessary.

NOTE: The soup can be prepared up to 2 days in advance and refrigerated, tightly covered. Stir well before serving.

....

While not the juiciest by far, plum tomatoes are frequently specified in recipes because they have the most pulp. That's why they're used for tomato sauce and for soups like this one.

Gazpacho Amarillo

ADAPTED FROM STEPHAN PYLES, DALLAS, TEXAS

Stephan Pyles has been a trailblazer of New Southwestern cooking, one of the first recognized offshoots of New American cuisine for more than twenty-five years. A fifth-generation Texan, he is also the author of five cookbooks. Of the many soups calling themselves gazpacho, this one is perhaps the most sophisticated. The color is vivid, too.

Serves 6 to 8

1½ cups freshly squeezed orange juice

9 large yellow tomatoes, peeled, seeded, and chopped

½ yellow bell pepper, seeds and ribs removed, chopped

½ cup chopped cantaloupe

½ cup chopped papaya

½ cup chopped mango

⅓ cup chopped chayote

1 small cucumber, peeled, seeded, and chopped

8 scallions, white parts only, chopped

3 to 4 serrano chiles, seeded

1 cup Chicken Stock (page 14), Vegetable Stock (page 16), or purchased stock

¼ teaspoon crushed saffron threads

3 tablespoons freshly squeezed lime juice

Salt and freshly ground black pepper to taste

Place the orange juice in a small saucepan over medium-high heat. Bring to a boil, lower the heat to medium, and reduce the juice until only ⅓ cup remains. Set aside.

Combine the tomatoes, bell pepper, cantaloupe, papaya, mango, chayote, cucumber, and scallions in a large mixing bowl. Set aside.

Purée the serrano chiles, stock, and saffron in a blender. Set aside for 10 minutes.

Combine the stock with half the tomato mixture in a blender or a food processor fitted with the steel blade. Purée until smooth. Pour the purée back into the mixing bowl with the remaining tomato mixture and add the reduced orange juice and lime juice. Season the soup to taste with salt and pepper.

Refrigerate the soup until cold, at least 4 hours but preferably overnight. Adjust the seasoning if necessary. To serve, ladle into chilled bowls.

NOTE: The soup can be prepared up to 2 days in advance and refrigerated, tightly covered. Stir well before serving.

. . . .

Chayote, also called mirliton, is a summer squash in the same family as zucchini, and it has become increasingly popular in Southern and Southwestern cooking. But it's difficult to find this squash that resembles a wrinkled green pear in other parts of the country. You can substitute peeled and seeded zucchini for it.

Grape and Avocado Gazpacho

ADAPTED FROM STRAIGHT WHARF RESTAURANT, NANTUCKET, MASSACHUSETTS

Amanda Lydon, who spent summers on Nantucket as a child, was my niece's roommate at Harvard and worked for me doing recipe testing for the summer of 1992. After earning a degree from Le Cordon Bleu, she went on with her partner, Gabriel Frasca, to take over the kitchen at this legendary restaurant. This is one of her signature soups. The pale green gazpacho combines mild cucumbers with sweet grapes and creamy avocado.

Serves 8 to 10

2 garlic cloves, peeled

1 pound green seedless grapes, pulled off the stem

1 ripe avocado, peeled, pitted, and diced

1 shallot, diced

3 large cucumbers, peeled, seeded, and chopped

3 cups white grape juice

¾ cup firmly packed cilantro leaves

2 cups croutons

½ cup white wine vinegar

½ cup extra-virgin olive oil

Salt and freshly ground black pepper to taste

2 cups chopped cucumber, for garnish

Combine the garlic, grapes, avocado, shallot, cucumbers, grape juice, cilantro, and croutons in a food processor fitted with the steel blade or in a blender. Purée until smooth. This may have to be done in batches. Scrape the mixture into a large mixing bowl, and stir in the vinegar and oil. Season the soup to taste with salt and pepper.

Refrigerate the soup until cold, at least 4 hours but preferably overnight. Adjust the seasoning if necessary. To serve, ladle into bowls, topping each serving with chopped cucumber.

NOTE: The soup can be prepared up to 2 days in advance and refrigerated, tightly covered. Stir well before serving.

....

Unlike fruits such as melons that once cut stop ripening, avocados are more user-friendly. If you cut one and it's not quite ripe, coat the cut edges with mayonnaise and put the avocado back together. It will continue to soften at room temperature.

Minted Honeydew Gazpacho

This chilled fruity soup is pale green and luscious, with just a hint of mint. If you use yogurt, it is also an excellent low-calorie diet dish. I take it to the beach, and it's a refreshing start to any meal on a hot summer day.

Serves 6 to 8

1 ripe honeydew melon, peeled, seeded, and diced

3 celery ribs, sliced

1 medium onion, diced

2 cucumbers, peeled, seeded, and diced

1 cup sour cream or plain nonfat yogurt

⅓ cup white wine vinegar

3 tablespoons chopped fresh mint, plus additional mint leaves for garnish

Salt and freshly ground white pepper to taste

Combine the melon, celery, onion, cucumber, sour cream, vinegar, and mint in a food processor fitted with the steel blade or in a blender. Purée until smooth. Season the soup to taste with salt and pepper. Refrigerate until cold, at least 4 hours but preferably overnight. Serve in chilled bowls, garnishing each serving with additional mint leaves.

NOTE: The soup can be prepared up to 2 days in advance and refrigerated, tightly covered. Stir well before serving.

....

Let your senses guide you to a ripe honeydew melon. First look at the rind; it should be a pale greenish yellow. If it's white, the melon may be past its prime, and if it's bright green, it isn't ready. Then look at the end that was attached to the vine. It should be smooth, which means the melon was heavy and ripe when detached. The final test is to sniff that end. What you're after is the sweet fragrance of honeydew, and a strong fragrance at that.

Watermelon Gazpacho

ADAPTED FROM STRAIGHT WHARF RESTAURANT, NANTUCKET, MASSACHUSETTS

There is a large farm on Nantucket that serves as the island's larder for the summer months, and it sets up a truck daily on Main Street. Second only to spying the first fresh corn of the season is spotting Bartlett's Farm's watermelons. I have yet to find melons as sweet and aromatic anywhere else. This vegetable and fruit combo is stunning, and the relish adds a bit of zing.

Serves 6 to 8

3 pounds ripe tomatoes, cored

1 pound seedless watermelon, rinds removed

1 pound cucumbers, peeled and seeded

2 tablespoons olive oil

2 tablespoons sherry vinegar

Salt and freshly ground black pepper to taste

3 scallions, white parts and 4 inches of green tops, thinly sliced

¼ cup chopped fresh cilantro

2 tablespoons freshly squeezed lime juice

¼ cup snipped fresh chives, for garnish

....

For a recipe like this one, if you're using English cucumbers, you don't have to seed them, but you should still peel them. The tone of this soup is blushing pink from the tomatoes and the watermelon, and the green peel from the cucumber makes it appear muddy.

Bring a large pot of water to a boil. Add the tomatoes and blanch them for 30 to 40 seconds, or until the skins loosen. Remove the tomatoes with a slotted spoon, and when cool enough to handle, peel the tomatoes and cut them in half crosswise.

Squeeze the tomatoes over a mixing bowl lined with a coarse sieve; you should collect about 1 cup of juice in the bowl. Coarsely chop enough tomatoes to make 2 cups of pulp, and finely dice the remaining tomatoes. Coarsely chop half of the watermelon and half of the cucumber, and finely dice the remainder.

Purée the coarsely chopped tomatoes, coarsely chopped watermelon, coarsely chopped cucumber, and tomato juice in a food processor fitted with the steel blade.

Transfer the mixture to a large mixing bowl and stir in the finely diced tomatoes, watermelon, and cucumber, along with the olive oil and vinegar. Season the soup to taste with salt and pepper. Refrigerate until cold, at least 4 hours but preferably overnight. Adjust the seasoning if necessary.

Just before serving, combine the scallions, cilantro, and lime juice in a small bowl. Season to taste with salt and pepper.

To serve, ladle the soup into bowls, sprinkling each serving with chives. Pass the scallion relish separately.

NOTE: The soup can be prepared up to 2 days in advance and refrigerated, tightly covered. Stir well before serving. Do not prepare the relish until just prior to serving.

Chilled Cardamom Melon Soup

ADAPTED FROM ROW 14 BISTRO & WINE BAR, DENVER, COLORADO

Cold fruit soups, traditional in many European cuisines, are showing up more regularly on American restaurant menus, too. I really like this one because the real star remains the sweet and aromatic melon. There are just enough other nuances of flavor to add complexity. This is a great soup to start a summer brunch.

Serves 4 to 6

1 ripe honeydew melon

½ cup heavy cream

¾ teaspoon ground cardamom

1 tablespoon freshly squeezed lemon juice

2 teaspoons honey

Salt and freshly ground black pepper to taste

Cut the melon in half, and scrape the seeds into a sieve set over a mixing bowl to catch all the juice that will escape. Peel and dice the melon, reserving ½ cup to use as a garnish.

Purée the melon and melon juice in batches in a blender or a food processor fitted with the steel blade. Combine the purée with the cream, cardamom, lemon juice, and honey. Whisk well. Season the soup to taste with salt and pepper, and chill until very cold. Serve in chilled bowls, garnishing each serving with the reserved melon.

NOTE: The soup can be prepared up to 2 days in advance and refrigerated, tightly covered. Stir well before serving.

....

While cardamom, a member of the ginger family, is native to the tropics, it takes a leading role in Scandinavian baking as well. But it's rarely called for in other recipes and it's rather expensive, so it makes little sense to buy a jar for this soup. While cardamom has a unique aroma and flavor, you can substitute equal parts of ground cinnamon and freshly grated nutmeg successfully.

Strawberry Gazpacho

While the strawberries add sweetness to chef Suzi Maitland's refreshing summer soup, that sweetness is balanced by acidic ingredients and bright flavors. Cooking the vegetables removes any roughness from the flavor and makes this is truly elegant soup.

Serves 6 to 8

2 tablespoons olive oil

3 tablespoons chopped fresh ginger

1 medium sweet onion, such as Vidalia or Bermuda, diced

2 celery ribs, diced

3 scallions, white parts only, sliced

3 tablespoons dry red wine

3 tablespoons freshly squeezed lime juice

1 quart Vegetable Stock (page 16) or purchased stock

½ teaspoon ground ginger

½ teaspoon ground coriander

3 cups sliced fresh strawberries, divided

Salt and freshly ground black pepper to taste

Heat the oil in a 4-quart soup pot over medium-high heat. Add the ginger, onion, and celery. Cook, stirring frequently, for 3 minutes, or until the onion is translucent. Add the scallions and cook for 2 minutes. Add the wine and lime juice and cook for 2 minutes, or until the liquids have almost evaporated.

Add the stock, ginger, and coriander, and bring to a boil over medium-high heat. Reduce the heat to low and simmer, uncovered, for 10 minutes, or until the vegetables are tender. Add 2½ cups of the strawberries and stir well. Remove the pot from the heat.

Allow the soup to cool for 10 minutes. Purée with an immersion blender or in a food processor fitted with the steel blade. If using a food processor, you may need to work in batches. Season to taste with salt and pepper. Refrigerate until cold, at least 4 hours but preferably overnight. Adjust the seasoning, if necessary.

To serve, ladle the soup into bowls, topping each serving with some of the remaining strawberry slices.

NOTE: The soup can be prepared up to 2 days in advance and refrigerated, tightly covered. Stir well before serving.

....

When you're selecting fresh ginger, look for large lobes with taut skin. Don't buy a chunk of this rhizome if the skin is shriveled or if it has a number of small projections, which you will trim off because they're too much bother to peel. Many supermarkets offer huge pieces of ginger in the produce section, but you can break off the amount you need.

Corn Zupetta with Lobster and Buffalo Mozzarella

ADAPTED FROM OSTERIA, PHILADELPHIA, PENNSYLVANIA

Both lobster and corn are inherently sweet, so it is a natural to join their flavors in a soup, as chef Jeff Michaud has done here. If the garnish of lobster, tomatoes, and mozzarella is increased, this starter soup can become a light lunch. Serve it with Focaccia (page 214).

Serves 6 to 8

SOUP

3 tablespoons unsalted butter

1 small onion, diced

1 garlic clove, minced

1 quart Corn Stock (page 19)

2 cups Lobster or Shrimp Stock (page 17) or purchased stock

3 cups fresh corn kernels (or substitute frozen corn kernels, thawed)

1 bay leaf

½ cup heavy cream

Salt and freshly ground black pepper to taste

GARNISH

¼ pound cooked lobster meat, diced

2 ripe plum tomatoes, cored, seeded, and chopped

2 ounces fresh buffalo mozzarella, diced

2 teaspoons chopped fresh chervil

2 teaspoons chopped fresh tarragon

2 teaspoons snipped fresh chives

2 tablespoons freshly squeezed lemon juice

Salt and freshly ground black pepper to taste

⅓ cup olive oil

Melt the butter in a 4-quart soup pot over medium heat. Add the onion and garlic, and cook, stirring frequently, for 3 minutes, or until the onion is translucent. Add the corn stock, lobster or shrimp stock, corn, and bay leaf. Bring to a boil over medium heat, reduce the heat to low, and simmer the soup, uncovered, for 15 minutes. Remove and discard the bay leaf, and stir in the cream.

Allow the soup to cool for 10 minutes. Purée with an immersion blender, or in a food processor fitted with the steel blade. If using a food processor, you may have to work in batches. Season to taste with salt and pepper. Refrigerate the soup until cold, at least 4 hours but preferably overnight. Adjust the seasoning if necessary.

While the soup chills, prepare the garnish. Combine the lobster, tomatoes, mozzarella, chervil, tarragon, and chives in a small bowl. Toss gently to combine. Combine the lemon juice and salt and pepper in a jar with a tight-fitting lid. Shake well, add the olive oil, and shake well again. Combine half of the dressing with the lobster mixture. To serve, ladle the chilled soup into chilled shallow bowls, and place some of the lobster mixture in the center. Drizzle the remaining dressing around the lobster.

NOTE: The soup can be prepared up to 2 days in advance and refrigerated, tightly covered. Stir well before serving. Do not make the garnish until just prior to serving.

Variation

Substitute diced shrimp or morsels of crab for the lobster.

Buffalo mozzarella, called *mozzarella di bufala* in Italian, is made from the milk of domestic water buffalo, which makes the cheeses higher in calcium, higher in protein, and lower in cholesterol than cow's milk cheese. Buffalo mozzarella from the Campania region bears the "Mozzarella di Bufala Campana" trademark and it was granted DOC status in 1993. This mozzarella is a snowy-white fresh, soft cheese with a mild flavor.

Cream of Watercress Soup

Fannie Merritt Farmer included cream of watercress soup in the 1918 edition of her cookbook, and by World War II it was a staple of ladies' luncheons and formal dinner parties alike. To update the concept, I've added a bit of fresh ginger to my version, which serves as a perfect foil to the peppery watercress.

Serves 6 to 8

3 tablespoons unsalted butter

2 leeks, white and light green parts only, thinly sliced and rinsed well

1 medium russet potato, peeled and chopped

3 cups Chicken Stock (page 14), Vegetable Stock (page 16), or purchased stock

2 tablespoons grated fresh ginger

1½ cups heavy cream

6 cups firmly packed fresh watercress

Salt and freshly ground white pepper to taste

⅓ cup crème fraîche, for garnish

Additional watercress leaves, for garnish

Heat the butter in a 4-quart soup pot over medium-high heat. Add the leeks and cook, stirring frequently, for 3 minutes, or until the leeks are translucent. Add the potato, stock, and ginger, and bring to a boil. Reduce the heat to low and simmer the soup, partially covered, for 15 minutes. Add the cream and watercress, and simmer for an additional 5 minutes, or until the vegetables are very tender.

Allow the soup to cool for 10 minutes. Purée with an immersion blender or in a food processor fitted with the steel blade. If using a food processor, you may have to work in batches. Season to taste with salt and pepper.

Refrigerate the soup until cold, at least 4 hours but preferably overnight. Adjust the seasoning if necessary. To serve, ladle the soup into bowls, topping each serving with crème fraîche and additional watercress leaves.

NOTE: The soup can be prepared up to 2 days in advance and refrigerated, tightly covered. Stir well before serving.

Variation

For a more complex flavor profile, substitute 3 cups of firmly packed fresh arugula leaves for 3 cups of the watercress.

....

Watercress has been elevated to the pantheon of superfoods in the past decade, according to work published in the *American Journal of Clinical Nutrition*. This plant that grows in wet areas has a high amount of antioxidants and reduced levels of DNA damage to blood cells, which potentially lowers the risk for cancer. A cup, which is only 4 calories, also contains a day's worth of vitamin K, necessary for blood clotting.

Fresh Pea Soup with Tarragon

Serving a cold soup made from fresh peas is an English tradition, but I like anise-scented tarragon better than the traditional mint. Unless you have fresh peas growing in your garden in the spring, I suggest using frozen peas for all dishes, especially this delicate soup. They have a far better flavor than those from the supermarket.

Serves 8 to 10

4 tablespoons (½ stick) unsalted butter

1 large onion, chopped

6 cups Chicken Stock (page 14), Vegetable Stock (page 16), or purchased stock

1¼ pounds russet potatoes, peeled and diced

3 (10-ounce) packages frozen peas, thawed

2 tablespoons chopped fresh parsley

2 tablespoons chopped fresh tarragon (or substitute 1 tablespoon dried)

1½ cups half-and-half

Salt and freshly ground black pepper to taste

¾ cup crème fraîche (or substitute sour cream)

Heat the butter in a 4-quart soup pot over medium-high heat. Add the onion and cook, stirring frequently, for 3 minutes, or until the onion is translucent.

Add the stock, potatoes, peas, parsley, and tarragon to the pot, and bring to a boil over high heat, stirring occasionally. Reduce the heat to low, and simmer, covered, for 15 to 20 minutes, or until the potatoes are very tender.

Allow the soup to cool for 10 minutes. Purée with an immersion blender or in a food processor fitted with the steel blade. If using a food processor, you may have to work in batches. Stir in the half-and-half, and season the soup to taste with salt and pepper.

Refrigerate the soup until cold, at least 4 hours but preferably overnight. Adjust the seasoning if necessary. To serve, ladle into bowls, topping each serving with crème fraîche.

NOTE: The soup can be prepared up to 2 days in advance and refrigerated, tightly covered. Stir well before serving.

Variation

Substitute ¼ cup firmly packed fresh mint leaves for the tarragon.

....

Cold foods, especially creamed soups, frequently need additional salt once chilled. The butterfat in the soup coats the taste buds, so more salt is needed for the flavors to emerge. That's why you should always taste a chilled soup before serving it. What might have seemed like the proper amount of seasoning when the soup was hot might not be enough once it chills.

Squash Blossom Soup

There are many recipes for stuffed squash blossoms in Italian cuisine. Chef Randy Evans uses the flowers' bright orange color and delicate flavor in this chilled soup, thickened with potato and flecked with mellow poblano chile, zucchini, and corn.

Serves 6 to 8

2 tablespoons unsalted butter

1 large sweet white onion, such as Vidalia or Bermuda, chopped

1 quart Vegetable Stock (page 16) or purchased stock

1 small russet potato, peeled and chopped

2 poblano chiles

25 large (3- to 4-inch) squash blossoms

1 cup whole milk

1 medium zucchini, cut into ¼-inch dice

1 large ear of corn, husked, kernels cut from the cob

½ cup crème fraîche

Salt and freshly ground white pepper to taste

....

All species of squash have edible blossoms that you can eat raw or cooked. Only pick male blossoms (female blossoms are the fruit producers) unless you want to reduce production. Male blossoms are easily distinguished from the female blossoms. The stem of the male blossom is thin and trim, while the stem of the female blossom is very thick. At the base of the female flower below the petals is where the squash is developing.

NOTE: The soup can be prepared up to 2 days in advance and refrigerated, tightly covered. Stir well before serving.

Heat the butter in a 4-quart soup pot over medium heat. Add the onion and cook, stirring frequently, until slightly browned, about 5 minutes. Remove half of the onion and set aside. Add the stock and potato to the pot and bring to a boil over medium-high heat. Reduce the heat to low, and simmer, partially covered, for 20 minutes.

While the soup simmers, prepare the chiles and squash blossoms. Light a gas or charcoal grill or preheat the oven broiler. Cut a small slit in the stem end of each pepper to prevent them from exploding. Grill or broil the peppers 6 inches from the heat, turning them gently with tongs until they are charred all over. Transfer the peppers to a platter and cover with an overturned mixing bowl. Allow the peppers to steam for 10 to 15 minutes. When the peppers are cool enough to handle, discard the stems, seeds, and ribs; pull off the charred skin. Chop the peppers and set aside.

Break off the stems of the squash blossoms, and then the little green sepals that come out from the base of the blossoms. Use your fingers to break loose the long pistil in the center of each flower and discard. With a very sharp knife, cut the blossoms crosswise into ¼-inch strips, including the bulbous base. Add half the blossoms to the broth and simmer 3 minutes.

Allow the soup to cool for 10 minutes. Purée with an immersion blender, or in a food processor fitted with the steel blade. If using a food processor, you may have to work in batches.

Add the peppers to the soup along with the milk and reserved onion. Bring to a simmer over medium heat and cook for 10 minutes. Add the zucchini and corn and simmer for 3 minutes, then add the remaining squash blossoms and simmer for 3 minutes longer. Stir in the crème fraîche, and season the soup to taste with salt and pepper. Refrigerate the soup until cold, at least 4 hours but preferably overnight. Adjust the seasoning if necessary.

Ukrainian Sorrel Soup (Schav)

This refreshing soup is made with sorrel and scallions, both of which are plentiful in the northern climates of Russia and Ukraine in the spring. It's sometimes called green borscht, and garnishing it with hard-cooked eggs and sour cream is traditional.

Serves 6 to 8

2 tablespoons unsalted butter

1 pound fresh sorrel leaves, stemmed

1 bunch scallions, white parts and 4 inches of green tops, sliced

6 cups Vegetable Stock (page 16), Chicken Stock (page 14), or purchased stock

1 tablespoon chopped fresh tarragon

2 tablespoons granulated sugar

3 tablespoons freshly squeezed lemon juice

2 large egg yolks

Salt and freshly ground black pepper to taste

3 to 4 diced hard-cooked eggs, for garnish

½ cup sour cream, for garnish

¼ cup chopped fresh dill, for garnish

Heat the butter in a 4-quart soup pot over medium heat. Add the sorrel and scallions and cook, stirring frequently, for 5 minutes, or until the sorrel wilts. Add the stock and tarragon and bring to a boil over medium-high heat. Reduce the heat to low and simmer, uncovered, for 20 minutes. Stir the sugar and lemon juice into the soup.

Beat the egg yolks in a mixing bowl with a whisk until thick and light yellow in color. Slowly beat about 1 cup of the hot soup into the egg yolks so they are gradually warmed up, and then return the egg and soup mixture to the pot. Place the pot over medium-low heat, and stir constantly, reaching all parts of the bottom of the pot, until the mixture reaches about 170°F on an instant-read thermometer; at this point it will begin to steam and thicken slightly. Do not allow the mixture to boil or the eggs will scramble. Season to taste with salt and pepper.

Refrigerate the soup until cold, at least 4 hours but preferably overnight. Adjust the seasoning if necessary. To serve, ladle into bowls, topping each serving with diced eggs, sour cream, and dill.

NOTE: The soup can be prepared up to 2 days in advance and refrigerated, tightly covered. Stir well before serving.

Sorrel is an herb, although we cook with it as if it were a green like arugula. While it's sometimes eaten raw, most often it's puréed into a soup or a sauce for fish or eggs. Sorrel has a somewhat sour flavor, and it can be difficult to find in some parts of the country. You can always substitute arugula or spinach; add a few tablespoons of fresh lemon juice to replicate the sourness.

Cold Beet Borscht

Beets have been experiencing a real renaissance in popularity this decade, and cold borscht is now popular anew. While the soup is slowly simmered, the fresh garnishes add flavor and textural interest to this classic of Eastern European soups.

Serves 6 to 8

SOUP

3 tablespoons unsalted butter

2 pounds beets, peeled and julienned

2 carrots, julienned

3 celery ribs, julienned

1 medium red onion, quartered and thinly sliced

2 garlic cloves, minced

1 bay leaf

2 whole cloves

5 whole peppercorns

8 cups Vegetable Stock (page 16), Chicken Stock (page 14), or purchased stock

Salt and freshly ground black pepper to taste

GARNISHES

1 large cooked Yukon Gold potato, peeled and cut into ½-inch dice

1 cucumber, peeled, seeded, and cut into ½-inch dice

4 scallions, white parts and 4 inches of green tops, thinly sliced

3 large hard-cooked eggs, diced

¼ cup chopped fresh dill

¼ cup snipped fresh chives

¾ cup sour cream or crème fraîche

Melt the butter in a 4-quart soup pot over medium heat. Add the beets, carrots, celery, onion, and garlic. Cook, stirring frequently, for 3 minutes, or until the onion is translucent. Place the bay leaf, cloves, and peppercorns in a tea infuser or wrap them in cheesecloth. Add the sachet and stock to the pot, and bring to a boil over medium-high heat, stirring occasionally.

Reduce the heat to low and simmer the soup, partially covered, for 45 minutes, or until the vegetables are tender but not mushy. Remove and discard the spice sachet, and season the soup to taste with salt and pepper.

Refrigerate the soup until cold, at least 4 hours but preferably overnight. Adjust the seasoning if necessary. Make sure all the garnishes are also well chilled.

To serve, ladle the soup into bowls, topping each serving with cubes of potato, cucumber, scallion, eggs, dill, chives, and sour cream.

NOTE: The soup can be prepared up to 2 days in advance and refrigerated, tightly covered. Stir well before serving.

....

Few people use leaf tea today; most of us use handy pre-measured tea bags. But a mesh tea infuser is still a handy item to keep around. I use them constantly to enclose spices that will need removal after a dish has finished cooking. Unlike cheesecloth, the tea infuser keeps the spices contained with no fear of falling apart.

Walla Walla Onion Soup with Tarragon Yogurt

ADAPTED FROM GIRL & THE GOAT, CHICAGO, ILINOIS

Chef Stephanie Izard, a winner on Bravo's *Top Chef* series and recipient of the James Beard Award in 2013 for Best Chef in the Great Lakes Region, named her restaurant for her last name. Izard is a species of goat native to the Pyrenees mountains. This soup enhances the sweetness of the onions with sweet white dessert wine, and then sharp Greek yogurt mixed with anise-flavored tarragon is added.

Serves 6 to 8

SOUP

2 tablespoons unsalted butter

1 tablespoon olive oil

3½ pounds Walla Walla, Vidalia, or Bermuda onions, thinly sliced

2 garlic cloves, minced

Salt and freshly ground black pepper to taste

1 cup sweet late-harvest white wine, such as Loupiac, Sauternes, or late-harvest Riesling

6 cups Vegetable Stock (page 16) or purchased stock

TOPPING

¾ cup plain Greek-style yogurt

3 tablespoons chopped fresh tarragon

2 tablespoons heavy cream

Heat the butter and oil in a 4-quart soup pot over medium heat. Add the onions and garlic, and toss to coat them evenly with the butter mixture. Cover the pot and cook, stirring occasionally, for 20 minutes, or until the onions have softened. Season the vegetables to taste with salt and pepper.

Add the wine to the pot, bring to a boil, and cook over medium-high heat for 5 minutes. Add the stock, and bring back to a boil. Lower the heat to medium-low and simmer, partially covered, for 20 minutes, or until reduced by one-fourth.

Allow the soup to cool for 10 minutes. Purée with an immersion blender, or in a food processor fitted with the steel blade. If using a food processor, you may have to work in batches. Season to taste with salt and pepper. Refrigerate the soup until cold, at least 4 hours but preferably overnight. Adjust the seasoning, if necessary.

While the soup chills, combine the yogurt, tarragon, and cream in a small bowl and stir well. Refrigerate until ready to use. To serve, ladle the soup into bowls, topping each serving with some of the yogurt mixture.

NOTE: The soup and the topping can be prepared up to 2 days in advance and refrigerated, tightly covered. Stir well before serving.

The grapes picked for late-harvest dessert wines are the last of the growing season. The sugars concentrate as the grapes ripen on the vine, sometimes with the help of the fungus botrytis, the so-called noble rot that creates the lushness of the wines from Sauternes in Bordeaux. For cooking, it's not necessary to spring for an expensive wine; save those to accompany dessert. Italian Vin Santo and French Loupiac are far less expensive and work well for cooked dishes.

Roasted Garlic Vichyssoise

Despite the French name, vichyssoise is actually an American invention. This chilled leek and potato soup was created by Chef Louis Diat during his tenure in the early-twentieth century at the Ritz-Carlton Hotel in New York. Diat named the soup after Vichy, the resort town near his boyhood home in France. The combination of delicate leeks and onions with creamy potatoes can't be beat, except by adding the nutty sweetness of roasted garlic.

Serves 6 to 8

2 heads fresh garlic

1 tablespoon olive oil

3 tablespoons unsalted butter

6 leeks, white parts only, chopped and rinsed well

2 pounds russet potatoes, peeled and diced

7 cups Chicken Stock (page 14) or purchased stock

1 cup heavy cream

Salt and freshly ground white pepper to taste

¼ cup snipped fresh chives, for garnish

....

You can substitute finely chopped green scallion tops for chives in any recipe. It's rare that you ever use a whole scallion, so the greens frequently go to waste.

Preheat the oven to 350°F. Cut 1 inch off the top of each garlic head, and rub the heads with the olive oil. Wrap them tightly in heavy-duty aluminum foil, and place them on a baking sheet. Roast the garlic for 45 minutes, or until tender. When cool enough to handle, break the heads apart into cloves and press the flesh out of the cloves. Set aside.

While the garlic bakes, melt the butter in a 4-quart soup pot over medium heat. Add the leeks and cook, stirring frequently, for 5 minutes, or until the leeks are translucent. Add the potatoes and stock, and bring to a boil over high heat. Reduce the heat to low, and simmer, partially covered, for 25 minutes, or until the potatoes are tender. Stir in the roasted garlic and the cream, and simmer 5 minutes.

Allow the soup to cool for 10 minutes. Purée with an immersion blender, or in a food processor fitted with the steel blade. If using a food processor, you may have to work in batches. Season to taste with salt and pepper. Refrigerate the soup until cold, at least 4 hours but preferably overnight. Adjust the seasoning if necessary. To serve, ladle the soup into bowls, topping each serving with some chopped chives.

NOTE: The soup can be prepared up to 2 days in advance and refrigerated, tightly covered. Stir well before serving.

Variations:

• Omit the garlic for a classic vichyssoise.

• Omit the cream, and increase the chicken stock by ¾ cup. Instead of puréeing the soup, mash some of it with a potato masher and serve it hot.

Dilled Cream of Cucumber Soup

Aromatic, fresh-tasting dill is the perfect accent for the delicate cucumber in this classic creamed summer soup. It's really essential to use fresh dill to achieve the right flavor balance. Serve some Popovers (page 230) on the side.

Serves 6 to 8

5 tablespoons unsalted butter, divided

3 English cucumbers, sliced

½ cup chopped fresh dill

5 cups Chicken Stock (page 14), Vegetable Stock (page 16), or purchased stock

¼ cup all-purpose flour

1½ cups half-and-half, heated

Salt and freshly ground black pepper to taste

Fresh dill sprigs, for garnish

....

English cucumbers, sometimes called hothouse cucumbers, are always wrapped in plastic in supermarkets. They're about twice the length of a traditional cucumber. Their true benefit to cooks is that the seeds are small and tender so they do not need seeding. If you're substituting conventional cucumbers, you should remove the seeds and also peel them, because the peel is most likely waxed.

Melt 2 tablespoons of the butter in a 4-quart soup pot over medium heat. Add the cucumbers and dill. Cook, stirring occasionally, for 5 minutes, or until the cucumbers become translucent and begin to soften.

Add the stock, and bring to a boil over high heat. Reduce the heat to low, and simmer, partially covered, for 15 to 20 minutes, or until the cucumbers are soft.

While the soup simmers, melt the remaining butter in a small saucepan over low heat. Stir in the flour and cook, stirring constantly, for 1 minute, or until the mixture turns slightly beige, is bubbly, and appears to have grown in volume. Increase the heat to medium, and slowly whisk in the half-and-half. Bring to a boil, whisking frequently. Add the mixture to the soup, and simmer for 2 minutes.

Allow the soup to cool for 10 minutes. Purée with an immersion blender, or in a food processor fitted with the steel blade. If using a food processor, you may have to work in batches. Season to taste with salt and pepper.

Refrigerate the soup until cold, at least 4 hours but preferably overnight. Adjust the seasoning if necessary. To serve, ladle the soup into bowls, topping each serving with some of the remaining dill.

NOTE: The soup can be prepared up to 2 days in advance and refrigerated, tightly covered. Stir well before serving.

4 *Vegetable Soups*

What distinguishes these soups from the ones in Chapter 2 is that these can indeed become a full meal rather than just a starter of a multi-course meal. While this group contains some puréed soups, most of the dishes are for broths with lots of vibrantly colored vegetables floating in them.

Many of us are working consciously to include more vegetables in our daily diets, and soups are a wonderful way to do it. You'll notice that because these are vegetarian soups, the first option given is for vegetable stock, but if you're not a strict vegetarian, feel free to use chicken stock. I think it gives soups a depth of flavor not found in a stock in which only vegetables simmered. And do keep in mind that, while these soups are vegetarian, many of them are not vegan, as they include dairy products and the occasional egg.

Rules for Reheating

You have to be careful when reheating a soup with fresh vegetables that it's only heated until hot and doesn't come back to a boil. Especially green vegetables, like green beans or garden peas, suffer tremendously from being simmered again. They turn an unappealing olive green and become mushy in texture. Also, remember that vegetable soups should always be reheated uncovered.

Vegetable Soup with Poached Eggs

This soup is based on a common vegetarian soup from the region around Bra in Italy. Adding a poached egg enriches the broth and makes it into a true meal. Serve this with a crusty loaf of Garlic and Cheese Bread (page 224).

Serves 6 to 8

2 tablespoons olive oil

1 large onion, diced

2 celery ribs, diced

1 carrot, diced

2 garlic cloves, minced

2 quarts Vegetable Stock (page 16), Chicken Stock (page 14), or purchased stock

3 tablespoons chopped fresh parsley

2 tablespoons chopped fresh oregano

2 tablespoons chopped fresh basil

2 teaspoons fresh thyme leaves

1 bay leaf

2 tablespoons tomato paste

3 medium redskin potatoes, diced

1 (4-inch) Parmesan rind (optional)

1 pound small zucchini, diced

2 tablespoons distilled white vinegar

6 to 8 large eggs

Salt and freshly ground black pepper to taste

....

Store eggs in the carton they come in to help prevent moisture loss and to keep the eggs from picking up other odors. Never rinse eggs until you're about to use them; water makes the shells porous and can cause the eggs to spoil faster and allow bacteria to enter.

Heat the oil in a 4-quart soup pot over medium-high heat. Add the onion, celery, carrot, and garlic. Cook, stirring frequently, for 3 minutes, or until the onion is translucent.

Stir in the stock, parsley, oregano, basil, thyme, bay leaf, tomato paste, potatoes, and Parmesan rind, if using. Bring to a boil over medium-high heat, then reduce the heat to low and simmer, covered, for 15 minutes, or until the vegetables are almost tender. Add the zucchini and simmer for an additional 10 to 12 minutes, or until the zucchini is tender.

While the soup simmers, prepare the poached eggs. Bring 3 inches of water and the vinegar to a boil in a deep 10-inch skillet. Reduce the heat so that the water barely simmers. Break cold eggs, one at a time, into a custard cup or saucer. Holding the cup close to the water's surface, slip the egg into the simmering water. Repeat with the rest of the eggs, adding them quickly so they will all cook in about the same time. Cook the eggs for 3 to 5 minutes, depending on desired doneness, keeping the water just barely simmering. Remove the eggs with a slotted spoon in the order you added them. Dip each in a bowl of cold salted water for 10 seconds to remove the vinegar and stop the cooking. Place the eggs gently onto a kitchen towel to drain, and trim off any loose whites.

Remove and discard the bay leaf and Parmesan rind, if used. Season the soup to taste with salt and pepper, and serve immediately. To serve, ladle into shallow bowls and top each serving with a poached egg.

NOTE: The soup can be prepared up to 2 days in advance and refrigerated, tightly covered. Reheat over low heat, stirring occasionally. Do not poach the eggs until just prior to serving.

Fideo Soup

This soup is a Mexican version of noodle soup; it's made with a thin pasta that is browned in oil before it is cooked, which adds a toasty note to this chile and tomato broth. It's garnished with an avocado, and if it is accompanied by a tossed salad, it could complete your meal.

Serves 6 to 8

½ cup olive oil

12 ounces fideo, vermicelli, or angel hair pasta, broken into 1-inch lengths

3 to 4 dried chipotle chiles, stemmed and seeded

2 pounds ripe plum tomatoes, cored and diced

8 garlic cloves, peeled

1 large onion, roughly chopped

2 teaspoons salt

6 cups Vegetable Stock (page 16), Chicken Stock (page 14), or purchased stock

Salt and freshly ground black pepper to taste

1 ripe avocado, peeled, seeded, and sliced, for garnish

½ cup chopped fresh cilantro, for garnish

Heat the olive oil in a 4-quart soup pot over medium-low heat. Cook the pasta, stirring frequently, for 5 to 7 minutes, or until golden brown. Watch carefully so that the pasta does not burn. Add the chiles and cook 2 minutes longer.

Combine the tomatoes, garlic, onion, salt, and ½ cup water in a blender. Purée until smooth.

Add the tomato purée and stock to the pot with the browned pasta. Cook over medium-low heat for 15 minutes, or until the noodles soften. Remove and discard the chiles, and season the soup to taste with salt and pepper. Serve immediately, garnishing each serving with avocado and cilantro.

NOTE: The soup can be prepared up to 2 days in advance and refrigerated, tightly covered. Reheat over low heat, stirring occasionally. Do not prepare the garnish until just prior to serving.

....

While battles rage over whether pasta was created in Italy or China, at some point in the seventeenth century it reached Spain and from there traveled to Central and South America. The most common form of pasta in Hispanic cultures is fideos, tightly woven coils resembling birds' nests. You should be able to find them with the Hispanic ingredients at the supermarket; if not, you can substitute thin spaghetti or angel hair pasta.

Tomato and Bread Soup *(Pappa al Pomodoro)*

ADAPTED FROM RESTAURANT NORA, WASHINGTON, DC

What I love about Nora Pouillon's version of this Tuscan dish is that she keeps its rustic character. She doesn't peel the tomatoes nor does she strain away the seeds. It's a straightforward and delicious recipe that's really quick to make, too. There's bread in the soup, so just serve a tossed salad on the side.

Serves 6 to 8

2 pounds ripe tomatoes, cored and coarsely chopped

4 cups Vegetable Stock (page 16), Chicken Stock (page 14), or purchased stock

¼ cup olive oil

3 garlic cloves, minced

5 cups firmly packed day-old country bread, diced

½ cup firmly packed fresh sliced basil

Salt and freshly ground black pepper to taste

Freshly grated Parmesan cheese, for garnish

Combine the tomatoes and stock in a 4-quart soup pot. Cook over medium-high heat, stirring occasionally, for 15 minutes, or until the tomatoes break down.

Heat the oil in a small skillet over medium-low heat. Add the garlic and cook, stirring frequently, for 30 to 45 seconds, or until the garlic begins to brown.

Stir the garlic and bread cubes into the soup and cook over medium-low heat, uncovered and stirring occasionally, for 10 minutes, or until the bread falls apart.

Stir in the basil and season the soup to taste with salt and pepper. Serve immediately, passing the Parmesan separately at the table.

NOTE: The soup can be prepared up to 2 days in advance and refrigerated, tightly covered. Reheat over low heat, stirring occasionally. Add stock or water if the soup needs thinning after reheating.

Variations

- Add 1 tablespoon grated orange zest along with the garlic.
- Substitute crushed red pepper flakes for the black pepper.

Don't be stingy with the salt in this dish. There's a large amount of very bland bread serving as the thickening agent and unless you salt the soup sufficiently the wonderful ripe tomato flavor won't sing in your mouth.

Provençal Vegetable Soup with Pistou

This soup is the Provençal version of Italian minestrone. It's enriched with a garlicky basil *pistou*, which is a sauce similar to Italian pesto but made without pine nuts. This soup is a great winter dish because it's made with dried *herbes de Provence* rather than a panoply of fresh herbs. Socca (page 232), made with garbanzo bean flour, is a great bread to serve alongside.

Serves 4 to 6

SOUP

1 cup dried cannellini or navy beans

3 tablespoons olive oil

1 large onion, diced

2 leeks, white parts only, thinly sliced and rinsed well

6 garlic cloves, minced

8 cups Vegetable Stock (page 16), Chicken Stock (page 14), or purchased stock

1 large carrot, diced

½ fresh fennel bulb, diced

1 celery rib, diced

1 (14.5-ounce) can petite diced tomatoes, undrained

3 tablespoons chopped fresh parsley

1 tablespoon *herbes de Provence*

1 bay leaf

1 cup ditalini

¼ pound green beans, trimmed, cut into ¾-inch pieces

1 small zucchini, diced

1 small yellow squash, diced

Salt and freshly ground black pepper to taste

PISTOU

3 garlic cloves, peeled

3 cups firmly packed fresh basil leaves

⅓ cup olive oil

¾ cup grated Parmesan cheese

Salt and freshly ground black pepper to taste

Rinse the beans in a colander and place them in a mixing bowl. Cover with cold, salted water and allow beans to soak overnight. Alternatively, place the beans into a saucepan of salted water and bring to a boil over high heat. Boil 1 minute. Turn off the heat, cover the pan, and soak the beans for 1 hour. With either soaking method, drain the beans, discard the soaking water, and cook or refrigerate the beans immediately.

Cover the beans with cold water and bring to a boil over medium-high heat. Reduce the heat to low and simmer, covered, for 30 minutes, or until cooked but still slightly crunchy. Drain and set aside.

Heat the oil in a 4-quart soup pot over medium-high heat. Add the onion, leeks, and garlic. Cook, stirring frequently, for 3 minutes, or until the onion is translucent. Add the cooked beans, stock, carrot, fennel, celery, tomatoes, parsley, herbes de Provence, and bay leaf. Bring to a boil, then reduce the heat to low and simmer the soup, uncovered, for 15 minutes.

While the soup simmers, bring a small pot of salted water to a boil over high heat. Cook the ditalini according to package directions until al dente. Drain and set aside.

Add the green beans, zucchini, and yellow squash to the soup pot and simmer for an additional 10 to 12 minutes, or until the vegetables are tender. Remove and discard the bay leaf, stir in the cooked pasta, and season the soup to taste with salt and pepper.

While the soup simmers, make the pistou. Combine the garlic and basil in a food processor fitted with the steel blade and chop it finely using on-and-off pulsing. Slowly add the olive oil and purée until smooth. Add the cheese and blend well. Season to taste with salt and pepper.

To serve, ladle the soup into low bowls and place 1 tablespoon of pistou in the center. Pass the remaining pistou separately.

NOTE: The soup can be prepared up to 2 days in advance and refrigerated, tightly covered. Reheat over low heat, stirring occasionally. The pistou can be prepared up to 1 day in advance and refrigerated. Press a sheet of plastic wrap directly into the surface to prevent discoloration.

Variation

If you want to make this soup in a hurry, substitute 1 (15-ounce) can of cannellini beans or garbanzo beans, drained and rinsed, for the dried beans.

....

Herbes de Provence, found in the spice section of many supermarkets and gourmet stores, is a dried blend of many herbs associated with the sunny cuisine of that region, including basil, thyme, fennel, rosemary, sage, and marjoram.

Southwestern Vegetable Soup

The chiles and aromatic spices enliven your taste buds when eating this soup. There's a richness to it that comes from mashing some of the potatoes to provide a thicker texture than a clear broth soup. Serve it with a jicama salad and some heated flour or corn tortillas.

Serves 4 to 6

3 tablespoons olive oil

1 large onion, diced

1 small poblano chile, seeds and ribs removed, chopped

2 garlic cloves, minced

1 jalapeño or serrano chile, seeds and ribs removed, finely chopped

1 tablespoon smoked Spanish paprika

2 teaspoons ground cumin

1 teaspoon dried oregano

5 cups Vegetable Stock (page 16), Chicken Stock (page 14), or purchased stock

¾ pound redskin potatoes, cut into 1-inch cubes

1 large carrot, diced

2 celery ribs, thinly sliced

1 (15-ounce) can red kidney beans, drained and rinsed

1 cup fresh corn kernels or frozen corn, thawed

¼ cup chopped fresh cilantro

Salt and freshly ground black pepper to taste

Lime wedges for garnish

Heat the oil in a 4-quart soup pot over high heat. Add the onion, poblano chile, garlic, and jalapeño chile. Cook, stirring frequently, for 3 minutes, or until the onion is translucent. Add the paprika, cumin, and oregano, and cook for 1 minute, stirring constantly.

Stir in the stock, and add the potatoes, carrot, and celery. Bring to a boil over high heat, then reduce the heat to low, cover the pot, and cook for 12 to 15 minutes, or until potatoes are tender.

Coarsely mash some of the potatoes with a potato masher. Stir in the beans, corn, and cilantro. Bring back to a boil and simmer, covered, for 3 minutes. Season the soup to taste with salt and pepper, and serve immediately, garnishing each serving with lime wedges.

NOTE: The soup can be prepared up to 2 days in advance and refrigerated, tightly covered. Reheat over low heat, covered, until hot, stirring occasionally.

Variation

Substitute sweet potatoes for the redskin potatoes, and omit the hot chile for a milder soup.

....

It's common to see jalapeño and serrano chiles given as recipe options in the same quantity, even though serrano peppers are much smaller. They are also much hotter, so the larger jalapeño and the smaller serrano produce the same amount of heat.

Onion Soup Gratinée

ADAPTED FROM AVILA MEDITERRANEAN CUISINE, BOSTON, MASSACHUSETTS

Chef Rodney Murillo developed this version of onion soup at this recently closed restaurant in Boston's theater district. It combines sweet onions with shallots and leeks, so the flavor is more complex than the classic French version of this perennial favorite. It has the bread and cheese on top, however, which makes it a complete meal.

Serves 6 to 8

6 tablespoons (¾ stick) unsalted butter

2 large sweet onions, such as Vidalia or Bermuda, diced

½ pound shallots, thinly sliced

3 leeks, white parts only, halved lengthwise, thinly sliced, and rinsed well

2 teaspoons granulated sugar

Salt and freshly ground black pepper, divided

¼ cup all-purpose flour

6 cups Beef Stock (page 15) or purchased stock, heated

1 quart Chicken Stock (page 14) or purchased stock, heated

2 tablespoons fresh thyme leaves

2 tablespoons chopped fresh parsley

1 bay leaf

6 to 8 (1-inch-thick) slices French bread

⅓ cup freshly grated Parmesan cheese

2 tablespoons sherry vinegar

3 to 4 ounces Gruyère cheese, thinly sliced

....

If you don't have ovenproof soup bowls, you can still enjoy the gooey toast topping. Arrange the toast slices on a baking sheet lined with heavy-duty aluminum foil, and top with the Gruyère. Broil until the cheese melts, and then transfer the toast to soup bowls with a wide spatula.

Heat the butter in a 4-quart soup pot over medium-high heat. Add the onions, shallots, and leeks. Toss to coat the vegetables with the butter, reduce the heat to low, and cover the pot. Cook the vegetables for 10 minutes, stirring occasionally. Uncover the pot, and sprinkle the vegetables with the sugar, salt, and pepper. Cook the vegetables over medium-high heat for 20 to 30 minutes, or until deeply browned. Stir the vegetables frequently toward the end of the cooking time, distributing the brown bits clinging to the bottom of the pot into the vegetables.

Stir in the flour, and cook over low heat for 2 minutes, stirring constantly. Stir in the beef stock, chicken stock, thyme, parsley, and bay leaf. Bring to a boil over high heat, then reduce the heat to low and simmer the soup, partially covered, for 1 hour.

While the soup cooks, preheat the oven to 450°F and cover a baking sheet with heavy-duty aluminum foil. Sprinkle the bread with the Parmesan cheese, and bake the slices for 5 to 8 minutes, or until browned. Remove from the oven, and set aside.

Preheat the oven broiler. Remove and discard the bay leaf from the soup, stir in the vinegar, and season to taste with salt and pepper.

To serve, ladle into ovenproof soup bowls and top each with a toast slice. Divide the Gruyère on top of the toast and broil 6 inches from the heating element for 1 to 2 minutes, or until the cheese melts and browns. Serve immediately.

NOTE: The soup can be prepared up to 2 days in advance and refrigerated, tightly covered. Reheat it over low heat, stirring occasionally. The toast can be made up to 2 days in advance and kept at room temperature. Do not top with cheese and broil until just before serving.

Tuscan Minestrone

Every Italian soup filled with vegetables is labeled with the moniker of minestrone, and this hearty version is part of that tradition. A tossed salad and some Crispy Herbed Breadsticks (page 220) can complete your meal.

Serves 6 to 8

¼ cup olive oil

1 medium onion, diced

1 large carrot, sliced

1 celery rib, sliced

3 garlic cloves, minced

2 cups shredded green cabbage

5 cups Vegetable Stock (page 16) or purchased stock

1 (28-ounce) can diced tomatoes, undrained

¼ cup chopped fresh parsley

3 tablespoons chopped fresh basil

2 teaspoons Italian seasoning

1 bay leaf

1 (4-inch) Parmesan rind (optional)

2 small zucchini, diced

¼ pound green beans, trimmed, cut into ¾-inch pieces

¼ pound small shells or other small pasta

Salt and freshly ground black pepper to taste

½ cup freshly grated Parmesan cheese, for garnish

Heat the olive oil in a 4-quart soup pot over medium-high heat. Add the onion, carrot, celery, and garlic. Cook, stirring frequently, for 3 minutes, or until the onion is translucent. Add the cabbage and cook for 1 minute.

Add the stock, tomatoes, parsley, basil, Italian seasoning, bay leaf, and Parmesan rind, if using. Bring to a boil over medium-high heat, stirring occasionally. Reduce the heat to low, and simmer, partially covered, for 30 minutes. Add the zucchini and green beans, and simmer for an additional 10 minutes. Remove and discard the bay leaf and Parmesan rind.

While the soup simmers, bring a large pot of salted water to a boil over high heat. Cook the pasta according to package directions until al dente, then drain. Add the pasta, and season the soup to taste with salt and pepper. Serve immediately, passing the Parmesan cheese separately.

NOTE: The soup can be prepared up to 2 days in advance and refrigerated, tightly covered. Reheat over low heat, stirring occasionally. Add stock or water if the soup needs thinning after reheating.

Variation

Substitute 1 (15-ounce) can garbanzo beans, drained and rinsed, for one of the zucchini.

....

Italian seasoning was one of the first pre-blended herb mixes on the market, and it's used not only in Italian food but also in most Mediterranean cooking. It's a mixture of basil, oregano, rosemary, and thyme, so any of these component ingredients can be substituted, or you can make the blend yourself.

¼ cup Italian seasoning = 2 tablespoons dried oregano, 1 tablespoon dried basil, 1 teaspoon dried thyme, 1 teaspoon dried rosemary, and 1 teaspoon dried marjoram.

Eastern European Sweet and Sour Cabbage Soup

This soup is another in the pantheon of foods that came to this country with the Jews from Eastern Europe in the late nineteenth and early twentieth centuries. It's hearty although low in calories, and it should be served with a crusty Limpa (page 218) or Pretzel Rolls (page 219).

Serves 6 to 8

2 tablespoons olive oil

1 medium onion, diced

4 garlic cloves, minced

1 carrot, chopped

7 cups Vegetable Stock (page 16) or purchased stock, divided

1 (15-ounce) can tomato sauce

1 (14.5-ounce) can diced tomatoes, undrained

3 tablespoons tomato paste

⅓ cup ketchup

½ cup firmly packed dark brown sugar

½ cup cider vinegar

2 tablespoons chopped fresh parsley

2 teaspoons fresh thyme leaves

1 bay leaf

1 (2-pound) head green cabbage

2 Golden Delicious apples, cored, peeled, and diced

½ cup raisins

Salt and freshly ground black pepper to taste

Sour cream, for garnish (optional)

· ·

Many recent studies have been conducted on cruciferous vegetables, of which all forms of cabbage as well as broccoli and kale are members. In terms of conventional nutrients, there is no collection that is as high in vitamin A carotenoids, vitamin C, folic acid, and fiber. This vegetable group also contributes a surprising amount of protein to our diets. Two-hundred calories of broccoli contribute 20 grams of protein.

Heat the oil in a 4-quart soup pot over medium-high heat. Add the onion, garlic, and carrot, and cook, stirring frequently, for 3 minutes, or until the onion is translucent. Add 3 cups of the stock, the tomato sauce, tomatoes, tomato paste, ketchup, brown sugar, vinegar, parsley, thyme, and bay leaf. Bring to a boil, reduce the heat to medium, and simmer, partially covered, for 20 minutes.

While the soup simmers, prepare the cabbage. Discard the core and dark green outer leaves. Cut the head into quarters and then cut each quarter into ⅓-inch slices. Set aside.

Remove and discard the bay leaf from the soup. Allow the soup to cool for 10 minutes. Purée with an immersion blender, or in a food processor fitted with the steel blade. If using a food processor, you may have to work in batches.

Bring the soup back to a boil over medium-high heat. Add the cabbage and the remaining stock and bring the soup back to a boil. Cook over medium-low heat for 30 minutes. Add the apples and raisins, and cook for an additional 20 to 25 minutes, or until the cabbage is tender. Season to taste with salt and pepper, and serve immediately, garnishing each serving with a dollop of sour cream, if using.

NOTE: The soup can be prepared up to 2 days in advance and refrigerated, tightly covered. Reheat over low heat, stirring occasionally.

Variation

This vegetarian soup can easily be transformed into a soup version of stuffed cabbage. Make some meatballs with a combination of ground beef and ground veal and cooked white rice. Brown the meatballs in a skillet over medium heat, and add them to the soup along with the apples and raisins.

Broccoli and White Cheddar Soup

ADAPTED FROM THE SOUPBOX, CHICAGO, ILLINOIS

The Soupbox opened its first location in Chicago in 1995, and it has become a fixture of the city's dining scene. Chef Dru Melton creates more than a dozen soups daily and garners rave reviews in the local and national press. This thick and luscious soup is a perfect candidate to serve in Bread Bowls (page 216).

Serves 6 to 8

4 tablespoons (½ stick) unsalted butter, divided

1 medium onion, diced

1 medium carrot, diced

2 heads broccoli, cut into florets, with stems peeled and cut into ½-inch dice

2 garlic cloves, minced

¼ cup all-purpose flour

1 quart Vegetable Stock (page 16), Chicken Stock (page 14), or purchased stock, heated and divided

2 cups whole milk

1 teaspoon fresh thyme leaves

1 teaspoon chopped fresh marjoram

6 ounces (about 3 cups) grated white cheddar cheese

Salt and freshly ground black pepper to taste

Heat 2 tablespoons of the butter in a 4-quart soup pot over medium-low heat. Add the onion, carrot, and broccoli stems. Cook, covered, for 10 minutes, or until the vegetables begin to soften. Add the garlic and broccoli florets, and cook for 2 minutes longer.

While the vegetables cook, heat the remaining butter in a small saucepan over medium-low heat. Stir in the flour and cook, stirring constantly, for 1 minute, or until the mixture turns slightly beige, is bubbly, and appears to have grown in volume. Increase the heat to medium, and slowly whisk in 1 cup of the stock. Bring to a boil, and simmer for 1 minute.

Add the thickened stock, remaining stock, milk, thyme, and marjoram to the pan with the vegetables and bring to a boil over medium heat, stirring occasionally. Reduce the heat to low, and simmer the soup for 20 minutes, or until the vegetables are tender.

Allow the soup to cool for 10 minutes. Purée with an immersion blender or in a food processor fitted with the steel blade. If using a food processor, you may have to work in batches.

Bring the soup back to a boil over medium heat. Add the cheese to the soup by ½-cup measures, stirring until the cheese melts before making the next addition. Season the soup to taste with salt and pepper, and serve immediately.

NOTE: The soup can be prepared up to 2 days in advance and refrigerated, tightly covered. Reheat over low heat, stirring occasionally. Add milk or cream if the soup needs thinning after reheating.

....

When you want to dress up a puréed soup, one way to do it is to save out some of the ingredients that are going to be puréed (in this case a few pieces of the broccoli florets) and add them as a garnish at the end.

Baked Potato Soup

I've never met a potato I didn't like. I think of them as their own food group. I developed this recipe many years ago in response to a reader request for a way to use up leftover mashed potatoes. But there never are any leftover potatoes in my house, so I revised the recipe to start from the beginning. The smoky nuances from the bacon, sharp cheese, and zesty sour cream and chives make this a filling and luscious meal.

Serves 6 to 8

4 large russet potatoes

½ pound thick-cut bacon, cut into ½-inch strips

¼ cup all-purpose flour

2 cups Chicken Stock (page 14) or purchased stock

3 cups light cream

2 teaspoons fresh thyme leaves

1 bay leaf

2 cups grated sharp cheddar cheese, divided

Salt and freshly ground black pepper to taste

½ cup sour cream or crème fraîche, for garnish

¼ cup snipped fresh chives, for garnish

....

A bonus of this recipe is that you've got eight pieces of potato skins to eat as snacks. If you want to make them pretty, scoop out the potato pulp with an ice cream scoop, leaving a ⅓-inch shell of pulp. Then brush the insides and outsides of the skins with melted butter, and crisp them upside down in a 350°F oven for 5 minutes. Turn them right-side up, add your favorite toppings (cheese, chopped scallions, crisp bacon, etc.), and bake them for an additional 5 to 7 minutes, or until the cheese melts.

Preheat the oven to 400°F. Scrub the potatoes and prick them all over with a metal skewer.

Bake the potatoes right on the oven rack for 45 to 55 minutes, or until a paring knife pierces them easily. Remove the potatoes from the oven, and slice them in half lengthwise. Scoop out the pulp and set aside.

Cook the bacon in a 4-quart soup pot over medium-high heat for 5 to 7 minutes, or until crisp. Remove the bacon from the pot with a slotted spoon, and drain on paper towels. Set aside. Discard all but 3 tablespoons of the bacon grease from the pot.

Stir in the flour and cook, stirring constantly, for 1 minute, or until the mixture turns slightly beige, is bubbly, and appears to have grown in volume. Increase the heat to medium, and slowly whisk in the stock and cream. Bring to a boil, whisking frequently. Reduce the heat to low, stir in the thyme and bay leaf, and simmer for 10 minutes.

Add the potato pulp to the soup and mash it with a potato masher to your desired consistency; the longer you mash it, the smoother it will become. Add 1⅓ cups of the cheese by ½-cup measures, stirring until the cheese melts before making the next addition.

Remove and discard the bay leaf. Season the soup to taste with salt and pepper and ladle it into bowls, garnishing each serving with the remaining cheese, bacon, sour cream, and chives. Serve immediately.

NOTE: The soup can be prepared up to 2 days in advance and refrigerated, tightly covered. Reheat it over low heat, stirring occasionally. Add milk or cream if the soup needs thinning after reheating.

Variation

Substitute jalapeño Jack cheese for the cheddar cheese, substitute cilantro for the chives, and add 2 tablespoons of canned chopped mild green chiles to the soup when adding the stock and cream.

Curried Cauliflower and Fennel Soup

ADAPTED FROM SLURP, SANTA FE, NEW MEXICO

Slurp operates from a silver trailer along a road in Santa Fe. The creaminess of this thick vegan soup comes from tropical coconut milk that tames the spices in the curry and blends nicely with the two white vegetables.

Serves 6 to 8

2 tablespoons vegetable oil

2 medium onions, diced

2 small fennel bulbs, diced

4 garlic cloves, minced

2 tablespoons curry powder or to taste

2 heads cauliflower, broken into 1-inch florets

3 cups Vegetable Stock (page 16) or purchased stock

2 (14-ounce) cans coconut milk

Salt and freshly ground black pepper to taste

Heat the oil in a 4-quart soup pot over medium-high heat. Add the onions and cook, stirring frequently, for 3 minutes, or until the onions are translucent. Add the fennel and cook, stirring frequently, for 7 to 10 minutes, or until the vegetables are golden brown. Add the garlic and curry powder and cook for 1 minute, stirring constantly.

Add the cauliflower and stock to the pot and bring to a boil over high heat. Reduce the heat to low and simmer the soup, partially covered, for 12 to 15 minutes, or until the cauliflower is tender.

Allow the soup to cool for 10 minutes. Purée with an immersion blender, or in a food processor fitted with the steel blade. If using a food processor, you may need to work in batches.

Return the soup to the pot and add the coconut milk. Bring it back to a simmer over medium heat, and simmer over low heat for 10 minutes. Season to taste with salt and pepper, and serve immediately.

NOTE: The soup can be prepared up to 2 days in advance and refrigerated, tightly covered. Reheat over low heat, stirring occasionally.

....

The easiest way to deal with a head of cauliflower is to trim the bottom and cut it into quarters. Then it is easy to cut out the core and break the cauliflower into florets. However, don't discard the core. Dice it into irregular 1- or 1½-inch pieces and cook them along with the florets.

Potato Soup with Gorgonzola and Prosciutto

This is a creamy and sophisticated soup drawn from the world of nouvelle Italian cooking. The potato soup is laced with flavorful Gorgonzola cheese, and then topped by bits of crunchy prosciutto. If you garnish it with toasted pine nuts, rather than prosciutto, you have a vegetarian soup. Serve it with Crispy Herbed Bread Sticks (page 220).

Serves 6 to 8

2 tablespoons olive oil

¼ pound prosciutto, cut into thin slivers

1 large onion, chopped

1 carrot, chopped

1 celery rib, chopped

3 garlic cloves, minced

½ cup dry white wine

4½ cups Vegetable Stock (page 16), Chicken Stock (page 14), or purchased stock

2 tablespoons chopped fresh parsley

1 tablespoon chopped fresh sage (substitute 1½ teaspoons dried)

1 bay leaf

1 pound russet potatoes, peeled and diced

6 ounces crumbled Gorgonzola cheese

1¼ cups half-and-half

Salt and freshly ground black pepper to taste

Heat the oil in a 4-quart soup pot over medium-high heat. Add the prosciutto, and cook for 2 to 3 minutes, or until the prosciutto is crisp. Remove the prosciutto from the pot with tongs, drain on paper towels, and set aside.

Add the onion, carrot, celery, and garlic to the pot and cook, stirring frequently, for 3 minutes, or until the onion is translucent. Add the wine, and cook for 2 minutes. Add the stock, parsley, sage, bay leaf, and potato. Bring to a boil over high heat, stirring occasionally.

Reduce the heat to low, and cook, covered, for 15 to 20 minutes, or until the vegetables are very soft. Remove and discard the bay leaf.

Remove 1 cup of the solids from the pot with a slotted spoon. Combine the solids and cheese in a food processor fitted with the steel blade or in a blender. Purée until smooth, and then stir the purée back into the soup. Stir in the half-and-half, season the soup to taste with salt and pepper, and serve immediately, sprinkling each serving with fried prosciutto.

NOTE: The soup can be prepared up to 2 days in advance and refrigerated, tightly covered. Reheat over low heat, stirring occasionally. Add milk or cream if the soup needs thinning after reheating.

....

There's a reason why bay leaves should always be discarded. Although they add a pungent and woodsy flavor and aroma to dishes, they can be quite a bitter mouthful if you accidentally eat one. That's also why bay leaves are always added whole. If they were broken into pieces, it would be a real scavenger hunt to retrieve them.

Creamy Onion and Potato Soup with Fried Shallots

I developed this soup because two of my favorite foods in the world are sweet caramelized onions and creamy potatoes. It's a great prelude to any winter meal, and the fried shallots add some crunch. It goes nicely with Focaccia (page 214).

Serves 6 to 8

4 tablespoons (½ stick) unsalted butter

2 tablespoons olive oil

3 large sweet onions, such as Vidalia or Bermuda, diced

1 teaspoon granulated sugar

Salt and freshly ground black pepper to taste

4 cups Vegetable Stock (page 16), Chicken Stock (page 14), or purchased stock

1 tablespoon chopped fresh parsley

1½ teaspoons fresh thyme

1½ pounds russet potatoes, peeled and diced

3 shallots, sliced and separated into rings

¼ cup cornstarch

¾ cup vegetable oil for frying

1 cup half-and-half

....

Onions just don't brown as well in a saucepan as they do in a skillet. What accelerates the browning is the evaporation of the water, and that's better done in a skillet with low sides than in a deep pot.

Melt the butter and oil in a large skillet over medium heat. Add the onions, sugar, salt, and pepper, and toss to coat the onions. Cover the skillet, and cook for 10 minutes, stirring occasionally. Uncover the skillet, and cook over medium-high heat for 20 to 30 minutes, or until the onions are browned. Transfer the onions to a 4-quart soup pot.

Add the stock, parsley, thyme, and potatoes to the pot, and bring to a boil over high heat, stirring occasionally. Reduce the heat to low, and simmer the soup, covered, for 15 to 20 minutes, or until the potatoes are very tender, stirring occasionally.

While the soup simmers, prepare the shallots. Combine the shallots and cornstarch in a plastic bag, and shake it to coat the rings. Remove the rings from the bag, and discard any remaining cornstarch. Heat the oil in a skillet over medium-high heat to a temperature of 375°F. Fry the shallots for 2 minutes, or until brown and crispy. Remove the shallots from the skillet with tongs and drain well on paper towels.

Allow the soup to cool for 10 minutes. Purée with an immersion blender, or in a food processor fitted with the steel blade. If using a food processor, you may have to work in batches. Stir in the half-and-half, and season the soup to taste with salt and pepper. Serve immediately, sprinkling each serving with some fried shallots.

NOTE: The soup can be prepared up to 2 days in advance and refrigerated, tightly covered. Reheat over low heat, stirring occasionally. Add milk or cream if the soup needs thinning after reheating. Do not prepare the shallots until just prior to serving.

Variation

Add 1 head roasted garlic to the soup; see page 80 for how to roast the garlic.

Moroccan Sweet Potato Soup

ADAPTED FROM SLURP, SANTA FE, NEW MEXICO

The bright-colored sweet potatoes in this soup are enlivened with harissa, a chile paste popular in North Africa. Serve this soup with Skillet Cornbread (page 223) or Socca (page 232).

Serves 6 to 8

¼ cup olive oil

2½ pounds sweet potatoes, peeled and cut into 2-inch chunks

3 shallots, peeled

2 quarts Vegetable Stock (page 16) or purchased stock

2 to 3 tablespoons harissa, or to taste

1 tablespoon honey

Salt and freshly ground black pepper to taste

Plain Greek yogurt or sour cream, for garnish

Chopped fresh cilantro, for garnish

Preheat the oven to 400°F, and line a baking sheet with heavy-duty aluminum foil. Pour the olive oil onto the foil, and then add the sweet potatoes and shallots, turning them in the oil to totally cover them. Roast the potatoes and shallots for 20 minutes, or until they are almost soft and lightly browned.

Transfer the potatoes and shallots to a 4-quart soup pot, and add the stock, harissa, and honey. Bring to a boil over medium-high heat, stirring occasionally. Reduce the heat to low, and simmer, uncovered, for 20 minutes, or until the potatoes are very tender.

Allow the soup to cool for 10 minutes. Purée with an immersion blender, or in a food processor fitted with the steel blade. If using a food processor, you may have to work in batches.

Season the soup to taste with salt and pepper, and serve immediately, placing a dollop of yogurt and a sprinkling of cilantro on each serving.

NOTE: The soup can be prepared up to 2 days in advance and refrigerated, tightly covered. Reheat over low heat, stirring occasionally. Add stock or water if the soup needs thinning after reheating.

....

In some parts of the country it's still difficult to find harissa, the fiery Moroccan red pepper paste. If you can't locate it, a good substitute is Chinese chile paste with garlic, with a bit of ground coriander and paprika added.

5 *Bean Soups*

Beans are justly praised for their nutritional value as well as their availability and economy, and dried beans play a role in almost all the world's cuisines, so there are soups here from a veritable United Nations of cuisines. Beans are a high source of fiber and protein, and they are low in fat and contain no cholesterol. They are also a good source of B vitamins, especially B6.

Before using dried beans, rinse them in a colander or sieve under cold running water, and pick through them to discard any broken beans or pebbles that might have found their way into the bag. When the beans are covered with water to soak, discard any that float to the top.

Dried beans should be cooked until they are no longer crunchy but still have texture. If beans are going to be precooked and then cooked further in a dish, such as in a chili, stop the initial cooking when they are still slightly crunchy. The other caveat of bean cookery is to make sure beans are cooked to the proper consistency before adding any acidic ingredient—such as tomatoes, vinegar, or lemon—because acid prevents beans from becoming tender.

Cooking beans is common sense: The larger the bean, the longer it will take to soften. But it's not necessary to presoak larger beans for a longer period of time than smaller beans. There's only so much softening that goes on at no or low heat.

Using Canned Beans

Here are the benefits of dry beans: They don't have the high sodium content of canned beans, you can monitor their texture, and you can flavor them as you wish. Here is the benefit of canned beans: They're ready to use because they're already cooked.

There is a basic arithmetic to dry and cooked beans: $\frac{2}{3}$ cup of dry beans, when cooked, is equal to 1 (15-ounce) can of cooked beans. So calculate accordingly. But add the canned beans at the end of the cooking time because they're already fully cooked.

Substituting Various Beans

Bean recipes are very tolerant to substitutions, and here's a guide to what can become a stand-in for another. Color, texture, and flavor are all criteria to consider, but this list can be used for guidance.

Bean	What to Substitute
Black (also called Turtle)	Kidney
Black-eyed Peas	Kidney
Cannellini	Navy
Cranberry	Kidney
Fava (broad beans)	Large Lima
Flageolet	Navy
Kidney (pink and red, pinto)	Navy
Lentils (red, brown, green)	Split peas
Split peas	Lentils

Curried Red Lentil Soup

ADAPTED FROM NEW RIVERS, PROVIDENCE, RHODE ISLAND

This is a vividly colored and aromatic soup developed by former owner Bruce Tillinghast that is thickened with a number of fresh vegetables in addition to the lentils. While it comes from a different part of the world, serve this with Socca (page 232) and the meal is complete.

Serves 6 to 8

3 tablespoons olive oil

1 large red bell pepper, seeds and ribs removed, chopped

1 medium onion, chopped

1 large carrot, chopped

1 celery rib, chopped

1 parsnip, chopped

2 tablespoons garam masala

2 tablespoons paprika

1 tablespoon ground cumin

1 teaspoon crushed fenugreek seeds

1 teaspoon turmeric

½ teaspoon cayenne

10 cups Vegetable Stock (page 16) or purchased stock

3 tablespoons tomato paste

1 bay leaf

3 tablespoons chopped fresh cilantro or parsley

3 cups red lentils, rinsed well

Salt and freshly ground black pepper to taste

¾ cup plain Greek yogurt, for garnish

Heat the oil in a 4-quart soup pot over medium-high heat. Add the bell pepper, onion, carrot, celery, and parsnip. Cook, stirring frequently, for 3 minutes, or until the onion is translucent. Stir in the garam masala, paprika, cumin, fenugreek seeds, turmeric, and cayenne. Cook for 1 minute, stirring constantly.

Add the stock, tomato paste, bay leaf, cilantro, and lentils. Bring to a boil, stirring occasionally. Reduce the heat to low and simmer the soup, partially covered, for 40 to 45 minutes, or until the lentils are very soft. Remove and discard the bay leaf.

Allow the soup to cool for 10 minutes. Purée half of the soup with an immersion blender, or in a food processor fitted with the steel blade. If using a food processor, you may have to work in batches. Return the puree to the soup. Season the soup to taste with salt and pepper, and serve immediately, garnishing each serving with a dollop of the yogurt.

NOTE: The soup can be prepared up to 2 days in advance and refrigerated, tightly covered. Reheat over low heat, stirring occasionally. Add stock or water if the soup needs thinning after reheating.

....

Aromatic fenugreek seeds, grown on the Indian subcontinent, are an integral part of most curry powder formulations. They can usually be found in Indian and Middle Eastern markets but rarely in standard supermarkets. If you can't find them, substitute yellow mustard seeds.

Lentil Soup with Plantains

ADAPTED FROM BORDER GRILL, SANTA MONICA, CALIFORNIA

One way to achieve depth of flavor in soups is to infuse the stock with flavor before the vegetables and other ingredients are added. That is the approach taken by Susan Feniger and Mary Sue Milliken in their version of lentil soup, served at their famed Los Angeles outpost of exciting Southwestern cuisine.

Serves 6 to 8

2 medium onions, divided

8 garlic cloves, peeled and divided

1½ (3-inch) cinnamon sticks

4 whole cloves

4 sprigs fresh thyme

2 quarts Vegetable Stock (page 16), Chicken Stock (page 14), or purchased stock

2 cups red lentils, rinsed well

¼ cup olive oil

2 ripe (black) plantains, peeled, cut in half, and diced

2 medium carrots, quartered lengthwise, and sliced into ½-inch pieces

Salt and freshly ground black pepper to taste

¼ teaspoon ground allspice

¾ cup chopped fresh cilantro, divided

....

Plantains are a cousin to our beloved banana, but this starchy fruit is always cooked and never served raw. Plantains are used in many savory tropical dishes the way that potatoes are added in Western cuisines. But unlike a potato, the flavor of the plantain changes as it matures. When the peel is green to yellow, the flavor of the flesh is bland and its texture is starchy. As the peel changes to brown or black, the flesh gains a sweeter flavor and more of a banana aroma, but it will still keep a firm shape when cooked.

Cut 1 onion into chunks and dice the other one. Mince 5 of the garlic cloves and keep the remaining 3 whole.

Place the onion chunks, whole garlic cloves, cinnamon sticks, and cloves in the center of a medium square of cheesecloth. Tie the ends together to form a package. Place the fresh thyme in another square of cheesecloth and tie the ends together to enclose.

Combine the stock with the spice and herb packages in a 4-quart soup pot. Bring to a boil over high heat, then reduce the heat to low, and simmer, uncovered, for 30 minutes. Stir in the lentils and continue cooking for 15 minutes, or until the lentils are cooked through but still firm. Remove and discard the spice package, leaving the thyme package.

While the lentils cook, heat the olive oil in a large skillet over medium heat. Add the diced onion, and cook for 15 minutes, or until lightly browned. Add the plantains and carrots, and season to taste with salt and pepper. Reduce the heat to medium-low and continue cooking for 15 minutes, or until the plantains are soft and golden. Stir in the minced garlic and allspice and cook about 5 minutes longer, being careful not to scorch the garlic.

Add the vegetables to the lentil mixture. Bring to a simmer and cook for 15 minutes, or until the vegetables are soft. Remove the pot from the heat. Remove and discard the thyme bundle. Stir in half of the chopped cilantro. Adjust the seasoning with salt and pepper. To serve, ladle the hot soup into bowls and garnish with the remaining chopped cilantro.

NOTE: The soup can be prepared up to 2 days in advance and refrigerated, tightly covered. Reheat over low heat, stirring occasionally. Add water if the soup needs thinning after reheating it. Do not prepare the garnish until just prior to serving.

Lentil Soup with Bacon

ADAPTED FROM CIRO, SUN VALLEY, IDAHO

Lentil soups are always hearty, and this one combines rich lentils with various forms of pork charcuterie, which gives it a smoky nuance. This is a natural recipe to serve in Bread Bowls (page 216), with a wedge salad alongside.

Serves 6 to 8

¾ pound brown lentils, rinsed well

3 tablespoons unsalted butter

½ cup olive oil, divided

4 strips bacon, cut into ½-inch pieces

⅓ cup all-purpose flour

1 medium onion, chopped

3 carrots, chopped

1 celery rib, chopped

3 ripe plum tomatoes, cored, seeded, and diced

5 cups Ham Stock (page 20), Beef Stock (page 15), or purchased stock

2 smoked ham hocks

½ pound kielbasa, diced

4 garlic cloves, peeled

3 tablespoons red wine vinegar

Salt and freshly ground black pepper to taste

3 tablespoons chopped fresh parsley, for garnish

....

It's possible to make this soup so that it can be enjoyed by people who avoid red meat but do eat poultry. Substitute smoked turkey wings for the ham hock, turkey bacon for the pork bacon, and a poultry sausage for the kielbasa.

Combine the lentils and 6 cups of water in a saucepan, and bring to a boil, covered, over high heat, stirring occasionally. Reduce the heat to low, and simmer the lentils for 40 minutes. Drain, and set aside.

Heat the butter and 2 tablespoons of the oil in a 4-quart soup pot over medium-high heat. Add the bacon and cook for 5 to 7 minutes, or until the bacon is crisp. Remove the bacon from the pot with a slotted spoon, and set aside.

Add the flour to the pot and cook over medium, stirring very frequently, for 13 to 15 minutes, or until the roux is dark brown. Add the onion, carrots, and celery, and cook for 3 minutes, stirring frequently.

Add ¾ of the drained lentils, tomatoes, stock, and ham hocks to the pot. Bring to a boil over medium-high heat, then reduce the heat to low and simmer, uncovered, for 30 minutes. Add the reserved lentils and simmer for 15 minutes. Add the reserved bacon and kielbasa, and simmer for 15 minutes. Remove the ham hocks, and when cool enough to handle, remove the meat from the ham hocks, discarding the skin and bones, and dice it. Set aside.

While the soup simmers, combine the remaining olive oil, garlic, and vinegar in a blender. Purée until smooth. Add the mixture to the soup, season to taste with salt and pepper, and ladle into bowls, garnishing each serving with ham hock meat and parsley.

NOTE: The soup can be prepared up to 2 days in advance and refrigerated, tightly covered. Reheat over low heat, stirring occasionally. Add water if the soup needs thinning after reheating it.

Split Pea Soup with Tasso Ham and Pickled Green Beans

ADAPTED FROM SOCIETY CAFÉ, LAS VEGAS, NEVADA

Society Café is one of the restaurants in the Wynn Las Vegas Resort and Casino that is open from breakfast to late into the evening, and always features soups on the menu from lunchtime on. This richly flavored version of a fairly traditional split-pea soup is garnished with spicy tasso ham and tart green beans that wake up the flavors in the soup.

Serves 6 to 8

SOUP

6 slices bacon, diced

1 large onion, diced

2 celery ribs, diced

2 carrots, diced

3 garlic cloves, minced

3 tablespoons tomato paste

1 smoked ham hock

1½ teaspoons fresh thyme leaves

2 bay leaves

1 pound green split peas, rinsed well

2 quarts Ham Stock (page 20), Chicken Stock (page 14), or purchased stock

Salt and freshly ground black pepper to taste

GARNISH

½ cup distilled white vinegar

2 tablespoons granulated sugar

2 teaspoons pickling spice

1 teaspoon mustard seed

1 teaspoon black peppercorns

1 tablespoon salt

¼ pound fresh green beans, trimmed

1 garlic clove, sliced

2 sprigs fresh dill

¼ pound tasso ham, chopped

Place a 4-quart soup pot over medium-high heat. Add the bacon and cook, stirring occasionally, for 3 to 4 minutes, or until the bacon renders its fat and begins to brown. Add the onion, celery, carrots, and garlic. Cook, stirring frequently, for 3 minutes, or until the onion is translucent.

Add the tomato paste, ham hock, thyme, bay leaves, split peas, and stock to the pot. Bring to a boil over medium-high heat, stirring occasionally. Reduce the heat to low, cover the pot, and cook for 35 to 40 minutes, or until the split peas have disintegrated. Stir frequently towards the end of the cooking time.

Remove and discard the ham hock and bay leaves. Allow the soup to cool for 10 minutes. Purée with an immersion blender or in a food processor fitted with the steel blade. If using a food processor, you may have to work in batches. Season to taste with salt and pepper.

While the soup simmers, prepare the garnish. Combine the vinegar, sugar, pickling spice, mustard seed, peppercorns, salt, and 1 cup water in a saucepan and bring to a boil over high heat, stirring occasionally. Simmer for 2 minutes.

Place the green beans, garlic, and dill in a container, and pour the mixture over them. Allow them to cool to room temperature in the brine, then drain them and cut the green beans into thin slices.

To serve, arrange some of the green beans and tasso in the bottom of soup bowls and ladle the hot soup over them.

NOTE: The soup and green beans can be prepared up to 2 days in advance and refrigerated, tightly covered. Reheat the soup over low heat, stirring occasionally. Add stock or water if the soup needs thinning after reheating.

Tasso is a heavily smoked ham with a peppery crust used frequently in Cajun cooking. You can substitute Canadian bacon for it, but a better substitute is andouille sausage, which has the same spicy flavor.

Yellow Split Pea Soup with Beer and Bacon

Canadians are fond of using yellow split peas in soups rather than the drab green variety. While both are species of field pea, I find that the yellow ones are milder and sweeter, and I use them for salads as well as soups. This soup is spiked with yeasty beer, and it goes wonderfully with Cheddar Beer Bread (page 226).

Serves 6 to 8

¼ pound bacon, diced

1 large carrot, chopped

1 large onion, chopped

2 garlic cloves, minced

1 celery rib, chopped

1 (12-ounce) can lager beer

4 cups Ham Stock (page 20), Chicken Stock (page 14), or purchased stock

1 pound yellow split peas, rinsed well

2 tablespoons chopped fresh parsley

2 teaspoons fresh thyme leaves

1 bay leaf

Salt and freshly ground black pepper to taste

Cook the bacon in a 4-quart soup pot over medium-high heat for 5 to 7 minutes, or until crisp. Remove the bacon from the pot with a slotted spoon, and drain on paper towels. Set aside. Discard all but 3 tablespoons of bacon grease from the pot.

Add the carrot, onion, garlic, and celery to the pot. Cook over medium-high heat, stirring frequently, for 3 minutes, or until the onion is translucent. Add the beer, stock, split peas, parsley, thyme, and bay leaf. Bring to a boil over medium heat, stirring occasionally.

Reduce the heat to low, cover the pot, and cook for 1 hour, or until the split peas have disintegrated. Remove and discard the bay leaf and season to taste with salt and pepper. Serve immediately, garnishing each serving with some of the reserved bacon.

NOTE: The soup can be prepared up to 2 days in advance and refrigerated, tightly covered. Reheat over low heat, stirring occasionally. Add stock or water if the soup needs thinning after reheating.

Even if the garbage disposal is running, never discard bacon grease down the sink. It's a surefire way to incur a visit from your plumber. I suggest saving it to use in cooking as a more flavorful option than butter or olive oil. If you're going to dispose of it, allow it to cool, pour it into an old cream container and place it with your garbage and not anything to be recycled.

French Split Pea Soup
(Potage Saint-Germain)

While I think of basic split pea soup as a hearty winter dish, this version is light enough to serve in the spring and summer, too. The combination of split peas with half-and-half, fresh peas, and other vegetables truly lightens the color, texture, and flavor.

Serves 6 to 8

2 cups dried split peas

7 cups Vegetable Stock (page 16), Chicken Stock (page 14), or purchased stock, divided

2 tablespoons unsalted butter

2 medium onions, chopped

1 carrot, chopped

2 celery ribs, chopped

1 cup shredded romaine or iceberg lettuce, rinsed and dried

1 cup frozen peas, thawed

2 tablespoons chopped fresh parsley

1 teaspoon fresh thyme leaves

1 bay leaf

1 cup half-and-half or whole milk

Salt and freshly ground black pepper to taste

....

Along with lentils, split peas are the one form of legume that does not benefit from any presoaking. They cook very quickly, but you should make sure the heat is very low because they have a tendency to scorch.

Place the split peas in a colander, and rinse them well under cold running water. Put the split peas and 5 cups of the stock in a 4-quart soup pot, and bring to a boil over medium-high heat, stirring occasionally. Reduce the heat to low, and simmer the split peas, covered, for 35 to 40 minutes, or until most of stock is absorbed.

While the split peas simmer, heat the butter in a skillet over medium-high heat. Add the onion, carrot, and celery, and cook, stirring frequently, for 3 minutes, or until the onion is translucent.

Add the remaining 2 cups stock, vegetable mixture, lettuce, frozen peas, parsley, thyme, and bay leaf to the split peas. Bring to a boil over medium-high heat, then reduce the heat to low, and simmer, covered, for 30 to 40 minutes, or until vegetables are tender and split peas have disintegrated.

Remove and discard the bay leaf. Allow the soup to cool for 10 minutes. Purée with an immersion blender, or in a food processor fitted with the steel blade. If using a food processor, you may need to work in batches. Return the soup to the pot, and stir in the half-and-half. Heat to a simmer, season the soup to taste with salt and pepper, and serve immediately.

NOTE: The soup can be prepared up to 2 days in advance and refrigerated, tightly covered. Reheat over low heat, stirring occasionally. Add stock or water if the soup needs thinning after reheating.

Cuban Black Bean Soup

Garlic and aromatic spices including cumin and coriander add sparkle to this thick and hearty vegetarian soup. Add a tossed salad and some Garlic and Cheese Bread (page 224), and the meal is complete.

Serves 6 to 8

1 pound dried black beans

¼ cup olive oil

1 large onion, diced

1 green bell pepper, seeds and ribs removed, finely chopped

6 garlic cloves, minced

1 or 2 jalapeño or serrano chiles, seeds and ribs removed, finely chopped

2 tablespoons ground cumin

1 tablespoon ground coriander

6 cups Vegetable Stock (page 16) or purchased stock

¼ cup chopped fresh cilantro

Salt and freshly ground black pepper to taste

Sour cream, for garnish (optional)

Lime wedges, for garnish (optional)

· ·

There's no question that chiles contain potent oils. However, there's no need to wear rubber gloves when handling them. I cut the chiles on a glass plate rather than on my wooden cutting board so the volatile oils do not penetrate it. What's most important is that you wash your hands thoroughly after handling chiles.

Rinse the beans in a colander and place them in a mixing bowl covered with cold, salted water. Allow the beans to soak overnight. Alternatively, place the beans into a saucepan of salted water and bring to a boil over high heat. Boil 1 minute. Turn off the heat, cover the pan, and soak the beans for 1 hour. With either soaking method, drain the beans, discard the soaking water, and cook or refrigerate immediately.

Heat the oil in a 4-quart soup pot over medium-high heat. Add the onion, bell pepper, garlic, and chiles. Cook, stirring frequently, for 3 minutes, or until the onion is translucent. Reduce the heat to low, and stir in the cumin and coriander. Cook, stirring constantly, for 1 minute.

Add the beans and stock, and bring to a boil over high heat, stirring occasionally. Reduce the heat to low, and simmer, partially covered, for 1 to 1¼ hours, or until the beans are soft.

Remove 2 cups of the beans with a slotted spoon, and purée them in a food processor fitted with the steel blade or in a blender. Be careful not to fill the blender too full when blending hot ingredients. Return the beans to the soup, stir in the cilantro, season the soup to taste with salt and pepper, and serve hot. Top with a dollop of sour cream and serve with lime wedges, if using.

NOTE: The soup can be prepared up to 2 days in advance and refrigerated, tightly covered. Reheat over low heat, stirring occasionally. Add stock or water if the soup needs thinning after reheating.

Cream of Black Bean Soup with Pasta
(Sopa de Frijol con Fideos)

ADAPTED FROM KOMALI, DALLAS, TEXAS

Abraham Salum's Mexican version of black bean soup balances the richness of the cream with spices, and then garnishes the soup with fresh vegetables and toasted cooked pasta. It uses cooked beans, which can clearly come from a can, so it's fast to make, too.

Serves 6 to 8

SOUP

¼ cup olive oil

2 tablespoons unsalted butter

1 small onion, diced

1 leek, white part only, halved, sliced, and rinsed well

4 garlic cloves, minced

1 chipotle chile in adobo sauce, finely chopped

3 fresh epazote leaves (or substitute ¼ cup chopped fresh cilantro)

2 quarts Chicken Stock (page 14) or purchased stock

3 cups cooked black beans (or substitute 2 [15-ounce] cans, drained and rinsed)

1½ cups heavy cream

Salt and freshly ground black pepper to taste

GARNISH

⅓ cup vegetable oil, divided

1 small onion, diced

1 garlic clove, minced

4 ripe plum tomatoes, cored, seeded, and chopped

¼ pound fideo, vermicelli, or angel hair pasta, broken into 1-inch lengths

1½ cups Chicken Stock (page 14) or purchased stock

Salt and freshly ground black pepper to taste

1 cup grated queso fresco (or substitute mild goat cheese or paneer)

1 avocado, peeled and thinly sliced

Heat the oil and butter in a 4-quart soup pot over medium-high heat. Add the onion, leek, and garlic. Cook, stirring frequently, for 3 minutes, or until the onion is translucent. Add the chile, epazote, stock, and beans. Bring to a boil over high heat, stirring occasionally. Reduce the heat to low, and simmer, partially covered, for 15 minutes, or until the vegetables are soft.

Allow the soup to cool for 10 minutes. Purée with an immersion blender, or in a food processor fitted with the steel blade. If using a food processor, you may have to work in batches. Add the cream to the soup, and season to taste with salt and pepper.

While the soup simmers, prepare the garnish. Heat 2 tablespoons of the oil in a saucepan over medium-high heat. Add the onion and garlic, and cook, stirring frequently, for 3 minutes, or until the onion is translucent. Add the tomatoes, and cook for 5 minutes, or until the tomatoes break apart.

Heat the remaining oil in a skillet over medium-low heat. Cook the pasta, stirring frequently, for 5 to 7 minutes, or until golden brown. Watch carefully so that the pasta does not burn. Remove the pasta from the pan with tongs, and drain on paper towels.

Add the pasta and stock to the tomato mixture, and bring to a boil over medium-high heat, stirring occasionally. Cover the pan, reduce the heat to low, and cook the pasta for 8 to 10 minutes, or until al dente and the liquid is absorbed. Add more stock or water if the pasta needs additional cooking time and the liquid has evaporated. Season the soup to taste with salt and pepper.

To serve, ladle the soup into bowls and top each serving with some of the fideo mixture, grated cheese, and avocado slices.

NOTE: The soup can be prepared up to 2 days in advance and refrigerated, tightly covered. Reheat over low heat, stirring occasionally. Add stock or water if the soup needs thinning after reheating. Do not prepare the garnish until just prior to serving.

....

Queso fresco, literally "fresh cheese," is a mild, grainy Mexican cheese traditionally made from raw cow's milk or a combination of cow and goat milk. It softens but doesn't melt when heated. It's becoming widely available, but if you can't find it, two substitutes are paneer, an Indian cheese, or mild goat cheese.

Black-Eyed Pea and Bacon Soup

ADAPTED FROM SOUTH CITY KITCHEN, ATLANTA, GEORGIA

South City Kitchen has been one of Atlanta's most popular restaurants for more than twenty years. Chef Chip Ulbrich creates sophisticated, updated versions of classic Southern cooking and this thick and hearty soup is one of his favorites. Serve it with Buttermilk Biscuits (page 227) or Skillet Cornbread (page 223).

Serves 6 to 8

2 pounds fresh black-eyed peas (or substitute frozen black-eyed peas, thawed)

¼ pound thick-cut bacon, diced

1 large onion, diced

3 garlic cloves, minced

1 tablespoon fresh thyme leaves

1 quart Chicken Stock (page 14) or purchased stock

2 cups heavy cream

Salt and freshly ground black pepper to taste

....

Black-eyed peas are a member of the cowpea family and are a bean, not a true pea. Imported to this continent from Africa in the seventeenth century, they became an important staple of the diet of slaves before the Civil War. George Washington Carver promoted the crop because it adds nitrogen to the soil. The beans were originally called *mogette*, which is French for "nun," because the black eye in the center of the bean was thought to resemble the headdress of a nun's habit.

Rinse the peas if fresh. Place the peas in a saucepan and cover with hot tap water by 3 inches. Bring to a boil over high heat, then reduce the heat to low, and simmer the peas, covered, for 10 to 15 minutes, or until almost tender. Drain the peas, reserving a few cups of the boiling liquid. If using frozen peas, cook them for 5 to 7 minutes.

Cook the bacon in a 4-quart soup pot over medium-high heat for 5 to 7 minutes, or until crisp. Remove the bacon from the pot with a slotted spoon, and drain on paper towels. Set aside. Add the onion, garlic, and thyme to the pot, and cook, stirring frequently, for 3 minutes, or until the onion is translucent.

Add the peas, stock, and cream to the pot and bring to a boil over medium-high heat. Reduce the heat to low, and simmer, partially covered, for 20 minutes. Remove one fourth of the solids from the soup with a slotted spoon and purée them in a food processor fitted with the steel blade or in a blender. Return the purée to the pot, and season the soup to taste with salt and pepper. Add some of the reserved pea-cooking water if the consistency needs thinning, and serve immediately, garnishing each serving with some of the bacon.

NOTE: The soup can be prepared up to 2 days in advance and refrigerated, tightly covered. Reheat over low heat, stirring occasionally. Add stock or water if the soup needs thinning after reheating.

Basque Bean and Cabbage Soup (Garbure)

Unlike many bean soups that are at least partially puréed, this soup from the Pyrenees Mountains is clear and flavored by vegetables and aromatic smoked paprika. It goes well with Crispy Herbed Bread Sticks (page 225).

Serves 6 to 8

1½ cups dried white navy beans

2 tablespoons olive oil

1 medium onion, diced

3 garlic cloves, minced

1 carrot, diced

1 celery rib, diced

2 tablespoons smoked Spanish paprika

2 quarts Vegetable Stock (page 16), Chicken Stock (page 14), or purchased stock

¼ cup chopped fresh parsley

2 teaspoons fresh thyme leaves

1 bay leaf

¾ pound redskin potatoes, scrubbed and cut into ¾-inch cubes

6 cups firmly packed shredded green cabbage

Salt and freshly ground black pepper to taste

• •

It's only in the past decade that I've discovered the wonders of smoked Spanish paprika, *pimentón de la vera dulce*. The peppers are smoked over oak fires that really permeate them with flavor before they are ground. Using this spice adds an instant grilled flavor to foods.

Rinse the beans in a colander and place them in a mixing bowl covered with cold, salted water. Allow the beans to soak overnight. Alternatively, place the beans into a saucepan of salted water and bring to a boil over high heat. Boil 1 minute. Turn off the heat, cover the pan, and soak the beans for 1 hour. With either soaking method, drain the beans, discard the soaking water, and cook or refrigerate immediately.

Heat the oil in a 4-quart soup pot over medium-high heat. Add the onion, garlic, carrot, and celery. Cook, stirring frequently, for 3 minutes, or until the onion is translucent. Add the paprika and cook for 1 minute, stirring constantly.

Add the beans, stock, parsley, thyme, and bay leaf. Bring to a boil over high heat, then reduce the heat to low, and simmer, partially covered, for 45 to 50 minutes, or until the beans are almost tender.

Add the potatoes and cabbage, and cook for an additional 20 to 25 minutes, or until the vegetables are tender. Remove and discard the bay leaf, season the soup to taste with salt and pepper, and serve immediately.

NOTE: The soup can be prepared up to 2 days in advance and refrigerated, tightly covered. Reheat over low heat, covered, until hot, stirring occasionally.

Variations:

• Omit the potatoes, and cook ¼ pound macaroni or other small pasta in boiling salted water until al dente. Add the pasta to the soup at the end of the cooking time.

• This version is vegetarian, but you can substitute Ham Stock (page 16) and add a few smoked ham hocks to the soup pot. Remove the meat from the ham hocks, discarding the skin and bones, dice the meat, and serve as part of the soup.

Senate Bean Soup

What could be more American than this soup, which has been on the menu every day in the Senate dining room for more than a century? The original version was proposed by a senator from Idaho, Fred Dubois; given his constituency, it called for mashed potatoes. While the current soup in the Senate does not include a potato, I really like the older version, especially after I added some herbs to it.

Serves 6 to 8

1 pound dried navy beans

2 tablespoons unsalted butter

1 large onion, chopped

1 celery rib, chopped

8 cups Ham Stock (page 20), Chicken Stock (page 14), or purchased stock

2 smoked ham hocks

¼ cup chopped fresh parsley

1 tablespoon fresh thyme leaves

1 bay leaf

1 large russet potato, peeled and diced

½ cup whole milk

Salt and freshly ground pepper to taste

....

Leftover mashed potatoes are rarely a problem in my house, but if you have some, you can use them in this recipe. One large russet potato makes about ¾ cup of mashed potatoes when cooked.

Rinse the beans in a colander and place them in a mixing bowl covered with cold, salted water. Allow the beans to soak overnight. Alternatively, place the beans into a saucepan of salted water and bring to a boil over high heat. Boil 1 minute. Turn off the heat, cover the pan, and soak the beans for 1 hour. With either soaking method, drain the beans, discard the soaking water, and cook or refrigerate immediately.

Heat the butter in a 4-quart soup pot over medium-high heat. Add the onion and celery and cook, stirring frequently, for 3 minutes, or until the onion is translucent. Add the drained beans, stock, ham hocks, parsley, thyme, and bay leaf. Bring to a boil over medium-high heat. Reduce the heat to low and simmer, partially covered, for 1¼ hours, or until the beans are tender. Remove the ham hocks, and when cool enough to handle, chop the meat and discard the skin and bones.

While the beans cook, cover the diced potato with salted water and bring to a boil over high heat. Reduce the heat to medium and boil for 12 to 15 minutes, or until the cubes are very tender. Drain the potato and combine it with the milk in a small bowl. Mash with a potato masher until smooth.

Stir the potato and diced ham into the soup, and simmer over low heat for 15 minutes. Remove and discard the bay leaf, season to taste with salt and pepper, and serve immediately.

NOTE: The soup can be prepared up to 2 days in advance and refrigerated, tightly covered. Reheat over low heat, stirring occasionally. Add stock or milk if the soup needs thinning after reheating.

Fava Bean Soup with Vegetables and Rosemary Lardo

ADAPTED FROM OSTERIA, PHILADELPHIA, PENNSYLVANIA

Accolades have been awarded to Osteria from its inception. In 2008 it received the James Beard Award for Best New Restaurant, and two years later, its chef, Jeff Michaud, won as Best Chef for the Mid-Atlantic Region. This glorious soup demonstrates that both honors were merited. The colorful vegetable garnish and silky lardo are wonderful additions to a flavorful, thick soup. Serve it with Focaccia (page 214).

Serves 6 to 8

SOUP

1 pound dried peeled fava beans

2 ounces pancetta, diced

1 medium onion, diced

1 carrot, diced

2 celery ribs, diced

6 cups Chicken Stock (page 14), Vegetable Stock (page 16), or purchased stock

¼ cup chopped fresh parsley

1 bay leaf

2 tablespoons sherry vinegar or to taste

¼ cup extra-virgin olive oil

Salt and freshly ground black pepper to taste

GARNISH

3 tablespoons olive oil

½ fresh fennel bulb, chopped

2 carrots, chopped

¼ pound Brussels sprouts, shredded

Salt and freshly ground black pepper to taste

¼ pound lardo

3 tablespoons chopped fresh rosemary

2 slices white bread, toasted and cut into quarters

Rinse the beans in a colander and place them in a mixing bowl covered with cold, salted water. Allow the beans to soak overnight. Alternatively, place the beans into a saucepan of salted water and bring to a boil over high heat. Boil 1 minute. Turn off the heat, cover the pan, and soak the beans for 1 hour. With either soaking method, drain the beans, discard the soaking water, and cook or refrigerate immediately.

Heat a 4-quart soup pot over medium-high heat. Add the pancetta and cook, stirring frequently, for 3 to 4 minutes, or until the fat begins to render. Add the onion, carrot, and celery, and cook, stirring frequently, for 3 minutes, or until the onion is translucent. Add the drained beans, stock, parsley, and bay leaf. Bring to a boil over high heat, stirring occasionally. Reduce the heat to low, and simmer, partially covered, for 35 to 40 minutes, or until the beans are tender. Remove and discard the bay leaf.

Allow the soup to cool for 10 minutes, then stir in the vinegar and olive oil. Purée with an immersion blender, or in a food processor fitted with the steel blade. If using a food processor, you may have to work in batches. Return the soup to the pot, and season to taste with salt and pepper.

For the garnish, heat the olive oil in a skillet over medium-high heat. Add the fennel and carrot and cook, stirring frequently, for 5 minutes, or until the vegetables begin to soften. Add the Brussels sprouts, and cook for 2 minutes. Season the soup to taste with salt and pepper.

Purée the lardo and rosemary in a food processor fitted with the steel blade or in a blender. Spread some of the mixture on top of each toast quarter.

To serve, reheat the soup and garnish vegetables if necessary. Ladle the soup into low bowls, place small dollops of the vegetables around the edge of the bowl, and place the toast in the center of the bowl.

NOTE: The soup can be prepared up to 2 days in advance and refrigerated, tightly covered. Reheat over low heat, stirring occasionally. Add stock or water if the soup needs thinning after reheating. Do not prepare the garnish until just prior to serving.

....

Peeled, dried fava beans are not as easy to find as those still in the peel, but I've discovered that Latino markets are a good source. Goya is a major packager of the beans, which produces a large line of Latino foods. If you can't find the favas peeled, it's better to substitute large lima beans than unpeeled fava beans in this recipe.

Garbanzo Bean Soup with Chorizo

ADAPTED FROM THE COLUMBIA, TAMPA, FLORIDA

The Columbia Restaurant has been a kingpin of Tampa dining since its opening in 1905. There are now five locations to complement the flagship in Ybor City, and this flavorful hearty soup is one of the dishes that led to its fame and is on all of its menus. I ate this soup many years ago on what was for Tampa a wintery day, and I couldn't wait to come home and replicate it.

Serves 6 to 8

¾ pound dried garbanzo beans

¼ pound bacon, diced

½ pound beef chuck, cut into ½-inch dice

3 quarts Ham Stock (page 20), Chicken Stock (page 14), or purchased stock, divided

Pinch of saffron

1 smoked ham hock

1 tablespoon smoked Spanish paprika

2 large russet potatoes, peeled and diced

½ pound cooked Spanish chorizo sausage, diced

Salt and freshly ground black pepper to taste

....

There are two totally different foods that call themselves chorizo. The Mexican version is a raw sausage and the Spanish version is a cured and cooked sausage. In a recipe like this one, if you can't find the Spanish chorizo, it's better to substitute an Italian cured sausage like coppa rather than the Mexican chorizo.

Rinse the beans in a colander and place them in a mixing bowl covered with cold, salted water. Allow the beans to soak overnight. Alternatively, place the beans into a saucepan of salted water and bring to a boil over high heat. Boil 1 minute. Turn off the heat, cover the pan, and soak the beans for 1 hour. With either soaking method, drain the beans, discard the soaking water, and cook or refrigerate immediately.

Cook the bacon in a 4-quart soup pot over medium-high heat for 5 to 7 minutes, or until crisp. Remove the bacon from the pot with a slotted spoon, and drain on paper towels. Set aside. Discard all but 2 tablespoons of bacon grease from the pot.

Heat the remaining bacon grease over medium-high heat. Add the beef and cook until well browned. Combine ½ cup of the stock and the saffron in a microwave-safe cup. Microwave on High (100 percent) for 30 to 40 seconds, or until the liquid heats. Stir well, crushing the saffron threads on the side of the cup.

Add the drained beans, remaining stock, saffron stock, ham hock, and paprika to the pot and bring to a boil over medium-high heat. Reduce the heat to low and simmer, partially covered, for 1 hour to 1¼ hours, or until the beans and beef are very tender.

Add the potatoes and chorizo to the pot, and bring to a boil over medium-high heat. Reduce the heat to low and cook the soup, uncovered, for 20 minutes, or until the potatoes are tender.

Remove the ham hock from the pot with a slotted spoon, and when cool enough to handle, discard the skin and bones and finely dice the meat. Season the soup to taste with salt and pepper, and serve immediately, garnishing each serving with some of the ham meat.

NOTE: The soup can be prepared up to 2 days in advance and refrigerated, tightly covered. Reheat over low heat, stirring occasionally. Add stock or water if the soup needs thinning after reheating.

Tuscan White Bean Soup with Sausage

This hearty soup is relatively fast to make because I developed the recipe using canned beans, which require no soaking. The combination of the mild beans with the hearty sausage is delicious. Serve this with a platter of grilled vegetables and some Focaccia (page 214).

Serves 6 to 8

¾ pound bulk Italian sausage (sweet or hot)

2 medium onions, diced

3 garlic cloves, minced

2 celery ribs, diced

1 large carrot, diced

1 (6-inch) rind from Parmesan cheese (optional)

3¾ cups Chicken Stock (page 14) or purchased stock, divided

2 (15-ounce) cans white beans, drained and rinsed, divided

¼ cup chopped fresh parsley

2 teaspoons fresh thyme leaves

1 bay leaf

½ pound Swiss chard, stemmed and thinly sliced

½ cup freshly grated Parmesan cheese

Salt and freshly ground black pepper to taste

Place a heavy 4-quart soup pot over medium-high heat. Add the sausage, breaking up lumps with a fork. Cook, stirring frequently, for 3 to 5 minutes, or until the sausage is browned and no longer pink. Remove the sausage from the pot with a slotted spoon, and set aside. Discard all but 2 tablespoons of the sausage fat from the pot.

Add the onion, garlic, celery, and carrot to the pot. Cook, stirring frequently, for 3 minutes, or until the onion is translucent. Add the sausage, Parmesan rind, if using, 3 cups of the stock, 1 can of the beans, parsley, thyme, and bay leaf to the pot. Bring to a boil over medium heat, and simmer, partially covered, for 20 minutes, or until the carrots are soft.

While the soup simmers, combine the remaining beans and stock in a blender or food processor fitted with the steel blade. Purée until smooth, and stir the purée into the soup.

Add the Swiss chard to the soup, and simmer for 5 minutes. Remove and discard the bay leaf and Parmesan rind (if using), and stir in the grated Parmesan. Season to taste with salt and pepper, and serve immediately.

NOTE: The soup can be prepared up to 2 days in advance and refrigerated, tightly covered. Reheat over low heat, stirring occasionally. Add stock or water if the soup needs thinning after reheating.

....

I always save the rinds from Parmesan cheese and use them for flavoring dishes such as soups and sauces. The rind will not melt into the dishes, but it will impart flavor. Remove and discard it before serving.

Italian Bean and Pasta Soup *(Pasta e Fagioli)*

Slightly browning the onions adds some sweetness to this hearty bean soup of beige beans marked with irregular red spots. The addition of pasta completes the protein, too. Serve this with Parmesan Breadsticks (page 228).

Serves 6 to 8

1 pound dried borlotti (cranberry) beans

⅓ cup olive oil, divided

2 medium onions, chopped

1 teaspoon granulated sugar

Salt and freshly ground black pepper to taste

2 carrots, chopped

2 celery ribs, chopped

3 garlic cloves, minced

2 quarts Vegetable Stock (page 16), Chicken Stock (page 14), or purchased stock

¼ cup chopped fresh parsley

2 tablespoons chopped fresh rosemary

1 teaspoon Italian seasoning

1 bay leaf

1 (3-inch) piece Parmesan rind (optional)

¼ pound small shells or other small pasta

½ to ¾ cup freshly grated Parmesan cheese

....

A display rack of pretty glass bottles over the stove is about the worst place to store dried herbs and spices because both heat and light are foes of these foods. Keep them in a cool, dark place to preserve their potency. The best test for freshness is to smell the contents. If you don't smell a strong aroma, you need a new bottle.

Rinse the beans in a colander and place them in a mixing bowl covered with cold, salted water. Allow the beans to soak overnight. Alternatively, place the beans into a saucepan of salted water and bring to a boil over high heat. Boil 1 minute. Turn off the heat, cover the pan, and soak the beans for 1 hour. With either soaking method, drain the beans, discard the soaking water, and cook or refrigerate immediately.

Heat ¼ cup olive oil in a 4-quart soup pot over medium heat. Add the onions, sugar, salt, and pepper, and toss to coat the onions. Cover the pot, and cook for 10 minutes, stirring occasionally. Uncover the pot, and cook over medium-high heat for 10 to 15 minutes, or until the onions are lightly browned.

Add the beans, carrots, celery, garlic, stock, parsley, rosemary, Italian seasoning, bay leaf, and Parmesan rind, if using. Bring to a boil over high heat, then reduce the heat to low, and simmer, covered, for 1½ to 2 hours, or until the beans are tender.

While the soup simmers, bring a large pot of salted water to a boil over high heat. Add the pasta and cook according to package directions until al dente. Drain and set aside.

Remove and discard the bay leaf and Parmesan rind, if using. Remove two-thirds of the solids from the pot with a slotted spoon, and purée them in a food processor fitted with the steel blade or in a blender.

Stir the purée back into the soup, and add the pasta and remaining olive oil. Season the soup to taste with salt and pepper, and serve immediately, passing grated Parmesan separately.

NOTE: The soup can be prepared up to 2 days in advance and refrigerated, tightly covered. Refrigerate the pasta separately. Reheat the soup over low heat, covered, until hot, stirring occasionally. Add stock or water if the soup needs thinning after reheating.

Tuscan Bean and Bread Soup *(Ribollita)*

ADAPTED FROM KAMASOUPTRA, PORTLAND, MAINE

Three siblings of the Jerome family from Scotland teamed up with Iowa native Drew Kinney to start this restaurant featuring only hearty, steaming bowls of soup. It emphasizes vegetarian, vegan, and gluten-free soups on its menus. With one location in the historic Public Market House and another in a shopping mall, the firm also sells wholesale to restaurants in northern New England. Ribollita, a classic Tuscan soup, literally means "reboiled," and it always includes stale bread.

Serves 6 to 8

2 cups dried white cannellini beans

½ cup olive oil, divided

1 large sweet onion, such as Vidalia or Bermuda, chopped

2 carrots, chopped

2 celery ribs, chopped

5 garlic cloves, minced

½ teaspoon crushed red pepper flakes or to taste

2 quarts Vegetable Stock (page 16), Chicken Stock (page 14), or purchased stock

2 tablespoons chopped fresh oregano

2 tablespoons chopped fresh basil

1 tablespoon chopped fresh rosemary

1 tablespoon fresh thyme leaves

1 (4-inch) Parmesan rind (optional)

1 (28-ounce) can crushed tomatoes in tomato purée, undrained

5 cups firmly packed chopped kale

2 tablespoons red wine vinegar

3 cups stale bread cubes, crusts trimmed off

Salt and freshly ground black pepper to taste

Freshly grated Parmesan cheese, for serving

Rinse the beans in a colander and place them in a mixing bowl covered with cold, salted water. Allow the beans to soak overnight. Alternatively, place the beans into a saucepan of salted water and bring to a boil over high heat. Boil 1 minute. Turn off the heat, cover the pan, and soak the beans for 1 hour. With either soaking method, drain the beans, discard the soaking water, and cook or refrigerate immediately.

Heat ¼ cup of the oil in a 4-quart soup pot over medium-high heat. Add the onion, carrots, celery, and garlic. Cook, stirring frequently, for 3 minutes, or until the onion is translucent. Stir in the crushed red pepper flakes and cook for 1 minute, stirring constantly.

Add the beans, stock, oregano, basil, rosemary, thyme, and Parmesan rind, if using. Bring to a boil over high heat, then reduce the heat to low, and simmer, uncovered, for 45 minutes, or until the beans are almost tender. Add the tomatoes, kale, and vinegar, and cook for another 15 to 20 minutes, or until the beans are tender. Remove and discard the Parmesan rind, if used.

Remove 1 cup of beans and transfer them to a food processor fitted with the steel blade or to a blender. Purée until smooth, and stir the purée back into the soup.

Add the bread, and simmer over low heat for 10 minutes, or until the bread disintegrates and thickens the soup. Season the soup to taste with salt and pepper, and serve immediately, passing Parmesan cheese separately.

NOTE: The soup can be prepared up to 2 days in advance and refrigerated, tightly covered. Reheat over low heat, stirring occasionally. Add stock or water if the soup needs thinning after reheating.

When you're thickening any soup or stew with stale bread, you can vary the flavor with your choice of bread. Both olive bread and herb bread create a more complex flavor and whole-grain bread adds even more heartiness.

Chili Soup with Beans

This dish is a soup version of chili con carne. It has all the same seasonings, plus nutritious beans. Serve it with warm corn or whole-wheat tortillas, and a crunchy slaw, preferably made with jicama.

Serves 6 to 8

3 tablespoons olive oil, divided

¾ pound ground chuck

1 large onion, diced

1 large green bell pepper, seeds and ribs removed, diced

1 celery rib, diced

3 garlic cloves, minced

2 tablespoons chili powder

2 tablespoons smoked Spanish paprika

2 teaspoons ground cumin

4 cups Beef Stock (page 15) or purchased stock

1 (14.5-ounce) can petite diced tomatoes, undrained

1 (4-ounce) can diced mild green chiles, drained

2 chipotle chiles in adobo sauce, drained and finely chopped

2 tablespoons tomato paste

2 (15-ounce) cans red kidney beans, drained and rinsed

Salt and freshly ground black pepper to taste

½ to ¾ cup grated cheddar cheese, for garnish

½ to ¾ cup sour cream or plain yogurt, for garnish

¼ to ½ cup chopped red onion, for garnish

Heat 1 tablespoon of the oil in a 4-quart soup pot over medium-high heat. Add the beef, breaking up lumps with a fork, and cook for 2 to 3 minutes, or until the beef browns and no pink remains. Remove the beef from the pot with a slotted spoon, and set aside. Discard the fat from the pot.

Heat the remaining oil in the pot over medium-high heat. Add the onion, bell pepper, celery, and garlic. Cook, stirring frequently, for 3 minutes, or until the onion is translucent. Add the chili powder, paprika, and cumin, and cook for 1 minute, stirring constantly.

Return the beef to the pot and add the stock, tomatoes, green chiles, chipotle chiles, and tomato paste. Stir well to dissolve the tomato paste, and bring to a boil over medium-high heat.

Reduce the heat to low, and simmer, covered, for 20 minutes. Add the beans, and cook for an additional 20 minutes. Season the soup to taste with salt and pepper, and serve immediately, passing bowls of cheddar, sour cream, and onion separately.

NOTE: The soup can be prepared up to 2 days in advance and refrigerated, tightly covered. Reheat over low heat, stirring occasionally.

Variation

Substitute ground turkey for the ground beef, and chicken stock for the beef stock.

....

Be careful when pushing your shopping cart up the Mexican aisle that you're buying is mild green chiles and not canned jalapeño chiles. The cans are always next to each other, and the mistake turns this mildly flavored dish into one needing a fire extinguisher.

Trieste Bean and Sauerkraut Soup (Jota)

Jota, pronounced *YOO-tah*, is all about the heartiness of beans, pork, potatoes, and sauerkraut. Yes, you just read sauerkraut as an ingredient in a soup from Italy. That's because there's a lot of Austro-Hungarian influence in the cooking of Friuli and Istria in the northeast corner of Italy; sauerkraut there is dubbed *capuzi garbi*. A square of Focaccia (page 214) completes the Italian theme of this comforting winter meal.

Serves 6 to 8

½ pound dried borlotti beans or red kidney beans

2 tablespoons olive oil

¼ pound pancetta, chopped

1 large onion, diced

1 large carrot, diced

3 garlic cloves, minced

2 smoked ham hocks

8 cups Ham Stock (page 20), Chicken Stock
   (page 14), or purchased stock

1 bay leaf

½ pound sauerkraut

2 medium russet potatoes, peeled and diced

2 cups diced cooked smoked ham

Salt and freshly ground black pepper to taste

1 cup chopped prosciutto, for garnish

½ cup freshly grated Parmesan cheese, for garnish

....

Always add salt to any dish made with smoked pork products at the very end of the cooking time. The level of salt already in the pork can vary widely; most of the time when I use ham stock I add almost no additional salt.

Rinse the beans in a colander and place them in a mixing bowl covered with cold, salted water. Allow the beans to soak overnight. Alternatively, place the beans into a saucepan of salted water and bring to a boil over high heat. Boil 1 minute. Turn off the heat, cover the pan, and soak the beans for 1 hour. With either soaking method, drain the beans, discard the soaking water, and cook or refrigerate immediately.

Heat the oil in a 4-quart soup pot over medium-high heat. Add the pancetta and cook, stirring frequently, for 3 to 4 minutes, or until the pancetta begins to crisp. Add the onion, carrot, and garlic and cook, stirring frequently, for 3 minutes, or until the onion is translucent.

Add the ham hocks, stock, and bay leaf, and bring to a boil over high heat. Reduce the heat to low and cook the soup, partially covered, for 50 minutes, or until the beans are beginning to become tender.

While the beans cook, drain the sauerkraut and place it in a colander. Run cold water over it for 3 minutes, then squeeze it dry with your hands.

Add the sauerkraut and potatoes to the soup and cook for 30 minutes, or until the potatoes are tender when pierced with a knife. Remove the ham hocks, and when cool enough to handle, pick the meat from them, discarding the skin and bones.

Use a potato masher to mash about one-third to half of the potatoes and beans in the soup. Bring the soup back to a simmer and add the reserved ham hock meat and the smoked ham. Simmer, partially covered, for 10 minutes. Remove and discard the bay leaf, season the soup to taste with salt and pepper, and serve immediately, garnishing each serving with chopped prosciutto and Parmesan.

NOTE: The soup can be prepared up to 2 days in advance and refrigerated, tightly covered. Reheat over low heat, stirring occasionally. Add stock or water if the soup needs thinning after reheating.

Spicy Creole Peanut Soup

ADAPTED FROM NEW RIVERS, PROVIDENCE, RHODE ISLAND

Peanut soups are part of many African cuisines that became rooted in this country in the eighteenth century, and this one is velvety smooth and rich. While we eat them like nuts, peanuts are technically a legume, which is why this soup is in this chapter. Virginia Koster added this soup to the New Rivers repertoire; she is a friend of former chef-owner Bruce Tillinghast and worked in his kitchen when visiting friends in Providence. Serve it with a wedge of Skillet Cornbread (page 223) and a crunchy coleslaw.

Serves 6 to 8

2 tablespoons vegetable oil

1 sweet onion, such as Vidalia or Bermuda, diced

3 celery ribs, diced

1 garlic clove, minced

1 tablespoon celery seed

2 tablespoons all-purpose flour

½ teaspoon cayenne

3 cups tomato juice or mixed vegetable juice, such as V-8

1 (16-ounce) jar smooth commercial peanut butter (not homemade or natural)

3 cups whole milk

1 tablespoon freshly squeezed lemon juice, or to taste

Salt and freshly ground black pepper to taste

Hot red pepper sauce to taste

½ cup chopped roasted peanuts, for garnish

½ cup chopped celery leaves, for garnish

Heat the oil in a 4-quart soup pot over medium-high heat. Add the onion, celery, and garlic, and cook, stirring frequently, for 3 minutes, or until the onion is translucent. Stir in the celery seed, flour, and cayenne. Cook, stirring constantly, for 1 minute, or until the mixture turns slightly beige, is bubbly, and appears to have grown in volume. Increase the heat to medium, and slowly whisk in the tomato juice. Bring to a boil, whisking frequently.

When the soup comes to a simmer, whisk in the peanut butter, and stir until it melts into the soup. Add the milk, reduce the heat to low, and simmer the soup, uncovered, for 15 minutes, stirring occasionally. Season to taste with the lemon juice, salt, pepper, and hot red pepper sauce. Serve immediately, garnishing each serving with peanuts and celery leaves.

NOTE: The soup can be prepared up to 2 days in advance and refrigerated, tightly covered. Reheat over low heat, stirring occasionally.

....

As much as I'm all in favor of natural foods, this soup really needs all the additives of commercial peanut butter, as well as the sugar, to make it successful.

6 Soups from the Sea

Selecting the Most Select

"This is some fine kettle of fish" is a phrase I hope you'll use often when cooking the recipes in this chapter. This eighteenth-century expression originally meant a difficult or awkward situation, and that holds true for these soups and stews, too.

While meats are added to the soup base at the onset of cooking, or soon thereafter, seafood is the last ingredient to be added to these recipes due to its short cooking time. Cubes of fish cook in three to five minutes, while it can take cubes of beef up to three hours to reach tenderness. In fact, overcooking is a common mistake cooks make when handling seafood.

Another difference, when cooking fish and seafood, is that it does not freeze well—either before or after cooking. The reason is that when food is frozen, the liquid inside its cells expands to form ice. This expansion punctures the delicate cell walls, which makes the fish and seafood mushy once thawed.

Though fish cooks quickly, it's the base that takes the time. My suggestion is to double (or even triple) the recipe for the base, and freeze the extra portions. Thaw it, add the fresh fish, and within ten minutes you'll be enjoying a delicious fish soup resulting from a long-simmered base enlivened by perfectly cooked fresh fish.

Most supermarkets still display fish on chipped ice in a case rather than pre-packaging it, and they should. Fish should be kept at a lower temperature than meats. When making your fish selection, keep a few simple guidelines in mind: Above all, do not buy any fish that actually smells fishy, indicating that it is no longer fresh or hasn't been cut or stored properly. Fresh fish has the mild, clean scent of the sea—nothing more. Look for bright, shiny colors in the fish scales, because, as a fish sits, its skin becomes more pale and dull looking. Then peer into the eyes: They should be black and beady. If they're milky or sunken, the fish has been dead too long. And if the fish isn't behind glass, gently poke its flesh. If the indentation remains, the fish is old.

Classic New England Clam Chowder

About fifteen years ago, I owned a catering service named Nantucket Cuisine when I lived on that island off of Cape Cod, and clients told me that the path to stardom was a spectacular clam chowder. I spent a few winter months developing this recipe, which indeed became one of my signature dishes. The secret is a lot of reduced clam juice, so the sweet flavor of the mollusks emerges from the creamy broth.

Serves 6 to 8

1 pound chopped fresh clams

4 (8-ounce) bottles clam juice

6 tablespoons (¾ stick) unsalted butter, divided

1 large onion, diced

2 celery ribs, diced

2 large redskin potatoes, scrubbed and cut into ¾-inch dice

3 tablespoons chopped fresh parsley

2 teaspoons fresh thyme leaves

2 bay leaves

¼ cup all-purpose flour

1 quart half-and-half, heated and divided

Salt and freshly ground black pepper to taste

....

In Melville's *Moby Dick*, Ishmael and Queequeg land on Nantucket and are sent to Hosea Hussey's Try Pots; the name comes from the black iron cauldron used aboard whale ships for melting blubber to liquid oil. Melville writes that the "fishiest of all fishy places was the Try Pots. Chowder for breakfast, and chowder for dinner, and chowder for supper."

Drain the clams, reserving the liquor. Refrigerate the clams until ready to use.

Combine the drained clam juice and bottled clam juice in a 4-quart soup pot, and bring to a boil over high heat. Boil over medium-high heat until reduced by two-thirds.

While the clam juice boils, heat 2 tablespoons of the butter in a small saucepan over medium-high heat. Add the onion and cook, stirring frequently, for 3 minutes, or until the onion is translucent.

Add the onion, celery, potatoes, parsley, thyme, and bay leaves to the reduced clam juice. Bring to a boil, reduce the heat to low, and simmer the soup for 10 to 12 minutes, or until the potatoes are tender.

Heat the remaining butter in a small saucepan over medium-low heat. Stir in the flour and cook, stirring constantly, for 1 minute, or until the mixture turns slightly beige, is bubbly, and appears to have grown in volume. Increase the heat to medium, and slowly whisk in 2 cups of the half-and-half. Bring to a boil, whisking frequently. Add the thickened roux, remaining half-and-half, and the clams to the soup. Bring to a boil over medium heat, reduce the heat to low, and simmer the soup for 2 minutes. Remove and discard the bay leaves, season the soup to taste with salt and pepper, and serve immediately.

NOTE: The soup can be prepared up to 2 days in advance and refrigerated, tightly covered. Reheat over low heat, stirring occasionally. Add additional milk if the soup needs thinning after reheating.

Manhattan Clam Chowder

Ann Cashion has been a force in the Washington food scene for almost thirty years, and she has continued to grow and adapt to the city's ever-sophisticating food scene. She now boasts a James Beard Award for Best Chef in the Mid-Atlantic Region, won in 2004, and her style of honest forthright cooking is visible in her version of clam chowder.

Serves 6 to 8

1 pound chopped fresh clams

3 slices thick-cut bacon, diced

2 tablespoons olive oil

3 large onions, diced

4 celery ribs, diced

3 garlic cloves, minced

3 tablespoons fresh thyme leaves, divided

3 (8-ounce) bottles clam juice

2 russet potatoes, peeled and cut into ½-inch dice

3 pounds ripe plum tomatoes, peeled, cored, seeded, and chopped (or substitute 3 [14.5-ounce] cans petite diced tomatoes, drained)

Salt and freshly ground black pepper to taste

Hot red pepper sauce to taste

12 to 18 littleneck clams, cleaned and scrubbed well, for garnish

¼ cup fresh chopped parsley, for garnish

Drain the clams, reserving the liquor. Refrigerate the clams until ready to use.

Cook the bacon in a 4-quart soup pot over medium-high heat for 5 to 7 minutes, or until crisp. Remove from the pot with a slotted spoon, and drain on paper towels. Set aside.

Add the olive oil, onions, celery, and garlic to the bacon grease in the pot. Cook, stirring frequently, for 3 minutes, or until the onions are translucent. Add the reserved clam juice, half of the thyme, the bottled clam juice, and the potatoes to the pot, and bring to a boil over medium-high heat, stirring occasionally. Reduce the heat to low, and simmer, partially covered, for 8 to 10 minutes, or until the vegetables are almost tender.

Add the tomatoes and remaining thyme to the pot, and simmer for 3 minutes. Add the chopped clams, and simmer for 3 minutes, or until the clams are cooked through. Season the soup to taste with salt, pepper, and hot red pepper sauce.

To serve, bring the soup back to a simmer. Add the whole clams and cook for 2 minutes, or until the clams open. Discard any clams that do not open. Ladle the soup into bowls, and top each with two whole clams and a sprinkling of bacon and parsley.

NOTE: The soup base can be prepared up to 2 days in advance and refrigerated, tightly covered. Reheat over low heat, stirring occasionally. Do not cook the whole clams until just prior to serving.

Cans of petite-cut diced tomatoes began appearing about five years ago, and they are such a boon when cooking foods like this soup because they are the perfect size to fit on a soupspoon. If you can't find them and use larger diced tomatoes, you should chop or dice them before adding them to the soup.

Maryland Cream of Crab Soup

ADAPTED FROM LEGAL SEA FOODS, BOSTON, MASSACHUSETTS

Legal Sea Foods began as a fish market in Cambridge, Massachusetts, in 1950. Eighteen years later, the Berkowitz family opened their first restaurant right next door. There are now Legal restaurants from Massachusetts to Virginia, with the bulk of them remaining in the home state. While New England clam chowder came first, this rich and velvety cream of crab soup has also been on the menu for decades.

Serves 8

1 quart Lobster or Shrimp Stock (page 17) or purchased stock

½ cup (1 stick) unsalted butter

1 medium onion, chopped

1 celery rib, chopped

½ cup all-purpose flour

2 teaspoons Old Bay seasoning, plus more for garnish

1 quart heavy cream

¼ cup freshly squeezed lemon juice

Salt and freshly ground white pepper to taste

1 pound jumbo lump crab meat, picked over

1 tablespoon snipped fresh chives for garnish

....

Pre-picked-over crabmeat from the seafood department is a tremendous time-saver, but it's far from perfect. The best way to ensure that no shell fragments find their way into a dish is to spread out the crab on a dark-colored plate. You'll see many fragments against the dark background and can pick them out easily. Then rub the morsels between your fingers to check for more, being careful not to break up large lumps. Unless you have a shellfish allergy, please don't substitute imitation crabmeat, actually made from pollock, for real crabmeat.

Place the stock in a saucepan over high heat. Bring to a boil, reduce the heat to medium-high, and boil until the liquid is reduced by half. Set aside.

Heat the butter in a 4-quart soup pot over medium heat. Add the onion and celery, and cook, stirring frequently, for 3 minutes, or until the onion is translucent. Reduce the heat to low. Stir in the flour and Old Bay and cook, stirring constantly, for 1 minute, or until the mixture turns slightly beige, is bubbly, and appears to have grown in volume. Increase the heat to medium, and slowly whisk in the reduced stock. Bring to a boil, whisking frequently. Reduce the heat to low, and simmer the soup for 2 minutes.

Stir in the cream, and bring the mixture back to a boil. Reduce the heat to low and simmer the soup, uncovered, for 15 minutes. Stir in the lemon juice and season the soup to taste with salt and pepper.

To serve, divide the crab meat into heated soup bowls and ladle the soup over it. Garnish each serving with chives and a sprinkling of Old Bay.

NOTE: The soup can be prepared up to 2 days in advance and refrigerated, tightly covered. Reheat over low heat, stirring occasionally. Add milk or cream if the soup needs thinning after reheating.

Creamy Clam Chowder
with Smoked Potatoes and Chorizo

ADAPTED FROM DOVETAIL, NEW YORK, NEW YORK

John Fraser serves this with a homemade croissant made with lots of black pepper, but you can add a healthy dose of pepper to the soup to replicate the flavor. Smoking the potatoes imparts the same nuance that most cooks achieve by adding bacon to chowder.

Serves 6 to 8

½ cup applewood chips

3 dozen Manila clams

½ cup kosher salt or sea salt

3 large redskin potatoes

1½ cups dry white wine

3 sprigs fresh thyme

1 bay leaf

1 tablespoon white peppercorns

¾ cup (1½ sticks) unsalted butter

2 carrots, diced

4 celery ribs, diced

1 large sweet onion, such as Vidalia or Bermuda, diced

2 leeks, white parts only, halved lengthwise, thinly sliced, and rinsed well

¼ cup all-purpose flour

3 cups heavy cream, heated

3 cups whole milk, heated

Juice of 1½ lemons

Freshly ground black pepper to taste

6 to 8 tablespoons chopped hard Spanish chorizo, for garnish

Light a charcoal or gas grill. If using a charcoal grill, soak the wood chips in cold water for 30 minutes. If using a gas grill, wrap the dry wood chips in a piece of heavy-duty aluminum foil (18 x 12 inches), create a packet to encase the chips, and poke holes in the top of the packet.

While the grill is heating, gently scrub the clams under cold running water with a vegetable brush. Place them in a mixing bowl, cover them with cold water, and stir in the salt. Let the clams sit for 30 minutes, then remove them from the bowl with a slotted spoon and transfer them to a heavy pot. Discard any clams that are not tightly shut.

When the grill is hot, cut the potatoes into 1-inch-thick slices. If using a charcoal grill, drain the chips and sprinkle them over the hot coals. If using a gas grill, place the packet on top of the burners. Smoke the potatoes for 5 minutes per side. When cool enough to handle, dice the potatoes and set aside.

Add the wine, thyme, bay leaf, and peppercorns to the pot with the clams. Place the pot over high heat and cook the clams for 5 to 7 minutes, tightly covered, or until they open. After three minutes, shake the pot without opening it to redistribute the clams. Discard any clams that didn't open, and remove the clams from the pot with a slotted spoon. Strain the broth through a sieve lined with cheesecloth or a paper coffee filter, and set aside. When cool enough to handle, remove the clams from their shells, and refrigerate until needed.

Heat the butter in a 4-quart soup pot over medium heat. Add the carrots, celery, onion, and leeks. Reduce the heat to low, cover the pot, and cook the vegetables for 10 minutes, or until almost tender.

Stir in the flour and cook, stirring constantly, for 1 minute, or until the mixture turns slightly beige, is bubbly, and appears to have grown in volume. Increase the heat to medium, and slowly whisk in the cream and milk. Bring to a boil over medium-high heat, stirring frequently. Reduce the heat to low, and simmer the soup for 20 minutes. Add the diced potatoes, reserved clam and lemon juice, and cook for an additional 10 minutes. Add the reserved clams, and season the soup to taste with salt and pepper. To serve, ladle the soup into bowls and sprinkle each serving with 1 tablespoon of the chorizo.

NOTE: The soup can be prepared up to 2 days in advance and refrigerated, tightly covered. Reheat over low heat, stirring occasionally. Add additional milk if the soup becomes needs thinning after reheating.

....

Clams should be kept at a temperature no colder than 45°F for more than a couple of hours or they will begin to open and lose their freshness. To clean clams, place them in a medium bowl and fill it with cold water an inch or two above the clams. Add 1 tablespoon of kosher salt or sea salt per quart of water, but do not use table salt; the iodine in table salt will kill the clams before they are cooked. Allow the clams to sit at room temperature for 30 minutes. Gently remove the clams individually from the bowl without disturbing the sediment at the bottom of the bowl. Run them under cold water and gently scrub the surface of the clam with a vegetable brush to remove any sand stuck to the shell.

Old Charleston She-Crab Soup

ADAPTED FROM SOUTH CITY KITCHEN, ATLANTA, GEORGIA

Along with soups made with oysters and terrapin, crab soups were once the elegant way to begin a dinner party in the southern states. She-crab soup is almost a cross between a bisque and a chowder; food historians say that it is an adaptation of an eighteenth-century soup brought to the colony by Scottish immigrants.

Serves 6 to 8

½ cup (1 stick) unsalted butter

1 medium onion, chopped

2 celery ribs, chopped

2 garlic cloves, minced

¼ cup all-purpose flour

1 cup Lobster or Shrimp Stock (page 17) or bottled clam juice

1 quart whole milk

1 cup heavy cream

1 tablespoon Worcestershire sauce

1½ tablespoons Old Bay seasoning

1 bay leaf

¼ teaspoon freshly grated nutmeg

½ cup dry sherry

½ pound lump crabmeat, picked over

Salt and freshly ground black pepper to taste

Hot red pepper sauce to taste

Melt the butter in a 4-quart soup pot over medium heat. Add the onion, celery, and garlic and cook, stirring frequently, for 5 minutes, or until the vegetables soften.

Stir in the flour and cook, stirring constantly, for 1 minute, or until the mixture turns slightly beige, is bubbly, and appears to have grown in volume. Increase the heat to medium, and slowly whisk in the stock. Bring to a boil, whisking frequently. Reduce the heat to low, and simmer the soup for 2 minutes. Stir in the milk, cream, Worcestershire sauce, Old Bay, bay leaf, and nutmeg. Bring to a boil over medium heat, then reduce the heat to low and simmer, uncovered, for 15 minutes.

Remove and discard the bay leaf. Allow the soup to cool for 10 minutes. Purée with an immersion blender, or in a food processor fitted with the steel blade. If using a food processor, you may have to work in batches.

Stir in the sherry and crab and bring the soup back to a simmer over medium heat. Reduce the heat to low and simmer the soup for 5 minutes. Season to taste with salt, pepper, and hot red pepper sauce. Serve immediately.

NOTE: The soup can be prepared up to 2 days in advance and refrigerated, tightly covered. Reheat over low heat, stirring occasionally. Add milk or cream if the soup needs thinning after reheating.

Blue crabs can be found along the Atlantic Coast from Georgia north to Maine. The only way to tell the difference between males and females is to look at their "apron" or abdomen covering. Females have a wider plate, while males have a thinner plate. Fishermen have names to designate the different ages and genders of these crabs. Males are called "Jimmies," young females are called "Sallies," and mature females are called "she crabs."

Crab and Oyster Chowder

ADAPTED FROM PIKE PLACE CHOWDER, SEATTLE, WASHINGTON

Each day Pike Place Chowder creates eight fresh chowders, and this one was awarded first place in the 2012 West Coast Chowder Cook-off. The creamy base is enlivened with the spices of fresh chorizo sausage as well as Old Bay seasoning. Serve it with Pretzel Rolls (page 219).

Serves 6 to 8

2 medium redskin potatoes, halved

1 pint fresh oysters, drained, liquor reserved

¾ cup (1½ sticks) unsalted butter

2 ounces fresh chorizo sausage, casings removed

3 leeks, white parts only, halved, thinly sliced, and well rinsed

⅓ cup all-purpose flour

1 tablespoon Old Bay seasoning

2 quarts half-and-half, heated

⅔ cup fresh corn kernels

¾ pound fresh crab meat, picked over

Salt and freshly ground black pepper to taste

1 ripe plum tomato, cored, seeded, and chopped, for garnish

¼ cup chopped fresh parsley, for garnish

Cover the potatoes with salted water and bring to a boil over high heat. Boil for 7 to 10 minutes, or until just tender. Drain the potatoes, and when cool enough to handle, cut them into ½-inch dice. Set aside.

Cut the oysters into bite-sized pieces, and refrigerate until ready to use.

Heat the butter in a 4-quart soup pot over medium heat. Crumble the chorizo into the pot, and cook for 2 minutes. Add the leeks and cook for 3 minutes, or until they are translucent. Stir in the flour and Old Bay. Cook, stirring constantly, for 1 minute, or until the mixture turns slightly beige, is bubbly, and appears to have grown in volume. Increase the heat to medium, and slowly whisk in the half-and-half. Bring to a boil, whisking frequently. Reduce the heat to low, and simmer, uncovered, for 10 minutes, stirring frequently.

Add the potatoes, oysters, corn, and crab to the soup. Simmer for 2 minutes, or until the oysters are cooked through. Season to taste with salt and pepper. To serve, ladle into bowls and sprinkle each serving with tomato and parsley.

NOTE: The soup can be prepared up to 2 days in advance and refrigerated, tightly covered. Reheat over low heat, stirring occasionally, but do not let it boil. Add additional half-and-half if the soup needs thinning after reheating. Place crab in bowls just prior to serving.

....

Oysters and clams turn into little bits of rubber if they're overcooked, which unfortunately is their fate much of the time. That's why it's important to cook these oysters for only the two minutes specified, and to not allow the soup to boil again if you're reheating it.

Gumbo J'herbes with Oysters

ADAPTED FROM HAVEN, HOUSTON, TEXAS

Houston, close to the Gulf of Mexico, has a heritage of Creole cooking as well as Southwestern cuisine, and that is what chef Randy Evans taps for this gumbo garnished with cornmeal-crusted oysters. To continue in the Creole tradition, serve this with Skillet Cornbread (page 223).

Serves 6 to 8

1 pint shucked fresh oysters, with liquor

½ cup vegetable oil (or substitute strained bacon grease), divided

¼ cup all-purpose flour

1 large onion, chopped

4 celery ribs, chopped

2 small green bell peppers, seeds and ribs removed, chopped

2 small turnips, peeled and chopped

8 scallions, white parts and 5 inches of green tops, chopped

4 garlic cloves, minced

4 cups firmly packed chopped fresh greens (some combination of collard greens, turnip greens, mustard greens, kale, spinach, escarole, and Swiss chard)

4 teaspoons fresh thyme leaves

2 teaspoons filé powder

6 cups Chicken Stock (page 14), Vegetable Stock (page 16), or purchased stock

4 teaspoons Worcestershire sauce

3 tablespoons chopped fresh parsley

2 bay leaves

¼ pound fresh okra, trimmed and sliced (about 1 cup)

Salt and freshly ground black pepper to taste

Hot red pepper sauce to taste

Vegetable oil for frying

1 cup yellow cornmeal

Chopped scallion greens, for garnish

Preheat the oven to 450°F. Drain the oysters, reserving the liquor. Refrigerate the oysters and liquor separately.

Combine 6 tablespoons of the olive oil and the flour in a 4-quart soup pot. Bake the roux for 20 to 30 minutes, or until walnut brown, stirring occasionally.

Remove the pot from the oven, and add the onion, celery, pepper, turnips, scallions, and garlic. Cook over low heat for 3 minutes, or until the onion is translucent. Add the greens, and cook for 5 minutes, or until the greens wilt. Stir in the thyme and filé powder. Whisk in the stock gradually, then add the reserved oyster liquor, Worcestershire sauce, parsley, and bay leaves. Bring to a boil over medium heat, stirring frequently. Reduce the heat to low, and simmer, partially covered, for 1 hour.

While the soup simmers, heat the remaining olive oil in a small skillet over medium heat. Add the okra, and cook, stirring frequently, for 3 to 4 minutes, or until the okra is crisp-tender. Add the okra to the soup, and cook for an additional 3 minutes. Remove and discard the bay leaves. Season the soup to taste with salt, pepper, and hot red pepper sauce.

For the garnish, heat 1 inch of vegetable oil in a deep-sided skillet over medium-high heat to a temperature of 350°F. Sprinkle the oysters with salt and pepper, and dredge them in the cornmeal. Fry the oysters for 1 minute per side, or until browned. Drain on paper towels.

To serve, ladle the hot soup into shallow bowls, and top each bowl with a few fried oysters and a sprinkling of scallion greens.

NOTE: The soup can be prepared up to 2 days in advance and refrigerated, tightly covered. Reheat over low heat, stirring occasionally. Do not prepare the garnish until just prior to serving.

. . . .

Filé powder, pronounced *FE-lay* like a fish fillet, is one of the key ingredients in traditional gumbo; in fact it's sometimes sold as "gumbo file". It's made from the dried and ground leaves of the sassafras tree and it serves as a thickening agent in gumbo, used either in tandem or in place of okra. It was introduced by the Choctaw Inidan tribes, and it adds an earthy, somewhat spicy flavor to dishes.

White Miso Soup with Mussels and Chiles

ADAPTED FROM RIOJA, DENVER, COLORADO

Chef-owner Jennifer Jasinski, winner of the James Beard Award for Best Chef in the Southwest in 2013, competed on *Top Chef Masters* on the Bravo cable network and is head of three restaurants in Denver. While Rioja was named for the Spanish wine, many of her menu items have an Asian influence, like this soup made with ginger, white miso, and mirin.

Serves 6 to 8

2 quarts Lobster or Shrimp Stock (page 17) or purchased stock

2 ounces fresh ginger, peeled and finely chopped

4 ounces (½ cup) white miso paste

¾ cup mirin

½ cup granulated sugar

1 jalapeño chile, stemmed and very thinly sliced

1 Fresno chile (or substitute 1 additional jalapeño chile), stemmed and very thinly sliced

3 tablespoons canola oil

¼ pound fresh hon shimeji mushrooms (or substitute oyster mushrooms), wiped with a damp paper towel and sliced if large

1½ pounds fresh mussels

Salt and freshly ground black pepper to taste

¼ cup firmly packed fresh cilantro leaves, for garnish

....

Hon shimeji are delicate mushrooms with tiny brown smooth caps that top slender ivory stems. They are always served cooked because they have a harsh and bitter flavor when raw. Hon shimeji hold their shape well when cooked, which is why chefs enjoy using them in soups and stir-fries.

Combine the stock, ginger, miso paste, and mirin in a 4-quart soup pot, and stir well. Bring to a boil over medium heat, then reduce the heat to low, and simmer, uncovered, for 30 minutes. Keep warm.

While the stock simmers, combine the sugar and ½ cup water in a small saucepan over medium heat. Bring to a boil, stirring occasionally. Add the jalapeño and Fresno chiles to the pan, and bring back to a boil. Turn off the heat, and allow the pepper slices to steep for 15 minutes. Remove the peppers from the pan with a slotted spoon and set aside. Discard the soaking liquid. Heat the oil in a large skillet over medium-high heat. Add the mushrooms and cook, stirring frequently, for 3 minutes, or until the mushrooms are tender. Set aside. Add the mushrooms to the stock.

Scrub the mussels well under cold running water. Scrape off any barnacles from the shells, and scrape off the beard with a paring knife. The mussels should close tightly when tapped on a counter. Discard any mussels that do not.

Add the mussels to the soup, and bring to a boil over high heat. Cover the pot and cook the mussels for 3 minutes, or until they open. Discard any that did not open. Season the soup to taste with salt and pepper.

To serve, arrange the mussels in low soup bowls, and ladle the broth and mushrooms over them. Garnish each serving with some of the chiles and the cilantro leaves, and serve immediately.

NOTE: The soup and chiles can be prepared up to 2 days in advance and refrigerated, tightly covered. Reheat the soup over low heat, stirring occasionally. Do not cook the mussels until just prior to serving.

Classic Oyster Stew

ADAPTED FROM THE HOPE CLUB, PROVIDENCE, RHODE ISLAND

Chef Jay Hollen has been making this stew on Fridays at this venerable private club for more than twenty years. I've added a few vegetables to further enrich the creamy broth.

Serves 6 to 8

½ cup (1 stick) unsalted butter

1 large leek, white part only, chopped and rinsed well

2 celery ribs, chopped

1 carrot, chopped

6 cups (1½ quarts) light cream

2 teaspoons Worcestershire sauce or to taste

½ teaspoon hot red pepper sauce or to taste

2 pints shucked fresh oysters, with liquor

Salt and freshly ground white pepper to taste

2 teaspoons paprika (optional)

Melt the butter in a 4-quart soup pot over medium-low heat. Add the leek, celery, and carrot. Cook, stirring frequently, for 5 to 7 minutes, or until the vegetables soften. Add the cream, Worcestershire sauce, and hot red pepper sauce. Heat over low heat to a simmer. Simmer for 2 minutes.

As the cream heats, strain the oysters, reserving their liquor, and set aside. Strain the oyster liquor through a sieve lined with a paper coffee filter.

Place the oysters and the strained liquor in a deep skillet over low heat. Heat until the liquor begins to come to a simmer and the edges of the oysters are curled. Do not allow them to boil or they will become rubbery.

Pour the oysters and their liquor into the pot with the soup, and season the soup to taste with salt and pepper. Divide the oysters among shallow soup bowls, and ladle the soup over them. Serve immediately, sprinkling each serving with paprika, if using.

NOTE: The soup can be prepared up to 2 days in advance and refrigerated, tightly covered. Reheat over low heat, stirring occasionally. Do not cook the oysters or add them to the soup until just prior to serving.

....

The only tricky part to making oyster stew is the proper cooking of the oysters. If they're not cooked enough, certain enzymes in them will still be active and they will cause the cream to curdle. But if they're overcooked it's like chewing little pillows of rubber bands. The best visual clues to perfection are to watch for the oyster liquor to just come to a simmer and for the oysters to look plump with curled edges.

Shrimp Ball Soup

These shrimp balls are like light fluffy clouds floating in a richly flavored simple stock. The "secret" is that the egg whites binding the shrimp mixture are beaten first into a meringue. This is a truly elegant way to start any Asian meal.

Serves 6 to 8

1½ pounds peeled and deveined shrimp

1½ teaspoons kosher salt, or to taste

1 teaspoon freshly ground white pepper, divided

1½ tablespoons vodka

1½ tablespoons heavy cream

2 teaspoons Asian sesame oil

3 large egg whites, at room temperature

¼ teaspoon cream of tartar

3 quarts Shrimp Stock (page 17) or purchased stock

2 ripe plum tomatoes, cored, seeded, and chopped

1 celery rib, chopped

. . . .

The trend of using small amounts of vodka in dishes has been growing exponentially over the last few years. The high percentage of alcohol in vodka means that it adds liquid to a recipe without adding water. In the case of pie crust, that causes less gluten formation, so the crust is more tender and flaky than one made with water. In the case of these shrimp balls, the vodka stabilizes the egg whites.

Combine the shrimp, salt, ⅓ teaspoon of the pepper, vodka, cream, and sesame oil in a food processor fitted with the steel blade or in a blender. Purée until smooth. Scrape the mixture into a large mixing bowl.

Place the egg whites in a grease-free mixing bowl and beat at medium speed with an electric mixer until frothy. Add the cream of tartar, raise the speed to high, and beat until stiff peaks form.

Fold the meringue into the shrimp mixture. Refrigerate for at least 1 hour, or until firm.

While the shrimp mixture chills, bring the stock to a boil in a 4-quart soup pot over high heat. Reduce the heat to medium, and reduce the stock by one-third. Add the remaining pepper, tomato, and celery to the pot, and simmer for 3 minutes.

Bring a large pot of salted water to a boil over high heat, then reduce the heat so that the water is just simmering. Form the shrimp mixture into 1-inch balls using a pastry bag or a tablespoon dipped in cold water. Cook the shrimp balls for 2 minutes, or until they have doubled in size and float to the surface of the simmering water.

Remove the shrimp balls from the water with a slotted spoon, and add them to the soup. Season to taste with salt and pepper, and serve immediately.

NOTE: The soup and the shrimp mixture can be prepared up to 1 day in advance and refrigerated, tightly covered. Reheat the soup over low heat, stirring occasionally. Do not cook the shrimp balls until just prior to serving.

Billi Bi

Mussels are mollusks that are frequently overlooked in cookbooks and on restaurant menus, and there's no reason why. They make a fabulous creamy soup with undertones of herbs and wine, thickened with some egg. You can serve this hot or cold, but I prefer it hot.

Serves 6 to 8

2 pounds mussels

2 shallots, diced

1 small onion, diced

3 parsley sprigs

1 sprig fresh thyme

1 bay leaf

6 to 10 black peppercorns

1 cup dry white wine or ¾ cup dry white vermouth

4 tablespoons (½ stick) unsalted butter, divided

3 tablespoons all-purpose flour

1 quart Lobster or Shrimp Stock (page 17) or purchased clam juice, heated

1 large egg yolk

1 cup heavy cream

Salt and freshly ground white pepper to taste

3 tablespoons chopped fresh parsley, for garnish

Scrub the mussels well under cold running water. Scrape off any barnacles from the shells, and scrape off the beard with a paring knife. The mussels should close tightly when tapped on a counter. Discard any mussels that do not.

Combine the mussels, shallots, onion, parsley, thyme, bay leaf, peppercorns, wine, and 1 tablespoon of the butter in a Dutch oven. Place the pot over high heat and cook the mussels, covered, for 5 to 8 minutes, or until the mussels open. Shake the pot a few times during the cooking to redistribute the mussels, but do not uncover the pot.

Remove the mussels from the pot with a slotted spoon. Discard any that did not open. When cool enough to handle, remove the meat from the mussel shells. Refrigerate if the soup will not be served as soon as it is completed.

Strain the liquid in a colander lined with a double layer of cheesecloth, pressing the solids to extract as much liquid as possible. Discard the solids, and set aside the liquid.

Heat the remaining butter in a 4-quart soup pot over medium heat. Stir in the flour and cook, stirring constantly, for 1 minute, or until the mixture turns slightly beige, is bubbly, and appears to have grown in volume. Increase the heat to medium, and slowly whisk in the stock and reserved mussel liquid. Bring to a boil, whisking frequently. Reduce the heat to low, and simmer over low heat for 5 minutes.

Beat the egg yolk with the cream, and whisk in about 1 cup of the hot soup. Then beat the yolk mixture back into the pot and turn off the heat. Do not allow the soup to boil. Season the soup to taste with salt and pepper.

To serve, reheat the mussels in the soup, if necessary. Ladle into bowls, sprinkling each serving with parsley.

NOTE: The mussels can be steamed up to 2 days in advance. Refrigerate the mussels and strained juice separately. Beginning with heating the remaining butter, complete the soup just prior to serving.

· ·

While this creamy mussel broth comes from the coast of Brittany, its name has been puzzling to food historians since the early-twentieth century, when it became popular at the famed Maxim's restaurant in Paris. Most authorities now agree that Chef Louis Barthe named the dish for American tin-plating magnate William B. (Billi Bi) Leeds, who spent much of his time in Paris and died there in 1908.

Shrimp Bisque

ADAPTED FROM EPICURE MARKET & CAFÉ, MIAMI BEACH, FLORIDA

The key to the flavor of this classic French soup, created by specialty chef Michael Love, is the richly-flavored shrimp stock. Serve this with an interesting bread like Pretzel Rolls (page 219) or Focaccia (page 214) and a tossed salad to transform it into a meal.

Serves 6 to 8

1 pound medium raw shrimp in shells

2 quarts Shrimp Stock (page 17) or purchased stock

4 tablespoons (½ stick) unsalted butter

1 leek, white and pale green part only, thinly sliced and rinsed well

2 carrots, diced

2 celery ribs, diced

1 garlic clove, minced

2 tablespoons tomato paste

Pinch of cayenne

2 tablespoons all-purpose flour

½ cup cream sherry

1 cup whole milk

1 cup heavy cream

Salt and freshly ground white pepper to taste

....

Cooking food gently in water or a sauce that is just at the boiling point and barely simmering is called poaching. This cooking method ensures tenderness, whether it's a poached egg or a fish steak.

Peel and devein the shrimp, reserving the shells and heads, if attached. Refrigerate until needed, tightly covered with plastic wrap.

Bring the shells and stock to a boil in a 4-quart soup pot over high heat. Reduce the heat to low, and simmer, uncovered, for 45 minutes, or until reduced by half. Skim the scum that rises to the top of the pot for the first 15 minutes of the cooking time. Strain the stock, pressing with the back of a spoon to extract as much liquid as possible. Set aside, and keep warm. Rinse out the pot.

Heat the butter in the pot over medium heat. Add the leeks, and cook for 5 minutes, or until the leeks soften. Add the carrots and celery and cook for an additional 5 minutes, or until the vegetables soften. Do not allow the vegetables to brown. Add the garlic, tomato paste, and cayenne. Cook for 1 minute, stirring constantly.

Stir in the flour and cook, stirring constantly, for 1 minute, or until the mixture turns slightly beige, is bubbly, and appears to have grown in volume. Add the sherry, and reduce by half. Add the shrimp stock and continue to whisk. Bring to a boil over medium-high heat. Reduce the heat to low, and simmer, uncovered, for 30 minutes. Add the milk and simmer the soup for 10 minutes.

Strain the soup, pressing the solids with the back of a spoon to extract as much liquid as possible. Return the liquid to the pot. Place the raw shrimp in a metal strainer and lower the strainer into the soup. Poach the shrimp for 2 minutes, or until still slightly translucent in the center. Remove the shrimp and set aside. Add the cream, and simmer the soup for 10 minutes. Season the soup to taste with salt and pepper. To serve, arrange 4 or 5 shrimp in each bowl, and ladle bisque over them.

NOTE: The soup can be prepared up to 2 days in advance and refrigerated, tightly covered.

Lobster Bisque

Lobster bisque, drawn from classic French cuisine, is an elegant first course for any meal and my version is rather classic. It's pink from both paprika and tomato, and laced with a bit of dry sherry. While the actual recipe is very simple, the key to its flavor is a rich stock made from lobster bodies and shells.

Serves 6 to 8

4 quarts Lobster Stock (page 17)

1 onion, sliced

1 head of garlic, cut in half crosswise

3 tomatoes, seeded and diced

2 tablespoons fresh tarragon

3 sprigs fresh thyme

3 sprigs fresh parsley

1 bay leaf

10 whole black peppercorns

¾ cup dry sherry, divided

4 tablespoons (½ stick) unsalted butter

¼ cup all-purpose flour

1 tablespoon mild paprika

1 tablespoon tomato paste

2 cups half–and-half

½ pound lobster meat, finely diced

Salt and freshly ground white pepper to taste

Combine the lobster stock with the onion, garlic, tomatoes, tarragon, thyme, parsley, bay leaf, peppercorns, and ½ cup of the sherry in a large saucepan. Bring to a boil over high heat, reduce the heat to medium, and boil until the liquid has reduced to 1 quart. Strain the stock, pushing on the solids with the back of a spoon to extract as much liquid as possible. Discard the solids, and set the liquid aside.

Heat the butter in a 4-quart soup pot over low heat. Stir in the flour and cook, stirring constantly, for 1 minute, or until the mixture turns slightly beige, is bubbly, and appears to have grown in volume. Stir in the paprika and tomato paste and cook for 1 minute, stirring constantly. Increase the heat to medium, and slowly whisk in the reserved stock and remaining sherry. Bring to a boil, whisking frequently. Reduce the heat to low, and simmer, stirring frequently, for 3 minutes. Whisk in the half-and half, and simmer for 2 minutes. Stir in the lobster meat, season the soup to taste with salt and pepper, and serve immediately.

NOTE: The soup can be prepared up to 2 days in advance and refrigerated, tightly covered. Reheat over low heat, stirring occasionally. Add milk or cream if the soup needs thinning after reheating. Place lobster in the soup bowl just prior to serving.

Lobster stock is a reason to make friends with your local fishmonger. Most fish markets today (if you're lucky enough to have one near you that sells only fish) frequently cook up lobsters to sell the meat at an exorbitant price. The shop will either give you the bodies if you're a good customer, or sell them to you at a nominal charge, like one dollar apiece.

Lobster Coconut Bisque with Sizzling Rice

ADAPTED FROM FEARING'S, DALLAS, TEXAS

While famed chef Dean Fearing serves this Asian soup as an appetizer, I usually add some diced lobster meat and serve it with a salad tossed with a rice vinegar dressing for a light supper. This is Dean's variation on the famed Thai chicken and coconut soup, and the rice adds texture as well as flavor.

Serves 6 to 8

BISQUE

2 tablespoons vegetable oil

1 large onion, chopped

2 garlic cloves, minced

1 tablespoon grated fresh ginger

1 lemongrass stalk, trimmed and chopped

1 celery rib, chopped

1 quart Lobster Stock (page 17) or purchased stock

2 (15-ounce) cans coconut milk

1 cup cooked white rice

1 tablespoon *tom kha* paste

2 kaffir lime leaves

1 teaspoon fish sauce

Salt and freshly ground black pepper to taste

Freshly squeezed lime juice to taste

¾ pound cooked lobster meat, diced (optional)

½ cup chopped fresh cilantro, for garnish

RICE

2 cups medium-grain white rice, rinsed well

2 tablespoons seasoned rice wine vinegar

2 tablespoons vegetable oil, divided

½ small onion, diced

1 garlic clove, minced

1 teaspoon grated fresh ginger

Salt and freshly ground black pepper to taste

¼ cup chopped carrot

½ cup chopped green bell pepper

¼ cup fresh peas

1 tablespoon reduced-sodium soy sauce

Heat the oil in a 4-quart soup pot over medium-high heat. Add the onion, garlic, ginger, lemongrass, and celery. Cook, stirring frequently, for 3 minutes, or until the onion is translucent. Add the stock, coconut milk, rice, and *tom kha* paste, and stir well. Bring to a boil over medium heat, stirring frequently. Reduce the heat to low and simmer the soup, uncovered, for 15 minutes, stirring frequently.

Allow the soup to cool for 10 minutes. Purée with an immersion blender, or in a food processor fitted with the steel blade. If using a food processor, you may have to work in batches.

Add the lime leaves and fish sauce and simmer for an additional 10 minutes. Remove and discard the leaves. Season the soup to taste with salt, pepper, and lime juice.

While the soup simmers, prepare the rice. Combine the rice and 2 ½ cups cold water in a saucepan, and bring to a boil over medium-high heat. Reduce the heat to low, and simmer the rice, uncovered, for 5 minutes. Cover the pot tightly and turn off the heat. Allow the rice to stand, covered, for 10 minutes.

Turn the rice out onto a baking sheet, breaking up lumps with a fork. Sprinkle the rice with the vinegar, and allow the rice to cool.

Heat 1 tablespoon of the oil in a skillet over medium-high heat, swirling to coat the pan evenly. Add the onion, garlic, and ginger, and season to taste with salt and pepper. Cook for 2 minutes, or until fragrant. Stir in the carrot, bell pepper, and peas. Cook for 2 minutes, and scrape the mixture into a mixing bowl.

Return the skillet to the heat and add the remaining 1 tablespoon of oil, swirling to coat the pan evenly. Add the rice, sprinkle with the soy sauce, and stir-fry for 2 minutes. Allow the rice to cook undisturbed for 2 minutes, or until it gets crunchy on the bottom. Stir in the vegetables, break up the rice clumps, and cook for 1 minute to reheat the vegetables. Season the rice to taste with salt and pepper.

To serve, divide the rice and lobster meat, if used, into bowls, and top with the bisque. Sprinkle with cilantro.

NOTE: The soup can be prepared up to 2 days in advance and refrigerated, tightly covered. Reheat over low heat, stirring occasionally. Do not prepare the sizzling rice or add the lobster meat, if using, until just prior to serving.

....

While ginger and lemongrass are relatively easy to find in most supermarkets, the same cannot be said for fresh kaffir lime leaves, an essential ingredient for many Thai dishes. You can substitute one teaspoon of grated lime zest for each two kaffir lime leaves listed in a recipe.

Seafood Okra Gumbo

ADAPTED FROM MR. B'S BISTRO, NEW ORLEANS, LOUISIANA

You can't be a restaurant in New Orleans and not have gumbo on the menu. Gumbo is said to have originated from bouillabaisse, the French fish soup, but it's really Louisiana in a bowl. It may have started as a fish soup, but it's evolved to include a roux and native ingredients such as filé powder, andouille sausage, rice, and okra. Serve this with Buttermilk Biscuits (page 227).

Serves 8 to 10

¼ cup vegetable oil

¼ cup all-purpose flour

1 green bell pepper, seeds and ribs removed, diced

1 medium onion, diced

2 celery ribs, diced

2 quarts Lobster or Shrimp Stock (page 17) or purchased stock

2 pounds okra, sliced into ½-inch slices

1½ pounds gumbo crab or blue crab, hard-shell tops and gills removed, halved, and claws cracked with back of a chef's knife

2 cups canned, crushed tomatoes in tomato purée

2 tablespoons filé powder

1 tablespoon kosher salt or to taste

6 garlic cloves, minced

2 bay leaves

1 teaspoon freshly ground black pepper

1 teaspoon crushed red pepper flakes

1 teaspoon chili powder

1 teaspoon dried thyme

2 pounds medium shrimp, peeled and deveined

1 pint oysters, with liquor

½ pound lump crabmeat, picked over

Hot red pepper sauce to taste

Cooked white rice, hot, for serving

3 scallions, white parts and 4 inches of green tops, thinly sliced, for garnish

Heat the oil in an 8-quart soup pot over high heat. Stir in the flour, reduce the heat to low, and cook the roux for 6 to 8 minutes, or until medium brown.

Add the bell pepper and cook for 30 seconds, stirring constantly. Add the onion and celery, and cook for 30 seconds, stirring constantly. Gradually add the stock, whisking to prevent lumps from forming. Add the okra, crab, tomatoes, filé, salt, garlic, bay leaves, black pepper, red pepper flakes, chili powder, and thyme and bring to a boil. Simmer, uncovered, for 1¼ hours, stirring occasionally.

Add the shrimp, oysters with their liquor, and crabmeat. Simmer the gumbo for 7 to 10 minutes, or until the edges of the oysters have curled. Adjust the seasoning with salt and hot sauce. To serve, ladle the gumbo over rice, and sprinkle with the scallions.

NOTE: The gumbo base can be prepared up to 2 days in advance and refrigerated, tightly covered. Reheat over low heat, stirring occasionally. Cook the seafood in the soup just prior to serving.

....

The actual term "gumbo" is derived from the African word for okra, which is *gombo*. Okra is a natural in soup because it thickens, transforming soup into more of a stew. Okra is now being touted as one of the "super-veggies" like kale and broccoli. A cup contains only 30 calories, and it is very high in vitamin K, vitmin C, calcium, folate, and fiber.

Mixed Seafood Soup *(Huatape de Mariscos)*

ADAPTED FROM KOMALI, DALLAS, TEXAS

Abraham Salum's Komali is an authetically Mexican restaurant in a sea of Tex-Mex. The restaurant's name is an Aztec word for the open griddle used to make tortillas. The food focuses on delicate flavors like those from tomatillos, used in this flavorful soup. Serve it with corn tortillas and a salad made with jicama.

Serves 6

10 tomatillos, husked, rinsed, and cored

2 tablespoons corn oil

1 small onion, diced

4 garlic cloves

3 avocado leaves (or substitute 2 bay leaves and 1 teaspoon crushed fennel seed)

3 serrano chiles, seeds and ribs removed, chopped

2 cups Lobster or Shrimp Stock (page 17) or purchased stock

¼ cup masa harina

12 peeled and deveined extra-large (16 to 20 per pound) raw shrimp

12 mussels, scrubbed and debearded

½ pound bay scallops

½ pound thick white-fleshed fish fillet, such as cod or snapper, diced

Salt and freshly ground black pepper to taste

Chopped onion, for garnish

Chopped fresh epazote or cilantro leaves, for garnish

....

Avocado leaves (*hojas de aguacate*) are used extensively in the cooking of Oaxaca and Puebla, and they give foods a mild licorice taste. You can usually find them dried in the Latino aisle of supermarkets, but to find them fresh—unless you live near the Mexican border—is more of a problem. Famed chef Rick Bayless suggests a combination of bay leaves and crushed fennel seed as a substitution.

Heat a large sauté pan over medium-high heat. Place the tomatillos in the pan and roast them, turning them gently with tongs, until they are golden brown and start to break down. Remove the pan from the heat and set aside.

Heat the oil in 4-quart soup pot over medium heat. Add the onion, garlic, and avocado leaves, and cook, stirring frequently, for 3 minutes, or until the onion is translucent. Add the tomatillos, chiles, and stock to the pot and bring to a boil over medium heat. Reduce the heat to low, and simmer, covered, for 10 minutes.

Allow the soup to cool for 10 minutes. Purée with an immersion blender, or in a food processor fitted with the steel blade. If using a food processor, this may have to be done in batches.

Stir the masa harina into ½ cup of cold water, and add that to the soup. Bring to a boil over medium heat, stirring frequently. Reduce the heat to low and simmer for 5 minutes.

Add the shrimp, mussels, scallops, and fish to the pot. Cover the pot and cook for 5 to 7 minutes, or until the mussels open. Discard any mussels that do not open. Season the soup to taste with salt and pepper, and serve immediately, garnishing each serving with some chopped onion and chopped epazote.

NOTE: The soup base can be prepared up to 2 days in advance and refrigerated, tightly covered. Reheat over low heat, stirring occasionally. Add stock or water if the soup needs thinning after reheating. Cook the seafood in the soup just prior to serving.

Johnny's Fish Chowder

ADAPTED FROM JOHNNY'S HALF SHELL, WASHINGTON, DC

This chowder contains a cornucopia of fresh vegetables, ranging from onion and turnip to summer squash, so it really fits the definition of a one-pot meal. Serve it with Focaccia (page 214).

Serves 6 to 8

2 slices bacon, diced

3 tablespoons olive oil

1 large onion, diced

2 celery ribs, diced

1 large turnip, peeled and diced

1 large redskin potato, diced

5 garlic cloves, minced

3 tablespoons fresh thyme leaves

4 cups Fish Stock (page 18) or purchased stock

6 large ripe tomatoes, peeled, seeded, and chopped (or substitute 1 [28-ounce] can diced tomatoes, drained)

1½ cups diced yellow summer squash

Salt and freshly ground black pepper to taste

1½ pounds fresh seafood (some combination of bite-sized pieces of firm-fleshed white fish, shrimp, diced clams, and shucked oysters)

¼ cup chopped fresh parsley, for garnish

Cook the bacon in a 4-quart soup pot over medium-high heat for 5 to 7 minutes, or until crisp. Remove the bacon from the pot with a slotted spoon, and drain on paper towels. Set aside.

Add the olive oil to the rendered bacon fat. Add the onion and celery and cook, stirring frequently, for 3 minutes, or until the onion is translucent. Add the turnip, potato, and garlic, and cook for 2 minutes.

Add the thyme, stock, and tomatoes, and bring to a boil over high heat. Reduce the heat to low and simmer, uncovered, for 10 minutes. Add the summer squash and cook for an additional 10 minutes, or until the potatoes are tender.

Season the soup to taste with salt and pepper. Add the seafood, and bring the soup back to a boil. Simmer the soup for 1 minute. Cover the pot and remove from the heat. Allow to sit for 5 minutes, then serve immediately, sprinkling each serving with parsley.

NOTE: The soup base can be prepared up to 2 days in advance and refrigerated, tightly covered. Reheat over medium heat, stirring occasionally, until it comes to a boil. Cook the seafood just prior to serving.

....

If you're buying fresh minced clams or oysters for a soup, always drain the seafood and add the juices to your fish or seafood stock. At that point they're free as well as flavorful.

Carolina Fish Muddle

ADAPTED FROM ZINGERMAN'S DELI, ANN ARBOR, MICHIGAN

Every culture and cuisine has its own thick and hearty fish stew, and this one hails from the Outer Banks of North Carolina. There's a smoky undertone from the bacon in the tomato broth, which is thick from the potatoes that literally fall apart while it cooks.

Serves 6 to 8

½ pound sliced bacon, diced

2 medium onions, diced

1 large leek, white part only, thinly sliced and rinsed well

2 carrots, diced

2 celery ribs, diced

1 garlic clove, minced

1 bay leaf

2 pounds fresh plum tomatoes, cored, seeded, and chopped (or substitute 1 [28-ounce] can diced tomatoes, undrained)

¼ pound unsliced bacon chunk

1 tablespoon fresh thyme leaves

¼ teaspoon crushed red pepper flakes

2 tablespoons chopped fresh parsley

5 cups Fish Stock (page 18) or purchased stock

½ pound pollock or other inexpensive white ocean fish, cut into 1-inch pieces

1½ pounds Yukon Gold or other waxy potatoes, peeled and cut into ½-inch dice

1 pound striped bass or other full-flavored ocean fish, cut into 1-inch chunks

1 pound cod or other flaky white ocean fish, cut into 1-inch chunks

Salt and freshly ground black pepper to taste

6 to 8 slices good crusty bread

Cook the diced bacon in a 4-quart soup pot over medium-high heat for 5 to 7 minutes, or until crisp. Remove the bacon from the pot with a slotted spoon, and drain on paper towels. Set aside. Reserve 3 to 4 tablespoons of the bacon fat, and set aside.

Add the onions, leek, carrots, and celery to the bacon grease remaining in the pot. Cook, stirring frequently, for 5 to 7 minutes, or until the vegetables soften. Add the garlic and bay leaf. Cook for 1 minute, stirring constantly.

Add the tomatoes, bacon chunk, thyme, red pepper flakes, and parsley. Cook, stirring frequently, for 5 minutes. Add the stock, pollock, and potatoes, and bring to a boil over medium-high heat, stirring occasionally.

Reduce the heat to low, and cook, partially covered, for 1½ hours, or until the potatoes and fish have fallen apart and the texture is very thick.

Add the striped bass and cod, and cook, covered, for 5 to 8 minutes, or until the fish is cooked through and flakes easily. Remove and discard the bay leaf and bacon chunk. Season the soup to taste with salt and pepper.

While the fish is cooking, toast the bread slices and rub each with some of the reserved bacon grease. To serve, ladle the muddle into low bowls, and top each with a toast slice. Sprinkle each bowl with some of the reserved bacon, and serve immediately.

NOTE: The soup base can be prepared up to 2 days in advance and refrigerated, tightly covered. Reheat over low heat, stirring occasionally. Do not add the fish or toast the bread until just prior to serving.

Variation

Poach 6 to 8 eggs and place them on top of the toast before serving.

....

With fillets, run your fingers in every direction along the top before cooking to feel for any pesky little bones. You can remove bones easily in two ways. Larger bones will come out if they're stroked with a vegetable peeler, and you can pull out smaller bones with tweezers. This is not a long process, but it's a gesture that will be greatly appreciated by all who eat the fish.

Salmon Congee

Congee is a rice chowder that's part of all Asian cuisines, and with the diversity of Chinese cuisines, there are many versions in that vast nation alone. Also called *jook*, congee always includes rice cooked in a large amount of stock so that it falls apart and thickens; the nature of the stock and other ingredients are what gives it a distinct flavor. In this case, delicate salmon is the star, and it cooks from the heat of the soup.

Serves 6 to 8

¾ pound skinless salmon fillet

3 tablespoons vodka

2 tablespoons soy sauce

¼ cup vegetable oil, divided

2 celery ribs, finely chopped

5 shallots, minced

1 large jalapeño or serrano chile, seeds and ribs removed, finely chopped

2 tablespoons grated fresh ginger

½ cup glutinous rice, rinsed well

⅓ pound raw peeled and deveined shrimp, finely chopped

10 cups Fish Stock (page 18) or purchased stock

3 tablespoons freshly squeezed lemon juice

Salt and freshly ground black pepper to taste

¼ cup chopped fresh Thai basil, for garnish

Combine the salmon, vodka, soy sauce, and 1 tablespoon oil in a heavy resealable plastic bag. Refrigerate for 30 minutes, turning the bag occasionally.

Heat the remaining oil in a 4-quart soup pot over medium-high heat. Add the celery, shallots, chile, and ginger. Cook, stirring frequently, for 3 minutes, or until the shallots are translucent. Add the rice, shrimp, and stock to the pot. Bring to a boil over high heat, reduce the heat to low, and simmer, covered, for 15 to 20 minutes, or until the rice is tender.

While the soup simmers, remove the salmon from the marinade and cut it into ¼-inch-thick slices against the grain. Discard the marinade.

Stir in the lemon juice, and season the soup to taste with salt and pepper. To serve, arrange the salmon slices on the bottom of heated soup bowls, and ladle the simmering soup over the top. Serve immediately, garnishing each plate with basil.

NOTE: The soup can be prepared up to 2 days in advance and refrigerated, tightly covered. Reheat over low heat, stirring occasionally. Do not marinate or slice the salmon until just prior to serving.

Don't be confused by the name. Glutinous rice, like all species of rice, contains no gluten. What distinguishes this rice, grown in Southeast Asia, is its sticky quality that comes from its chemical composition. The two components of starch are amylose and amylopectin, and glutinous rice has almost none of the former while the latter is what makes it so sticky. Glutinous rice is ground into a flour that is cooked into a gel for some dishes.

Seafood Minestrone with Herb Oil

This hearty soup contains the large variety of vegetables found in other Italian minestrone soups. But the herb oil drizzled over it before serving adds both aroma and flavor. Serve it with a crusty loaf of Garlic and Cheese Bread (page 224).

Serves 4 to 6

SOUP

¼ pound small shells or other small pasta

3 tablespoons olive oil

1 large onion, diced

2 garlic cloves, minced

1 large carrot, sliced

½ fennel bulb, trimmed, and diced

2 cups firmly packed shredded green cabbage

5 cups Fish Stock (page 18) or purchased stock

1 (14.5-ounce) can diced tomatoes, undrained

2 tablespoons chopped fresh parsley

1 tablespoon chopped fresh oregano

2 teaspoons fresh thyme leaves

1 bay leaf

1 medium zucchini, diced

½ (15-ounce) can white cannellini beans, drained and rinsed

1 pound thick white firm-fleshed fish fillets, rinsed and cut into 1-inch cubes

Salt and freshly ground black pepper to taste

½ cup freshly grated Parmesan cheese, for garnish

HERB OIL

¾ cup firmly packed fresh parsley leaves

2 garlic cloves, minced

2 teaspoons Italian seasoning

⅓ cup olive oil

Salt and freshly ground black pepper to taste

Bring a large pot of salted water to a boil. Add the pasta and cook according to package directions until al dente. Drain and set aside.

While the water heats, heat the olive oil in a 4-quart soup pot over medium-high heat. Add the onion, garlic, carrot, fennel, and cabbage. Cook, stirring frequently, for 3 minutes, or until onion is translucent. Add the stock, tomatoes, parsley, oregano, thyme, and bay leaf. Bring to a boil over high heat, stirring occasionally.

Reduce the heat to low, and simmer, partially covered, for 10 minutes. Add the zucchini and cannellini beans, and cook for 5 to 7 minutes, or until the vegetables are almost tender. Add the fish, cover the pot, and cook for 3 to 5 minutes, or until fish is cooked and flakes easily. Remove and discard the bay leaf, add the pasta, and season to taste with salt and pepper.

While the soup simmers, prepare the herb oil. Combine the parsley, garlic, Italian seasoning, and oil in a food processor fitted with the steel blade or in a blender. Purée until smooth. Season to taste with salt and pepper, and scrape the mixture into a bowl.

To serve, ladle the soup into bowls, and pass the herb oil and Parmesan cheese separately.

NOTE: The soup base can be prepared up to 1 day in advance and refrigerated, tightly covered. Reheat over low heat, covered, until hot, stirring occasionally. Cook the fish and add the pasta just prior to serving.

Variation

Substitute 3 (6-ounce) cans light tuna, drained, for the fish.

....

Fresh fennel, sometimes called anise in supermarkets, has a slight licorice taste but the texture of celery—both raw and cooked. You can always substitute 2 celery ribs for each ½ fennel bulb specified in a recipe.

Smoked Salmon Chowder

ADAPTED FROM PIKE PLACE CHOWDER, SEATTLE, WASHINGTON

The Northwest is known for its smoked salmon, and that tantalizing flavor is augmented with smoked salt here so it really comes through. Serve this chowder with Popovers (page 230) and a salad of raw fennel dressed with lemon juice.

Serves 8 to 10

1½ pounds cold-smoked salmon

1 tablespoon smoked salt

½ pound (2 medium) redskin potatoes, halved

¾ cup (1½ sticks) unsalted butter

1 large sweet onion, such as Vidalia or Bermuda, diced

3 celery ribs, diced

4 garlic cloves, minced

½ cup all-purpose flour

6 cups half-and-half, heated

½ cup tomato paste

1 (8-ounce) package cream cheese, at room temperature, diced

¾ cup capers, drained and rinsed

Salt and coarsely ground black pepper to taste

....

There are eight species of salmon. They're divided by those that live in the Atlantic Ocean and their brethren who live in the northern parts of the Pacific Ocean. All the Atlantic salmon belong to the genus *Salmo*, while Pacific salmon belong to the genus *Oncorhynchus*. The ones from the Pacific are far more varied with names including Chinook, chum, coho, and sockeye.

Break the salmon into bite-sized pieces and arrange them in a mixing bowl. Sprinkle with the smoked salt, and cover with 3 cups of cold water. Refrigerate for at least 8 hours, or preferably overnight. Drain, reserving the soaking water.

Cover the potatoes with salted water and bring to a boil over high heat. Boil the potatoes for 7 to 10 minutes, or until just tender. Drain the potatoes, and when cool enough to handle, cut into ½-inch dice. Set aside.

Heat the butter in a 4-quart soup pot over medium heat. Add the onion, celery, and garlic. Cook, stirring frequently, for 3 minutes, or until the onion is translucent. Stir in the flour and cook, stirring constantly, for 1 minute, or until the mixture turns slightly beige, is bubbly, and appears to have grown in volume. Slowly whisk in the reserved salmon soaking water and half-and-half. Bring to a boil, whisking frequently. Whisk in the tomato paste and cream cheese. Reduce the heat to low, and simmer, uncovered, for 10 minutes, stirring frequently.

Stir in the capers and salmon, and simmer for 5 minutes. Season the soup to taste with salt and pepper, and serve immediately.

NOTE: The soup can be prepared up to 2 days in advance and refrigerated, tightly covered. Reheat it over low heat, stirring occasionally. Add additional milk if the soup becomes needs thinning after reheating.

7 Chicken and Other Poultry Soups

Chicken goes with soup the way bread goes with butter. The words are permanently linked in our minds and in our bowls. Chicken soups are the ultimate comfort food. You don't see Jack Canfield and Mark Victor Hansen writing books titled *Gazpacho for the Soul*, do you?

It doesn't matter if the temperature in the air is the same 101°F that your thermometer is registering for your fever. If you're sick, you want a steaming bowl of chicken soup.

That's true around the world, too. That's why the recipes in this chapter run the gamut from Asian to Hispanic cuisines and from soups based on clear broth to soups rich with cream.

Health Benefits

There is evidence to support the idea that chicken stock really does have medicinal qualities; perhaps your grandma was right all along. In 2000, University of Nebraska Medical Center researcher Dr. Stephen Rennard published a study printed in the international medical journal *Chest*—the Cardiopulmonary and Critical Care Journal—stating that chicken soup contains a number of substances, including an anti-inflammatory mechanism, that ease the symptoms of upper respiratory tract infections. Other studies showed that the chicken soup was equally medicinal if made without vegetables; it was the chicken itself that helped.

Another study, conducted by researchers at Mount Sinai Hospital in Miami and published in *Chest* in 1998, also suggests that chicken soup

has more than just a placebo effect. They looked at how chicken soup affected airflow and mucus in the noses of 15 volunteers who drank cold water, hot water, or chicken soup. In general, the warm fluids helped increase the movement of nasal mucus, but chicken soup did a better job than the hot water. Chicken soup also improves the function of protective cilia, the tiny hair-like projections in the nose that prevent contagions from entering the body, according to a 1998 *Coping with Allergies and Asthma* report.

Using Up the Leftovers

Hearty chicken and turkey soups are a favorite way to stretch leftovers (the summer reruns of the food world) to feed a crowd, and some of the recipes in this chapter are written to use cooked chicken or turkey. If you don't have any leftovers, you can buy half of a rotisserie chicken at the supermarket.

But a bigger problem arises if a recipe calls for cooking the chicken and you want to use one you've already cooked. If it's a small amount of chicken—like a pound of boneless breast or thigh meat—feel free to use what you have on hand, but add it at the end of the cooking time rather than at the beginning.

If a recipe calls for a lot of chicken, however, like the Chicken Soup with Matzo Balls (page 164), it's better to save that recipe for another time and choose one of the other temptations.

Chicken Soup with Matzo Balls

ADAPTED FROM ZINGERMAN'S DELI, ANN ARBOR, MICHIGAN

No soup cookbook would be complete without a great recipe for "Jewish penicillin" and here it is, from a legendary deli near the campus of the University of Michigan. What makes this soup so wonderful is the richness of the broth; it begins with chicken stock and then chicken and vegetables are cooked in the stock. The secret to the fluffy lightness of the dumplings is baking soda. There is no substitute for matzo meal, but it's available with the kosher foods in the ethnic aisle of almost all supermarkets.

Serves 6 to 8

MATZO BALLS

3 large eggs, lightly beaten

⅓ cup Chicken Stock (page 14) or purchased stock

⅓ cup rendered chicken fat, melted (or substitute vegetable oil)

1 teaspoon baking soda

Salt and freshly ground black pepper to taste

¾ cup matzo meal

SOUP

10 cups Chicken Stock (page 14) or purchased stock

1 whole bone-in chicken breast with skin and bones or 4 bone-in chicken thighs with skin, or some combination

2 carrots, thickly sliced

2 celery ribs, thickly sliced

1 parsnip, thickly sliced

3 tablespoons chopped fresh parsley

2 teaspoons fresh thyme leaves

1 bay leaf

Salt and freshly ground black pepper to taste

For the matzo balls, combine the eggs, stock, chicken fat, baking soda, salt, and pepper in a mixing bowl, and whisk well. Add the matzo meal, and whisk well again. Scrape the sides of the mixing bowl, and refrigerate the mixture for 40 minutes.

While the mixture chills, make the soup. Combine the stock, chicken, carrots, celery, parsnip, parsley, thyme, and bay leaf in a 4-quart soup pot. Bring to a boil over high heat. Reduce the heat to low, and simmer, uncovered, for 45 to 50 minutes, or until the chicken is cooked through and no longer pink. Skim the scum that rises to the top of the pot for the first 15 minutes of the cooking time.

Remove the chicken from the soup with tongs, and when cool enough to handle, discard the skin and bones, and cut the meat into bite-size pieces. Return the meat to the soup, remove and discard the bay leaf, and season the soup to taste with salt and pepper. Tilt the pot slightly and spoon the fat off the top of the soup.

To cook the matzo balls, bring a large pot of salted water to a boil over high heat. Form the batter into balls the size of large walnuts using two spoons dipped in cold water or your wet fingers. Drop the balls into the boiling water, cover the pot, and bring to a boil. Reduce the heat to low, and simmer for 30 to 40 minutes, or until cooked through. Do not uncover the pot at all while the matzo balls are cooking.

Remove the matzo balls from the pot with a slotted spoon, and add them to the soup. To serve, divide the soup into bowls, and top with matzo balls. Serve immediately.

NOTE: The soup and matzo balls can be prepared up to 2 days in advance and refrigerated, tightly covered. Store the matzo balls in the soup, and reheat over low heat, stirring occasionally.

Variations:

- Add 3 tablespoons chopped fresh dill to the matzo ball batter.

- Add ⅓ cup chopped scallions (white parts and 3 inches of green tops) to the matzo ball batter.

....

Rendered chicken fat, called *schmaltz* in Yiddish, was an essential ingredient for kosher cooks a century ago, because margarine hadn't been invented and the rules of kosher cooking dictate that meats and dairy—in this case butter—cannot be mixed. Chicken fat is easy enough to keep on hand. Instead of discarding the layer of fat from the top of your chicken stock, spoon it off and save it.

Herbed Chicken Soup with Dumplings

ADAPTED FROM THE SOUPBOX, CHICAGO, ILLINOIS

While Jewish delis might boast about their matzo balls, there are a lot of restaurants in the Midwest and South that have light, fluffy steamed dumplings as their chicken soup's claim to fame. Once you've tried this soup, which is a great way to use up leftover chicken (or turkey after Thanksgiving), you'll see why.

Serves 6 to 8

SOUP

2 tablespoons olive oil

1 large onion, diced

1 large carrot, diced

3 celery ribs, diced

2 garlic cloves, minced

2 quarts Chicken Stock (page 14) or purchased stock

2 teaspoons fresh thyme leaves

1 tablespoon chopped fresh rosemary

3 cups diced cooked chicken

Salt and freshly ground pepper to taste

¼ cup chopped fresh parsley, for garnish

DUMPLINGS

1½ cups all-purpose flour

1 tablespoon baking powder

½ teaspoon salt

3 tablespoons unsalted butter, cut into small bits

½ cup whole milk

1 large egg, lightly beaten

Heat the oil in a 4-quart soup pot over medium heat. Add the onion, carrot, and celery, and cook, stirring frequently, for 3 minutes, or until the onion is translucent. Add the garlic and cook for 2 minutes. Add the chicken stock, thyme, and rosemary and bring to a boil over high heat. Reduce the heat to low and simmer the soup, uncovered, for 15 minutes.

While the soup simmers, make the dumplings. Combine the flour, baking powder, and salt in a mixing bowl. Cut in the butter using a pastry blender, two knives, or your fingertips until the mixture resembles coarse crumbs. Add the milk and egg, and stir to blend. Knead the dough gently on a lightly floured counter.

Stir the chicken into the soup and season the soup to taste with salt and pepper. Form the dumpling dough into 12 to 16 portions, and place the dumplings on top of the soup. Cover the pot tightly, and cook the dumplings over medium-low heat for 15 to 20 minutes, or until the dumplings are puffed and cooked through. Do not uncover the pot while the dumplings are steaming.

To serve, arrange the dumplings in bowls and ladle the soup around them. Sprinkle each serving with parsley, and serve immediately.

NOTE: The soup can be prepared up to 2 days in advance and refrigerated, tightly covered. Do not make the dumpling dough until just prior to serving.

....

The formulation of dumpling dough is almost identical to the biscuit dough used to top a fruit cobbler. Both use baking powder as the leavening agent, but the difference is that dumplings are steamed while cobblers are baked. To confuse matters more, if dumplings are steamed on top of fruit, the resulting dessert is termed a "slump."

Chicken and Giant Noodle Soup

ADAPTED FROM THE GAGE, CHICAGO, ILLINOIS

The Gage, which opened in 2007, is housed in a historic building consisting of three facades designed by master Chicago architect Louis Sullivan. After twenty years in the restaurant business in their native Ireland, the Lawless family moved to Chicago in 1997 and opened a string of casual yet innovative restaurants; the Gage is their most recent venture. This meal-in-a-bowl chicken soup is flavored with myriad fresh herbs. Serve it with Popovers (page 230).

Serves 8 to 10

¼ cup rendered chicken fat (or substitute bacon grease or olive oil)

4 celery ribs, diced

2 carrots, diced

2 medium onions, diced

5 garlic cloves, minced

2 tablespoons fresh thyme leaves

2 tablespoons chopped fresh marjoram

2 tablespoons chopped fresh basil

½ cup chopped fresh parsley

3 tablespoons snipped fresh chives

1 (3½-to 4-pound) chicken or 2½ pounds chicken pieces with bones and skin (some combination of breasts and thighs)

4 quarts Chicken Stock (page 14) or purchased stock

1 tablespoon black peppercorns

1 tablespoon turmeric

1 teaspoon smoked Spanish paprika

Salt and freshly ground black pepper to taste

½ pound wide egg noodles

Heat the chicken fat in a 6-quart soup pot over medium-high heat. Add the celery, carrots, onions, and garlic. Cook, stirring frequently, for 3 minutes, or until the onions are translucent. Stir in the thyme, marjoram, basil, parsley, and chives. Cook for 2 minutes, stirring frequently. Remove half the contents of the pot, and set aside.

Add the chicken, stock, peppercorns, turmeric, and paprika to the pot, and bring to a boil over high heat. Reduce the heat to low and simmer, uncovered, for 1 hour, or until the chicken is tender. Skim the scum that rises to the top of the pot for the first 15 minutes of the cooking time. Remove the chicken from the pot with tongs, and set aside. Strain the stock, pressing with the back of a spoon to extract as much liquid as possible from the solids. Return the stock to the pot.

Bring the stock back to a boil, and reduce by one-third. Add the remaining vegetable mixture, and cook for an additional 15 to 20 minutes, or until the vegetable are tender and the stock has reduced by an additional one-fourth. Season the soup to taste with salt and pepper.

While the stock reduces, cook the egg noodles according to package instructions until al dente. When the chicken is cool enough to handle, remove it from the bones, and discard the bones and skin. Cut the chicken meat into bite-sized pieces. To serve, divide the noodles and chicken meat into bowls, and ladle the soup over them.

NOTE: The soup can be prepared up to 2 days in advance and refrigerated, tightly covered. Reheat it over low heat, stirring occasionally. Refrigerate the noodles separately from the soup if cooked in advance.

....

Adding the vegetables to soup at different times maximizes the flavor and enhances the texture, too.

Italian Chicken Soup with Barley, Beans, and Swiss Chard

Barley is an ancient grain, and it creates a thick and robust chicken soup, flavored with many vegetables and herbs as well as delicate cannellini beans. Serve it with a loaf of crusty Garlic and Cheese Bread (page 224) and a tossed salad.

Serves 4 to 6

3 tablespoons olive oil

1 pound boneless, skinless chicken thighs, cut into ¾-inch cubes

1 large onion, diced

3 garlic cloves, minced

2 celery ribs, sliced

2 medium carrots, sliced

1 red bell pepper, seeds and ribs removed, diced

¾ cup pearl barley, rinsed well

5 cups Chicken Stock (page 14) or purchased stock

1 (15-ounce) can cannellini beans, drained and rinsed

1 (14.5-ounce) can diced tomatoes, undrained

1 (8-ounce) can tomato sauce

3 tablespoons chopped fresh parsley

2 tablespoons chopped fresh oregano

2 tablespoons chopped fresh basil

1 bay leaf

8 leaves Swiss chard, stemmed and thinly sliced

⅔ cup freshly grated Parmesan cheese

Salt and freshly ground black pepper to taste

Heat the oil in a 4-quart soup pot over medium-high heat. Add the chicken, and cook for 2 minutes, or until the chicken is opaque. Add the onion, garlic, celery, carrots, and bell pepper, and cook, stirring frequently, for 3 minutes, or until the onion is translucent.

Add the barley, stock, beans, tomatoes, tomato sauce, parsley, oregano, basil, and bay leaf. Stir well. Bring to a boil, then reduce the heat to low and simmer, partially covered, for 25 minutes. Stir in the Swiss chard and simmer the soup for an additional 10 to 15 minutes, or until chicken is cooked through and no longer pink and the vegetables are tender.

Stir the Parmesan cheese into the soup, and cook for 5 minutes. Remove and discard the bay leaf, season the soup to taste with salt and pepper, and ladle into bowls.

NOTE: The soup can be prepared up to 2 days in advance and refrigerated, tightly covered. Reheat over low heat, covered, until hot, stirring occasionally.

Variation

Substitute 1 (10-ounce) package frozen leaf spinach, thawed and pressed in a colander to extract as much liquid as possible, for the Swiss chard. Add it along with the Parmesan cheese at the end of the cooking time.

....

One of the improvements made in the past decade to processed food is the availability of no-salt-added tomato products; however, the same cannot be said for canned beans, all of which are relatively high in sodium. If you're watching sodium in your diet, cook ⅔ cup dried beans and then make this recipe.

Tortilla Soup

While some chefs call it tortilla soup because they add slivers of fried corn tortillas as a garnish, famed Southwestern chef Dean Fearing purées them right into the soup, too. Though born in Kentucky, Fearing has been one of the leaders of New Southwestern Cuisine for more than thirty years. He served as executive chef at the justly lauded Mansion on Turtle Creek in Dallas for twenty years before starting his namesake restaurant at the nearby Ritz-Carlton Hotel.

Serves 6 to 8

SOUP

7 dried ancho chiles

3 tablespoons olive oil

6 (6-inch) corn tortillas, chopped

8 garlic cloves, minced

2 cups puréed fresh onion

6 cups puréed fresh tomatoes

3 jalapeño or serrano chiles, seeds and ribs removed, chopped

2 tablespoons ground cumin

1 tablespoon chopped fresh epazote (or substitute 3 tablespoons chopped fresh cilantro)

1½ teaspoons ground coriander

1 large bay leaf

9 cups Chicken Stock (page 14) or purchased stock

Salt and cayenne to taste

Freshly squeezed lemon juice to taste

GARNISHES

Vegetable oil for frying

6 (6-inch) corn tortillas, cut into thin strips

½ pound smoked chicken, diced

1 large avocado, peeled, seeded, and cut into small cubes

¾ cup shredded cheddar

6 tablespoons chopped green cabbage

3 tablespoons chopped radish

2 jalapeño or serrano chiles, seeds and ribs removed, finely chopped

Preheat the oven to 400°F. Cover a baking sheet with heavy-duty aluminum foil, and roast the ancho chiles for 2 to 3 minutes, or until lightly toasted. When cool enough to handle, discard the stems, break the chiles apart, and discard the seeds. Set aside.

Heat the olive oil in a 4-quart soup pot over medium heat. Add the tortillas and garlic and cook, stirring frequently, for 3 to 4 minutes, or until the tortillas are crisp and the garlic is golden brown. Add the onion purée and cook, stirring occasionally, for 5 minutes, or until reduced by half. Add the tomato purée, roasted chiles, fresh chiles, cumin, epazote, coriander, bay leaf, and stock.

Bring to a boil over medium-high heat, stirring occasionally. Reduce the heat to low, and simmer for 40 minutes. Skim the fat from the surface, if necessary.

Allow the soup to cool for 10 minutes. Purée with an immersion blender, or in a food processor fitted with the steel blade. If using a food processor, you may have to work in batches. Season the soup to taste with salt, cayenne, and lemon juice.

While the soup simmers, heat 2 inches of vegetable oil in a skillet over medium-high heat to a temperature of 365°F. Fry the tortilla strips until crisp, remove them from the skillet with tongs, and drain well on paper towels.

To serve, arrange some smoked chicken, avocado, cheddar, cabbage, radish, chiles, and tortilla strips in the bottom of warmed soup bowls, and ladle the hot soup over it. Serve immediately.

NOTE: The soup can be prepared up to 2 days in advance and refrigerated, tightly covered. Reheat over low heat, stirring occasionally. Do not prepare the garnishes until just prior to serving. Add stock or water if the soup needs thinning after reheating.

Raw epazote has a pungent flavor similar to that of fennel or tarragon, but even stronger, with hints of mint and citrus thrown in for good measure. It's frequently added to bean dishes in Latin America because of its carminative properties—it prevents gas from forming. It's still difficult to find fresh epazote in most supermarkets, even in the Southwest, so cilantro is a common substitute.

Thai Chicken Soup with Rice Noodles

Fiery chile, creamy coconut milk, and aromatic ginger flavor this Asian soup that is sold in all parts of Thailand. The coconut milk balances the more assertive flavors. Because the noodles are made from rice rather than wheat, this soup is appropriate for gluten-free diets.

Serves 6 to 8

4 ounces medium rice noodles

2 tablespoons vegetable oil

6 scallions, white parts and 4 inches of green tops, cut into ¾-inch lengths

3 garlic cloves, minced

1 Thai or jalapeño chile, seeds and ribs removed, finely chopped

1 tablespoon grated fresh ginger

2 teaspoons grated lemon zest

6 cups Chicken Stock (page 14) or purchased stock

1 cup reduced-fat coconut milk

3 tablespoons fish sauce

2 tablespoons freshly squeezed lemon juice

3 to 4 cups diced cooked chicken

3 ripe plum tomatoes, cored, seeded, and diced

1 cup firmly packed shredded bok choy leaves

Salt and freshly ground black pepper to taste

¼ cup firmly packed fresh cilantro leaves, for garnish

Bring a large pot of salted water to a boil over high heat. Add the noodles, and cook according to package directions until al dente. Drain and set aside.

While the water heats, heat the oil in a 4-quart soup pot over medium-high heat. Add the scallions, garlic, chile, ginger, and lemon zest, and cook, stirring frequently, for 3 minutes, or until the scallions are translucent.

Add the stock, coconut milk, fish sauce, and lemon juice, and bring to a boil over medium-high heat, stirring occasionally. Add the chicken, tomatoes, and bok choy, and cook for an additional 3 minutes. Stir in the noodles, season to taste with salt and pepper, and serve immediately, sprinkling each serving with cilantro.

NOTE: The soup can be prepared up to 2 days in advance and refrigerated, tightly covered; refrigerate the noodles separately. Reheat over low heat, covered, until hot, stirring occasionally.

Variations:

• Substitute medium egg noodles or a small pasta like ditalini for the rice noodles.

• Substitute 1 pound raw peeled and deveined shrimp for the cooked chicken and substitute Shrimp Stock (page 17) for the chicken stock.

....

If you're cooking a soup that contains pasta or egg noodles and plan to refrigerate it before serving it, don't add the pasta when you cook it. The pasta can absorb more liquid and become "soggy." If you are going to refrigerate leftovers after serving the soup, it's worth the few minutes it takes to pull out the pasta with a slotted spoon or tongs and refrigerate it separately.

Yucatan Chicken and Lime Broth

ADAPTED FROM BORDER GRILL, SANTA MONICA, CALIFORNIA

Famed chefs Mary Sue Milliken and Susan Feniger opened the first Border Grill in Santa Monica in 1990. This citrusy soup is garnished similarly to Tortilla Soup (page 170), but it has unique flavor.

Serves 6 to 8

SOUP

2 whole small (¾- to 1-pound) bone-in chicken breasts with skin attached

3 quarts Chicken Stock (page 14) or purchased stock

Salt to taste

1½ teaspoons black peppercorns, cracked

1½ teaspoons dried oregano

10 garlic cloves, smashed but unpeeled

2 tablespoons olive oil

1 medium onion, halved and cut lengthwise into fine julienne strips

1 small green bell pepper, seeds and ribs removed, cut into fine julienne strips

2 medium tomatoes, cored, seeded, cut into fine julienne strips

2 limes, juiced

2 strips grapefruit zest, each 3 x 1 inches

GARNISHES

½ cup vegetable oil

8 (6-inch) corn tortillas, cut into ¼-inch strips

3 serrano chiles, stemmed, seeded if desired, and minced (optional)

1 ripe avocado, peeled, seeded, and cut into chunks

2 limes, cut in wedges

....

It's important when removing the zest from a citrus fruit to make sure you get none of the white pith below the thin zest layer. The zest contains all the aromatic citrus oils, but the pith is extremely bitter and even a small amount of it can diminish the flavor of any dish.

Place the chicken breasts and stock in a 4-quart soup pot and bring to a boil over high heat. Reduce the heat to low, and skim off any scum that rises to the top in the first 15 minutes of the cooking. Add the salt, peppercorns, oregano, and garlic to the stock. Cook for an additional 15 to 20 minutes, or until the chicken is tender.

Remove the chicken from the pot with tongs, and transfer it to a platter. When the chicken is cool enough to handle, remove and discard the skin and bones. Shred the meat into strips and reserve.

Strain the stock through a sieve, pressing with the back of a spoon to extract as much liquid as possible. Discard the solids, and reserve the stock.

Heat the olive oil in the pot over medium-low heat. Add the onion and cook, stirring frequently, for 3 minutes, or until the onion is translucent. Add the pepper and cook 5 minutes longer. Add the tomatoes, shredded chicken, reserved chicken stock, lime juice, and grapefruit zest. Bring to a boil, reduce the heat to low, and simmer the soup for 10 minutes. Remove and discard the grapefruit zest, and season the soup to taste with salt and pepper.

While the soup simmers, prepare the garnishes. Heat the olive oil in a medium skillet over medium-high heat. Add the tortilla strips and fry for 2 minutes, or until crisp. Remove the strips from the skillet with tongs, drain on paper towels, and set aside.

To serve, ladle the hot soup into bowls and scatter the fried tortilla strips, chile rings, if using, and avocado over each serving. Pass the lime wedges separately.

NOTE: The soup can be prepared up to 2 days in advance and refrigerated, tightly covered. Reheat it over low heat, stirring occasionally. Prepare the garnish just prior to serving.

New Mexico Green Chile Chicken Soup

ADAPTED FROM SLURP, SANTA FE, NEW MEXICO

Authentic New Mexican chiles are zesty but not very hot, so you can achieve a real depth of flavor, as Rebecca Chastenet does in this soup. Serve it with some warmed corn tortillas on the side.

Serves 6 to 8

3 tablespoons olive oil

1 pound boneless, skinless chicken breast, cut into ½-inch cubes

1 large onion, diced

5 garlic cloves, minced

4 New Mexico green Hatch chiles, seeds and ribs removed, chopped (or substitute poblano chiles or Anaheim chiles)

1 (14.5-ounce) can diced tomatoes, undrained

2 quarts Chicken Stock (page 14) or purchased stock

1 large russet potato, peeled and diced

Salt and freshly ground black pepper to taste

¼ cup chopped fresh cilantro, for garnish

Heat the oil in a 4-quart soup pot over medium-high heat. Add the chicken and cook for 2 minutes, or until is opaque. Remove from the pot with a slotted spoon and set aside. Add the onion, garlic, and chiles, and cook, stirring frequently, for 3 minutes, or until the onion is translucent.

Add the tomatoes and stock and bring to a boil over medium-high heat, stirring occasionally. Add the potato, and simmer the soup, uncovered, for 10 minutes. Add the chicken and cook for an additional 10 to 15 minutes, or until the chicken is cooked through and no longer pink. Season the soup to taste with salt and pepper, and serve immediately, garnishing each serving with cilantro.

NOTE: The soup can be prepared up to 2 days in advance and refrigerated, tightly covered. Reheat over low heat, stirring occasionally.

....

The firepower of fresh chiles is judged on the Scoville scale, named for American pharmacist Wilbur Scoville who developed it in 1912. The number of Scoville heat units (SHU) indicates the amount of capsaicin, the chemical compound that stimulates the nerve endings in the skin, in a pepper. The higher the Scoville rating, the hotter the pepper will be. New Mexico green chiles, poblano chiles, and Anaheim chiles are all listed in the 1,000 to 2,500 zone, while serrano chiles start around 10,000. A general rule is the smaller the chile, the hotter the chile.

Italian Turkey Soup

I've often said that ground turkey is the hamburger of the twenty-first century. This quick soup scented with fresh herbs is a wonderful way to enjoy it. Serve it with Crispy Herbed Breadsticks (page 220) and a tossed salad with vinaigrette dressing.

Serves 4 to 6

2 tablespoons olive oil

1 large sweet onion, such as Vidalia or Bermuda, diced

1 carrot, diced

1 orange or yellow bell pepper, seeds and ribs removed, diced

2 garlic cloves, minced

¾ pound ground turkey

1 quart Chicken Stock (page 14) or purchased stock

1 (14.5-ounce) can diced tomatoes, drained

½ cup chopped fresh parsley, divided

1 tablespoon chopped fresh rosemary

1 tablespoon chopped fresh basil

1 bay leaf

1 (3-inch) piece Parmesan rind (optional)

4 cups firmly packed chopped fresh kale

Salt and freshly ground black pepper to taste

¾ cup freshly grated Parmesan cheese

Heat the oil in a 4-quart soup pot over medium-high heat. Add the onion, carrot, bell pepper, and garlic. Cook, stirring frequently, for 3 minutes, or until the onion is translucent. Crumble the turkey into the pot and cook for 2 minutes, or until it turns white.

Add the stock, tomatoes, 3 tablespoons of the parsley, rosemary, basil, bay leaf, and Parmesan rind, if using. Bring to a boil, stirring occasionally, then reduce the heat to low and simmer the soup, uncovered, for 15 minutes. Add the kale and simmer, covered, for 15 minutes, or until the vegetables are tender.

Remove and discard the bay leaf and the Parmesan rind, if using. Season the soup to taste with salt and pepper, and serve immediately, sprinkling each serving with some of the remaining parsley. Pass the Parmesan cheese separately.

NOTE: The soup can be prepared up to 2 days in advance and refrigerated, tightly covered. Reheat over low heat, stirring occasionally.

Variations

- Substitute ground beef for the ground turkey and substitute beef stock for the chicken stock.
- Add 1 cup cooked ditalini to the soup just prior to serving.

....

Kale, eaten both cooked and raw, is now one of the most touted superfoods around, even more so than its cousins in the cabbage family. Cooked kale is especially hailed for its ability to lower cholesterol, support the body's system for detoxification, and provide protection from developing cancers, including those of the colon, breast, and prostate.

Greek Lemon Egg Soup *(Kotosoupa Avgolemono)*

There's a satiny texture to this soup from the custard liaison and the bright flavors of dill and lemon, which enliven the broth. This recipe comes from Jim Botsacos, the former chef of my favorite Greek restaurant in New York, and the author of *The New Greek Cuisine*. In his original version, the avgolemono is a separate sauce preparation, because he uses it on many menu items, but I've simplified the recipe to make the addition just an added step.

Serves 8 to 10

STOCK

2 tablespoons olive oil

2 large onions, diced

10 cups Chicken Stock (page 14) or purchased stock

10 black peppercorns

2 bay leaves

10 sprigs fresh parsley

10 sprigs fresh dill

1 head garlic, papery skin removed and cut in half crosswise

1 whole bone-in chicken breast with skin and bones or 4 bone-in chicken thighs with skin, or some combination

SOUP

4 large eggs, lightly beaten

½ cup freshly squeezed lemon juice

2 teaspoons grated lemon zest

¼ cup chopped fresh dill

2 scallions, white parts and 4 inches of green tops, thinly sliced on the diagonal

Salt and freshly ground black pepper to taste

1¼ cups shredded arugula or other baby greens

Heat the oil in a 4-quart soup pot over medium heat. Add the onions, and cook, covered, stirring occasionally, for 10 minutes, or until the onions soften. Add the stock, peppercorns, bay leaves, parsley, dill, garlic, and chicken. Bring to a boil over high heat. Reduce the heat to low, and simmer, uncovered, for 45 to 50 minutes, or until the chicken is cooked through and no longer pink. Skim the scum that rises to the top of the pot in the first 15 minutes of the cooking time.

Remove the chicken from the soup with tongs, and when cool enough to handle, discard the skin and bones and cut the meat into bite-sized pieces. Strain the broth through a strainer, pressing the solids with the back of a spoon to extract as much liquid as possible. Discard the solids and return the soup to the pot. Skim off any fat from the surface, add the chicken meat, and bring the stock to a boil over high heat. Turn off the heat, and take the pot off the stove.

Whisk the eggs, lemon juice, and lemon zest together in a mixing bowl until light and frothy. Slowly whisk 1 cup of the soup broth into the eggs, then return the mixture to the soup pot. Stir it in, cover the pot, and allow the soup to sit for 3 minutes to thicken. Stir in the dill and scallions. Season to taste with salt and pepper, and add additional lemon juice if needed. Serve immediately, garnishing each serving with some of the arugula.

NOTE: The soup can be prepared up to 2 days in advance and refrigerated, tightly covered. Reheat over low heat, stirring occasionally, but do not allow it to boil or the eggs will scramble.

....

It's easier to remove the zest from citrus fruits before the juice is extracted because the skin is taut. Remove all the zest, not just the amount specified in a recipe, and store it refrigerated in a small plastic bag.

Greek Lemon Chicken Soup with Spinach

ADAPTED FROM SLURP, SANTA FE, NEW MEXICO

Here is a very straightforward adaptation of this Greek classic, thickened with eggs and dotted with bright green spinach leaves. Serve it with Socca (page 232) or Focaccia (page 214).

Serves 6 to 8

½ cup long-grain rice

3 tablespoons olive oil

2 medium onions, diced

2 carrots, diced

2 celery ribs, diced

2 quarts Chicken Stock (page 14) or purchased stock

1 (8-ounce) boneless, skinless chicken breast, diced

1 tablespoon dried oregano

⅓ cup freshly squeezed lemon juice or to taste

2 teaspoons grated lemon zest

2 cups firmly packed baby spinach leaves

2 large eggs

1 large egg yolk

Salt and freshly ground black pepper to taste

....

If you added beaten eggs directly to simmering soup you'd have egg drop soup. The process of heating beaten eggs with some of the hot liquid it will thicken is called "tempering." Make sure the eggs are whisked very well; clumps of white or yolk will not blend evenly. Take the pot of hot liquid off the heat, and whisk about one-fourth of it into the eggs. Now go in the other direction and, while whisking constantly, add the heated egg mixture back into the pot. Turn the heat on very low and cook until the liquid thickens, but if you see bubbles start to form, turn off the heat.

Combine the rice and 2 cups salted water in a small saucepan and bring to a boil over high heat. Reduce the heat to low, and cook, uncovered, for 15 to 18 minutes, or until tender. Drain and set aside.

Heat the oil in a 4-quart soup pot over medium-high heat. Add the onions, carrots, and celery. Cook, stirring frequently, for 5 to 7 minutes, or until the vegetables soften. Add the stock, chicken, oregano, lemon juice, and lemon zest to the pot and bring to a boil over high heat. Reduce the heat to low and simmer, uncovered, for 10 minutes. Add the rice and spinach to the soup, and cook for 3 minutes. Take the pot off the stove.

Whisk the eggs and egg yolk together in a mixing bowl until light and frothy. Slowly whisk 1 cup of the soup broth into the eggs, then return the mixture to the soup pot. Stir it in, cover the pot, and allow the soup to sit for 3 minutes to thicken. Season to taste with salt and pepper, and add additional lemon juice if needed. Serve immediately.

NOTE: The soup can be prepared up to 2 days in advance and refrigerated, tightly covered. Reheat over low heat, stirring occasionally, but do not allow it to boil or the eggs will scramble.

Smoked Chicken and Arugula Soup

ADAPTED FROM HAVEN, HOUSTON, TEXAS

Chef Randy Evans, who opened Haven in 2009, was studying to be a doctor at Baylor University when he traded the knives of an operating room for those in a kitchen. Haven is the ultimate farm to table restaurant in Texas, and the smoky nuance of the chicken is a wonderful contrast to the zesty, bright green arugula in this soup. Limpa (page 218) goes well with this soup.

Serves 6 to 8

2 tablespoons unsalted butter

1 tablespoon vegetable oil

2 garlic cloves, minced

1 large onion, diced

1 celery rib, diced

3 tablespoons all-purpose flour

2 quarts Chicken Stock (page 14) or purchased stock

½ pound arugula, chopped, divided

2 cups firmly packed, diced, cooked smoked chicken

Salt and freshly ground black pepper to taste

Additional arugula leaves, for garnish

Heat the butter and oil in a 4-quart soup pot over medium heat. Add the garlic, onion, and celery. Cook, stirring frequently, for 3 minutes, or until the onion is translucent. Stir in the flour and cook over low heat, stirring constantly, for 1 minute, or until the mixture turns slightly beige, is bubbly, and appears to have grown in volume. Increase the heat to medium, and slowly whisk in the stock. Bring to a boil, whisking frequently.

Add three-fourths of the arugula and bring to a boil, simmer for 30 minutes. Allow the soup to cool for 10 minutes. Purée with an immersion blender, or in a food processor fitted with the steel blade. If using a food processor, you may have to work in batches.

Stir in the remaining arugula and the smoked chicken. Bring to a boil over medium heat. Reduce the heat to low and simmer for 2 minutes. To serve, ladle the soup into warmed bowls and garnish each serving with additional arugula leaves.

NOTE: The soup can be prepared up to 2 days in advance and refrigerated, tightly covered. Reheat over low heat, stirring occasionally.

....

If you have leftover chicken or turkey that isn't smoked, you can get some of the same flavor in the finished soup by substituting bacon grease for the butter and oil and then adding a few drops of liquid smoke to the finished soup.

Gumbo Ya-Ya

ADAPTED FROM MR. B'S BISTRO, NEW ORLEANS, LOUISIANA

Thick, rich, and spicy is what this chicken gumbo is all about. Here's what Cindy Brennan, one of the owners of Mr. B's Bistro, wrote about this soup: "We were first introduced to this rich, dark-roux gumbo from one of our early chefs, Jimmy Smith, who grew up eating it in Cajun country. Its name is said to come from women who would cook the gumbo all day long while talking, or 'ya-ya-ing.'" Serve it with Buttermilk Biscuits (page 227) or Skillet Cornbread (page 223).

Serves 6 to 8

1 cup (2 sticks) unsalted butter

1½ cups all-purpose flour

1 red bell pepper, seeds and ribs removed, diced

1 green bell pepper, seeds and ribs removed, diced

1 medium onion, diced

1 celery rib, diced

2½ quarts Chicken Stock (page 14) or purchased stock

½ pound andouille sausage, cut into ¼-inch slices

1 tablespoon Creole seasoning

½ teaspoon crushed red pepper flakes

½ teaspoon chili powder

½ teaspoon dried thyme

2 garlic cloves, minced

1 bay leaf

3 cups firmly packed diced cooked chicken

Salt and freshly ground black pepper to taste

Hot red pepper sauce to taste

2 to 3 cups cooked white rice, hot, for serving

Preheat the oven to 450°F. Combine the butter and flour in a 4-quart soup pot. Bake the roux, stirring occasionally, for 30 to 45 minutes, or until it reaches a deep mahogany brown.

Remove the pot from the oven, and place it over medium heat. Add the red and green bell peppers and cook for 30 seconds, stirring constantly. Add the onion and celery, and cook for 30 seconds, stirring constantly. Gradually add the stock, whisking to prevent lumps from forming. Add the andouille, Creole seasoning, red pepper flakes, chili powder, thyme, garlic, and bay leaf. Bring to a boil, then reduce the heat to low, and simmer, uncovered, for 45 minutes, skimming off any fat and stirring occasionally.

Add the chicken and simmer 15 minutes. Remove and discard bay leaf. Season to taste with salt, pepper, and hot sauce, and ladle the gumbo over the rice. Serve immediately.

NOTE: The soup can be prepared up to 2 days in advance and refrigerated, tightly covered. Reheat over low heat, stirring occasionally. Add stock or water if the soup needs thinning after reheating.

....

There are many national brands of Creole seasoning on the market today, packaged by such superstar chefs as Paul Prudhomme and Emeril Lagasse. But here is a formulation to mix it yourself: Blend 3 tablespoons of paprika with 2 tablespoons each of kosher salt and granulated garlic and 1 tablespoon each of freshly ground black pepper, cayenne, dried oregano, dried thyme, and onion powder. Keep it in a cool dark place in an airtight container.

Thai Coconut Chicken Soup *(Gai Tom Kha)*

One of the wonders of authentic Thai cooking is the brightness of the flavors, and that is what appeals to me most about this soup. I developed this recipe using ingredients that can be found in any American supermarket because the traditional ingredients are still too exotic to find unless you have access to an Asian grocery. I've listed the authentic ingredients in parenthesis in case you're lucky enough to find them.

Serves 6 to 8

1 pound boneless skinless chicken breasts

3 cups Chicken Stock (page 14) or purchased stock

1 (14-ounce) can reduced-fat coconut milk

1 tablespoon grated lime zest (or 5 kaffir lime leaves, cut into thin shreds)

2 tablespoons grated fresh ginger (or 3 table- spoons shredded fresh galangal)

2 lemongrass stalks, only the tender inner parts, finely chopped

⅓ cup freshly squeezed lime juice

¼ cup Thai or Vietnamese fish sauce

2 tablespoons firmly packed light brown sugar

2 teaspoons Thai red curry paste

Salt and freshly ground black pepper to taste

¼ cup chopped fresh cilantro, for garnish

Pound the chicken breasts to an even thickness of ½ inch. Place the chicken on a sheet of plastic wrap, and place it in the freezer for 10 to 15 min- utes, or until firm. Cut the chicken into 2-inch strips, and then cut the strips against the grain into slices. Refrigerate until ready to use.

Combine the stock, coconut milk, lime zest, ginger, lemongrass, lime juice, fish sauce, brown sugar, and curry paste in a 3-quart soup pot, and bring to a boil over medium-high heat, stirring occasionally. Reduce the heat to low, and simmer for 5 minutes.

Add the chicken to the soup and cook, stirring frequently, for 3 minutes, or until the chicken is cooked through and no longer pink. Season the soup to taste with salt and pepper, if necessary. Serve immediately, sprinkling some cilantro on each serving.

NOTE: The soup can be prepared up to 2 days in advance and refrigerated, tightly covered. Reheat over low heat, stirring occasionally.

....

Thais use fish sauce (*nam pla*) at the table the way we use salt and pepper in Western cuisines; they sprinkle it on just about everything. While anchovies are usually fermented with salt to form this reddish-brown liquid, it can sometimes squid or other fish. If people have a fish allergy, they should avoid fish sauce and substitute light soy sauce with a bit of miso stirred in.

Mulligatawny

Mulligatawny, which means "pepper water" in Tamil, is a creamy Anglo-Indian dish that became popular in England during the era of the Raj. It's thickened with rice and contains some sweet apples as a foil to the spices.

Serves 6 to 8

4 tablespoons (½ stick) unsalted butter

1¼ pounds boneless, skinless chicken thighs, cut into ¾-inch cubes

Salt and freshly ground black pepper to taste

1 medium onion, diced

2 carrots, diced

1 celery rib, diced

3 garlic cloves, minced

2 tablespoons grated fresh ginger

3 tablespoons garam masala or to taste

1 teaspoon ground cumin

9 cups Chicken Stock (page 14) or purchased stock

1 cup reduced-fat coconut milk

2 Golden Delicious apples, peeled, cored, and diced

½ cup short-grain sushi rice

1 tablespoon cider vinegar

⅔ cup heavy cream

Salt and freshly ground black pepper to taste

½ cup toasted chopped cashews, for garnish

¼ cup chopped fresh cilantro, for garnish

Heat the butter in a 4-quart soup pot over medium-high heat. Add the chicken and cook, stirring frequently, for 2 minutes, or until the chicken is opaque. Remove the chicken from the pot with a slotted spoon and set aside. Add the onion, carrots, celery, garlic, and ginger. Cook, stirring frequently, for 3 minutes, or until the onion is translucent. Stir in the garam masala and cumin and cook for 1 minute, stirring constantly.

Return the chicken to the pot, and add the stock, coconut milk, apple, and rice. Bring to a boil over medium-high heat, stirring occasionally. Skim the scum that rises to the top of the pot for the first 15 minutes of the cooking time, if necessary.

Reduce the heat to low, and simmer the soup, uncovered, for 30 minutes, or until the chicken and vegetables are tender.

Stir in the vinegar and cream, and bring back to a simmer. Season the soup to taste with salt and pepper, and serve immediately, garnishing each serving with cashews and cilantro.

NOTE: The soup can be prepared up to 2 days in advance and refrigerated, tightly covered. Reheat over low heat, stirring occasionally. Add milk or cream if the soup needs thinning after reheating.

....

There is virtually no difference in flavor or consistency between regular coconut milk and the reduced-fat version. However, there is a big difference in calories and fat. Changing the heavy cream to half-and-half truly diminishes the soup, but you can save some fat calories by using the lighter coconut milk.

Creamy Chicken and Wild Rice Soup

ADAPTED FROM THE SOUPBOX, CHICAGO, ILLINOIS

There is a nutty flavor to wild rice that goes well with fresh herbs like the ones in this creamy soup. Serve it with Irish Soda Bread (page 225) and a creamy coleslaw.

Serves 6 to 8

½ cup (1 stick) unsalted butter, divided

1 medium onion, diced

1 medium carrot, diced

2 celery ribs, diced

2 garlic cloves, minced

1 cup uncooked wild rice, rinsed well

1 quart Chicken Stock (page 14) or purchased stock, divided

¼ cup all-purpose flour

3 cups whole milk

2 cups cooked diced chicken

2 teaspoons chopped fresh sage

2 teaspoons fresh thyme leaves

Salt and freshly ground black pepper to taste

Heat 4 tablespoons of the butter in a 4-quart soup pot over medium-low heat. Add the onion, carrot, and celery. Cook, covered, for 10 minutes, or until the vegetables soften. Add the garlic, and cook for 2 minutes longer.

Add the wild rice and 3 cups of the stock to the pot, and bring to a boil over high heat. Reduce the heat to low, and simmer, covered, for 35 minutes.

While the soup simmers, heat the remaining butter in a small saucepan over medium-low heat. Stir in the flour and cook, stirring constantly, for 1 minute, or until the mixture turns slightly beige, is bubbly, and appears to have grown in volume. Increase the heat to medium, and slowly whisk in the remaining stock. Bring to a boil, and simmer for 1 minute.

Add the thickened stock, milk, chicken, sage, and thyme to the pot with the vegetables and bring to a boil over medium heat, stirring occasionally. Reduce the heat to low, and simmer for 20 minutes, or until the wild rice is puffed and tender. Season the soup to taste with salt and pepper, and serve immediately.

NOTE: The soup can be prepared up to 2 days in advance and refrigerated, tightly covered. Reheat over low heat, stirring occasionally. Add milk or cream if the soup needs thinning after reheating.

....

Wild rice, native to the Chippewa Indian lands in the lake country of Minnesota, is America's only native species and is a distant cousin of Asian rice. It is really an aquatic grass, *Zizania aquatica*, and was named "wild rice" because the visual similarity to familiar rice fields. It contains more protein than most rice, and is processed by first fermenting it to develop the characteristic nutty flavor, then roasted, which accounts for the brown color.

Southwest Chicken, Corn, and Sweet Potato Chowder

There's an inherent sweetness in both sweet potatoes and corn, which in this soup is balanced by the fiery touch provided by the chiles. Chipotle chiles are smoked jalapeño chiles, and the adobo sauce in which they're packed is similar to a hot red pepper sauce. Some warm corn tortillas and a salad with avocado will complete the meal.

Serves 4 to 6

1 pound boneless, skinless chicken thighs

3 tablespoons unsalted butter

1 green bell pepper, seeds and ribs removed, chopped

1 large onion, diced

2 garlic cloves, minced

2 large sweet potatoes, peeled and cut into ¾-inch dice

1 quart Chicken Stock (page 14) or purchased stock

2 canned chipotle chiles in adobo sauce, finely chopped

2 teaspoons adobo sauce

1 (15-ounce) can creamed corn

1 cup fresh corn kernels (or substitute frozen corn, thawed)

2 cups half-and-half

Salt and freshly ground black pepper to taste

3 tablespoons chopped fresh cilantro, for garnish

Rinse the chicken and pat it dry with paper towels. Cut into ¾-inch dice.

Heat the butter in a 4-quart soup pot over medium-high heat. Add the chicken, and cook for 2 minutes, or until the chicken is opaque. Add the pepper, onion, and garlic. Cook, stirring frequently, for 3 minutes, or until the onion is translucent. Add the sweet potatoes, stock, chipotle chiles, and adobo sauce to the pot, and stir well.

Bring to soup to a boil, then reduce the heat to low and simmer, covered, for 30 to 35 minutes. Add the creamed corn, corn, and half-and-half, and simmer for 5 minutes, or until the chicken is cooked through and no longer pink and vegetables are tender. Season to taste with salt and pepper, and serve immediately, sprinkling each serving with cilantro.

NOTE: The soup can be prepared up to 2 days in advance and refrigerated, tightly covered. Reheat over low heat, stirring occasionally. Add milk or cream if the soup needs thinning after reheating.

Variation

For a less spicy soup, substitute 1 (4-ounce) can chopped mild green chiles, drained, for the chipotle chiles and adobo sauce.

....

What gives creamed corn its thick texture is the natural starches from the corn cobs. While canned creamed corn is thickened with modified starch, homemade creamed corn is made by scraping the cobs to glean all the milk and starch. Then the corn is simmered with a bit of cream and butter and seasoned with salt and pepper. When it's fresh corn season, make it yourself and experience sheer bliss.

Cream of Chicken Soup with Mushrooms

ADAPTED FROM CIRO, SUN VALLEY, IDAHO

This is a soup that the whole family will enjoy. It's straightforward and delicious with just the right balance of milk and stock to cream to make it luxurious but not too rich. Serve it with crunchy Gougères (page 231) on the side.

Serves 6 to 8

3 ounces egg noodles

4 tablespoons (½ stick) unsalted butter

1 medium onion, diced

1 celery rib, diced

1 garlic clove, minced

½ pound fresh mushrooms, wiped with a damp paper towel and thinly sliced

¼ cup all-purpose flour

1 quart Chicken Stock (page 14) or purchased stock

3 cups whole milk

1 cup heavy cream

2 cups firmly packed diced cooked chicken

Salt and freshly ground black pepper to taste

Cook the egg noodles according to package directions until al dente. Drain and set aside.

Heat the butter in a 4-quart soup pot over medium-high heat. Add the onion, celery, and garlic. Cook, stirring frequently, for 3 minutes, or until the onion is translucent. Add the mushrooms, and cook for 5 minutes, or until the mushrooms soften and the liquid in the pot evaporates.

Reduce the heat to low. Stir in the flour and cook, stirring constantly, for 1 minute, or until the mixture turns slightly beige, is bubbly, and appears to have grown in volume. Increase the heat to medium, and slowly whisk in the stock and milk. Bring to a boil, whisking frequently. Reduce the heat to low, and simmer for 10 minutes.

Add the cream, chicken, and noodles. Bring back to a simmer, and then remove the pot from the heat. Season the soup to taste with salt and pepper, and serve immediately.

NOTE: The soup can be prepared up to 2 days in advance and refrigerated, tightly covered. Reheat over low heat, stirring occasionally.

....

The point of cooking the flour for a roux before adding the liquid is to coat the protein particles so the resulting sauce or soup doesn't taste pasty. To accomplish this, the flour has to combine with fat and not water. That's why it's important to allow the moisture that will emerge from the mushrooms as they cook to evaporate before adding the flour to the pot.

Turkey Chili

INSPIRED BY *CLINTON ST. BAKING COMPANY COOKBOOK* BY DEDE LAHMAN,
NEIL KLEINBERG, AND MICHAEL HARLAN TURKELL (LITTLE, BROWN 2010)

Chef Neil Kleinberg's dish is a cross between a soup and a stew. It is eaten with a spoon, but it's really thick and satisfying with a complex flavor profile. This is one of the dishes that can be most successfully served in Bread Bowls (page 216).

Serves 8 to 10

2 tablespoons olive oil

1 medium Spanish onion, diced

2 medium carrots, diced

3 celery ribs, diced

1 medium red bell pepper, seeds and ribs removed, diced

5 garlic cloves, minced

1 pound ground turkey

1½ tablespoons chili powder

1½ teaspoons dried oregano

1½ teaspoons ground cumin

½ teaspoon dried thyme

½ teaspoon crushed red pepper flakes

2 bay leaves

2 dashes hot red pepper sauce

1 tablespoon tomato paste

1 chipotle pepper in adobo sauce, drained and finely chopped

3 cups crushed tomatoes

2 cups Chicken Stock (page 14) or purchased stock

1 (15-ounce) can red kidney beans, drained and rinsed

Salt and freshly ground black pepper to taste

Shredded sharp cheddar cheese, for garnish

Guacamole, for garnish

Crushed tortilla chips, for garnish

Sour cream, for garnish

Heat the oil in a 4-quart soup pot over medium-high heat. Add the onion, carrots, celery, pepper, and garlic. Cook, stirring frequently, for 5 to 7 minutes, or until the vegetables are soft and slightly browned. Add the turkey, and break up lumps with a spoon. Cook for 2 minutes, or until it lightens in color. Add the chili powder, oregano, cumin, thyme, red pepper flakes, bay leaves, hot sauce tomato paste, and chipotle pepper. Cook for 1 minute, stirring constantly.

Stir in the tomatoes and stock, and bring to a boil, stirring occasionally. Reduce the heat to low, and simmer, uncovered, for 15 minutes. Add the kidney beans, and simmer for 5 minutes. Remove and discard the bay leaves, and season the soup to taste with salt and pepper. Serve immediately, passing bowls of shredded cheddar, guacamole, crushed tortilla chips, and sour cream separately.

NOTE: The soup can be prepared up to 2 days in advance and refrigerated, tightly covered. Reheat over low heat, stirring occasionally.

....

Cooking dried herbs and spices before liquid is added to a recipe helps to bring out their flavors and aromas and takes away any "raw" taste. This process is especially important for mixtures like chili powder and curry powder.

8   *Meaty Soups*

These are all stick-to-the-ribs sorts of soups that are a whole meal when served with crispy bread and a tossed salad to add additional crunch, because the vegetables in the soups are all soft. In this chapter, you'll find recipes from a number of different cuisines, ranging from Vietnamese and Chinese to Mexican and Spanish.

Because these soups are made with meats many have rather long cooking times. But they all freeze well, so it makes sense to do a whole batch and have them around for winter "dinner insurance."

The Benefits of Browning

For red meats like beef, browning is the initial step to a delicious dish; it's an optional step for poultry and pork, and totally unnecessary for fish and seafood. What browning accomplishes is called the Maillard reaction, named for an early-twentieth century chemist, Louis Camille Maillard, who discovered it. A chemical reaction that takes place on the surface of meats creating the development of flavor, it takes place when food reaches 285°F, and that can only be done in a hot pan before cooking. Otherwise, the temperature of the meat only reaches 212°F, which is the simmering temperature of the soup.

Browning seals in juices as it makes foods more visually appealing, too. Here are some tips for browning foods to be braised:

- Dry food well. Moisture causes splatters, which messes up the stove, and can burn the cook.

- Preheat the pan. You have to wait until the fat is very hot, or the food will not brown.

- Don't crowd the pan. For food to brown it needs room for the steam to escape that's created when the cold food hits the hot pan.

All meats *not* coated with flour can be browned under the broiler as well as in a pan. Flour needs the fat in the pan to cook it properly. But you want to preheat the broiler for at least 10 or 15 minutes to create the brown crust.

Beef and Beet Borscht

Roasting the beets intensifies their innate sweetness, and also turns this traditional Eastern European soup a bright crimson red. Serve it with a loaf of Limpa (page 218) or Pretzel Rolls (page 219).

Serves 6 to 8

1 pound fresh beets

1 pound boneless chuck roast, trimmed and cut into ¾-inch dice

Salt and freshly ground black pepper to taste

2 tablespoons vegetable oil

1 large onion, diced

1 large carrot, chopped

2 garlic cloves, minced

6 cups firmly packed shredded green cabbage

6 cups Beef Stock (page 15) or purchased stock

1 (14.5-ounce) can diced tomatoes, undrained

2 tablespoons tomato paste

3 tablespoons chopped fresh parsley

1 pound redskin potatoes, scrubbed and cut into 1-inch cubes

3 tablespoons freshly squeezed lemon juice

3 tablespoons granulated sugar

¾ cup sour cream, for garnish

....

The pigment that gives beets their rich, purple-crimson color—betacyanin—is also a powerful cancer-fighting agent. Beets' potential effectiveness against colon cancer, in particular, has been demonstrated in several studies. They are also high in manganese and folate.

Preheat the oven to 425°F. Cut the leaves off the beets, leaving the stems attached. Scrub the beets gently, and wrap them in a double layer of heavy-duty aluminum foil. Place the foil packet on a baking sheet, and bake the beets for 1 to 1¼ hours, or until they are tender when pierced with the tip of a knife. When the beets are cool enough to handle, peel and cut them into ½-inch dice.

While the beets bake, rinse the beef and pat it dry with paper towels. Sprinkle the beef with salt and pepper.

Heat the oil in a 4-quart soup pot over medium-high heat. Add the beef, and brown it well on all sides. Remove the beef from the pot with a slotted spoon, and set aside. Add the onion, carrot, and garlic to the pot, and cook, stirring frequently, for 3 minutes, or until the onion is translucent. Add the cabbage, and cook for 2 minutes, or until the cabbage wilts.

Return the beef to the pot, and add the stock, tomatoes, tomato paste, and parsley. Bring to a boil over medium-high heat, reduce the heat to low, and simmer, covered, for 1½ hours, adding the beets to the pot when they are ready.

Add the potatoes, lemon juice, and sugar to the pot, and boil for an additional 30 minutes, or until the beef and potatoes are tender. Season the soup to taste with salt and pepper, and serve immediately, garnishing each serving with sour cream.

NOTE: The soup can be prepared up to 2 days in advance and refrigerated, tightly covered. Reheat over low heat, stirring occasionally.

Barley Mushroom Soup

We can thank the nineteenth-century immigration of Eastern European Jews for this hearty and warming winter soup, as well as for borscht and matzo ball soup. Barley grew well in the cold climate of Russia and Poland, and mushrooms could be harvested in the fall and dried for use all winter. This is truly a meal in a bowl, with nothing else needed. It is also an excellent soup to serve in Bread Bowls (page 216) or with a crusty loaf of Limpa (page 218).

Serves 6 to 8

¼ cup chopped dried porcini mushrooms

2 quarts Beef Stock (page 215) or purchased stock, divided

2 tablespoons vegetable oil

¾ pound beef chuck or brisket, cut into ½-inch cubes

1 large sweet onion, such as Vidalia or Bermuda, diced

2 carrots, sliced

2 celery ribs, sliced

2 garlic cloves, minced

1 pound fresh cremini mushrooms, wiped with a damp paper towel and sliced

¼ cup all-purpose flour

1 cup whole hulled barley, rinsed well

¼ cup chopped fresh parsley, divided

2 teaspoons fresh thyme

1 bay leaf

Salt and freshly ground black pepper to taste

....

The difference between whole hulled barley and pearled barley is the same as that between brown rice and white rice. The latter has been milled to remove the outer coating, so it is not as nutritious nor does it contain as much fiber. If you are substituting pearled barley in this or any other recipe, the cooking time will be about 40 minutes, rather than the 1 to 1¼ hours listed.

Combine the dried mushrooms and ¾ cup stock in a microwave-safe container. Microwave on High (100 percent power) for 1 to 1½ minutes, or until the stock boils. Soak the mushrooms in the stock, pushing them down into the liquid with the back of a spoon, for 10 minutes. Drain the mushrooms, reserving the stock. Strain the stock through a sieve lined with a paper coffee filter or a paper towel. Set aside.

Heat the oil in a 4-quart soup pot over medium-high heat. Add the beef, and brown on all sides. Remove the beef from the pot with a slotted spoon and set aside. Add the onion, carrots, celery, and garlic to the pot. Cook, stirring frequently, for 3 minutes, or until the onion is translucent. Add the fresh mushrooms, and cook, stirring frequently, for 5 to 7 minutes, or until the mushrooms begin to soften. Stir in the flour, and cook for 3 minutes, stirring constantly.

Add the beef, remaining stock, reserved mushroom stock, soaked dried mushrooms, barley, 2 tablespoons of the parsley, thyme, and bay leaf to the pot. Bring to a boil over medium-high heat, stirring occasionally.

Reduce the heat to low, cover the pot, and cook the soup for 1 to 1¼ hours, or until the barley is tender. Remove and discard the bay leaf, season the soup to taste with salt and pepper, and serve immediately, sprinkling each serving with the remaining parsley.

NOTE: The soup can be prepared up to 2 days in advance and refrigerated, tightly covered. Reheat over low heat, stirring occasionally. Add stock or water if the soup needs thinning after reheating.

Ropa Vieja

ADAPTED FROM BORDER GRILL, SANTA MONICA, CALIFORNIA

Ropa vieja literally translates as "old clothes," and traditional versions of this Cuban dish are made from whatever simple stew might be left over and is then joined with leftover vegetables and some broth. This updated version from Border Grill is served with warm tortillas, fried plantains, and a fresh tomato salsa. It's a satisfying meal, although not too heavy to enjoy during warmer months.

Serves 4 to 6

SOUP

2 poblano chiles

1 red bell pepper

1 pound pork loin or skirt steak, cut into bite-sized strips

Salt and freshly ground black pepper to taste

2 tablespoons olive oil

Salt and freshly ground black pepper to taste

1 large onion, halved and thinly sliced

4 garlic cloves, minced

2 teaspoons ground cumin

2 celery ribs, diced

1 medium carrot, diced

1 quart Chicken Stock (page 14) or purchased stock

1 (15-ounce) can black beans, drained and rinsed

6 tablespoons red wine vinegar

½ bunch cilantro, chopped

GARNISH

2 ripe plantains, for garnish

Oil for frying

Flour or corn tortillas, warmed, for garnish

Fresh tomato salsa, for garnish

Cut a small slit in the cap end of the poblano chiles and bell pepper. Roast the peppers over a gas flame or under the oven broiler. Keep turning so that their skin chars evenly. Transfer the peppers to a heavy resealable plastic bag and allow them to steam for 10 to 15 minutes. When cool enough to handle, pull off the charred skin by hand and dip the peppers in water to remove any blackened bits. Once peeled, discard the stems, seeds, and ribs. Cut the peppers into fine julienne strips, and set aside.

Season the meat to taste with salt and pepper. Heat the oil in a large skillet over medium-high heat. Cook meat until browned on all sides and just cooked through. Remove the meat from the pan with a slotted spoon, and set aside.

Add the onion to the skillet and cook, stirring frequently, for 10 minutes, or until golden. Add the garlic and cumin and cook for 1 minute, stirring constantly. Stir in the celery, carrot, poblano chiles, and bell pepper, and cook for 2 minutes. Scrape the mixture into a 4-quart soup pot, and add the stock and beans. Bring to a boil over high heat, then reduce the heat to low, and simmer for 10 minutes. Add the reserved meat to the pot along with any accumulated juices. Stir in the vinegar and cilantro and cook just to heat through. Adjust the seasoning, if necessary.

While the soup simmers, prepare the plantains. Cut the plantains into 1-inch pieces. Heat 2 inches of oil in a saucepan over medium-high heat to a temperature of 365°F. Fry the plantains for 5 minutes, or until they begin to brown. Remove the plantains from the pan with a slotted spoon and drain well on paper towels. Flatten the plantains with the bottom of a metal can or small saucepan to half their height. Heat the oil to 385°F and fry the plantains again for 3 minutes, or until browned. Drain again and keep warm. To serve, ladle the hot soup into bowls, and pass the tortillas, plantains, and salsa separately.

NOTE: The soup can be prepared up to 2 days in advance and refrigerated, tightly covered. Reheat over low heat, stirring occasionally. Do not prepare the garnish until just prior to serving.

....

This dish is perfect for using up leftover pot roast, beef brisket, or roasted pork butt. Just shred the cooked meat with a fork and add it to the soup at same time as the vinegar and cilantro.

Mexican Albondigas Soup with Chorizo Meatballs

Filled with healthful vegetables and legumes, this soup is enriched by the flavorful meatballs made of earthy and spicy chorizo sausage. Serve it with corn tortillas and a tomato salad.

Serves 6 to 8

SOUP

2 tablespoons olive oil

1 large onion, diced

2 garlic cloves, minced

1 jalapeño or serrano chile, seeds and ribs removed, finely chopped

2 carrots, sliced

2 celery ribs, sliced

8 cups Chicken Stock (page 14) or purchased stock

1 (14.5-ounce) can diced tomatoes, undrained

2 small zucchini, diced

1 (15-ounce) can garbanzo beans, drained and rinsed

Salt and freshly ground black pepper to taste

MEATBALLS

1/4 cup olive oil

3 garlic cloves, peeled

1 cup firmly packed fresh cilantro leaves

1 pound ground pork

1/2 pound chorizo, removed from casings if necessary

1 large egg, lightly beaten

1/2 cup plain breadcrumbs

Salt and freshly ground black pepper to taste

Nonstick cooking spray

Heat the oil in a 4-quart soup pot over medium-high heat. Add the onion, garlic, and chile, and cook, stirring frequently, for 3 minutes, or until the onion is translucent. Add the carrots, celery, stock, and tomatoes, and bring to a boil over medium-high heat. Reduce the heat to low, and simmer the soup, covered, for 15 minutes. Add the zucchini and garbanzo beans, and simmer for an additional 10 minutes, or until the vegetables are tender. Keep the soup hot.

While the soup simmers, make the meatballs. Preheat the oven to 450°F, line a rimmed baking sheet with heavy-duty aluminum foil, and spray the foil with nonstick cooking spray.

Combine the oil, garlic, and cilantro in a blender or food processor fitted with a steel blade, and purée until smooth. Combine the purée, pork, chorizo, egg, and breadcrumbs in a mixing bowl, and mix well. Season to taste with salt and pepper. Form the mixture into 1-inch meatballs, and arrange the meatballs on the prepared pan. Spray the tops of the meatballs with nonstick cooking spray.

Bake the meatballs for 8 to 10 minutes, or until cooked through. Add the meatballs to the soup, and simmer for 5 minutes. Season the soup to taste with salt and pepper, and serve immediately.

NOTE: The soup can be made up to 2 days in advance and refrigerated, tightly covered. Reheat over low heat, covered.

....

Chorizo, pronounced *chore-EAT-zoh*, is a highly-seasoned pork sausage flavored with garlic, chili powder, and other spices. It's used in both Mexican and Spanish cooking; if you can't find it, look for its cousin from the Iberian peninsula, linguiça, pronounced *ling-GWE-sah*.

Scotch Broth

While there are many wonderful soups that are based on beef, there are very few that use lamb, a meat I adore for its innate rich flavor, and traditional Scotch broth is one of them. Along with Scotch eggs and Dundee cake, this soup is one of the best-known dishes of Scottish cuisine. Vegetables and barley in a richly flavored broth join the lamb. My version contains some herbs not usually found in historic versions.

Serves 6 to 8

2 tablespoons vegetable oil

1¼ pounds boneless lamb shoulder, cut into ¾-inch cubes

1 large onion, diced

2 garlic cloves, minced

5 cups Beef Stock (page 15) or purchased stock

1 quart Vegetable Stock (page 16) or purchased stock

3 tablespoons chopped fresh parsley

2 bay leaves

1 tablespoon fresh thyme leaves

2 carrots, diced

2 parsnips, diced

½ rutabaga, diced

⅔ cup pearl barley, rinsed well

Salt and freshly ground black pepper to taste

Heat the oil in a 4-quart soup pot over medium-high heat. Add the lamb shoulder and cook, stirring frequently, until the lamb is browned on all sides. Add the onion and garlic, and cook, stirring frequently, for 3 minutes, or until the onion is translucent.

Add the beef stock, vegetable stock, parsley, bay leaves, and thyme to the pot, and bring to a boil over medium-high heat. Reduce the heat to low. Skim the scum that rises to the top of the pot in the first 15 minutes of the cooking time. Cook, partially covered, for 1 hour. Add the carrots, parsnips, rutabaga, and barley. Bring the soup back to a boil and simmer, covered, for 45 minutes to 1 hour, or until the lamb and vegetables are tender. Remove and discard the bay leaves, and season the soup to taste with salt and pepper. Serve immediately.

NOTE: The soup can be prepared up to 2 days in advance and refrigerated, tightly covered. Reheat over low heat, stirring occasionally. Add stock or water if the soup needs thinning after reheating.

In the eighteenth century, James Boswell recounted Dr. Samuel Johnson's first encounter with Scotch broth in his famed biography, *The Life of Samuel Johnson*. After Johnson had eaten a few bowls of the soup, Boswell asked if he'd never had it before. "No, sir," Johnson replied, "but I don't care how soon I eat it again." But the tradition remains in Scotland today to eat Scotch broth for good luck on New Year's Day.

Vietnamese Rice Chowder with Pork *(Chao)*

Vietnamese cuisine is known for its soups, most especially *pho*. But I discovered this comforting rice chowder, similar to a congee, at a restaurant in my neighborhood. It's subtle and the nuances of flavor from the fried shallots and scallions add complexity to the dish.

Serves 6 to 8

2 thick or 3 thin scallions

2 quarts Chicken Stock (page 14) or purchased stock

3 tablespoons finely julienned of fresh ginger

1 cup short-grain (sushi) rice

¼ pound ground pork

1 tablespoon Vietnamese fish sauce (*nuoc cham*)

½ teaspoon granulated sugar

4 teaspoons vegetable oil, divided

1 shallot, minced

1 to 2 tablespoons chopped fresh cilantro

Salt and freshly ground white pepper to taste

••

It's always important to use the rice specified in a recipe because each of the thousands of species, all of which came from one parent in India many millennia ago, are different. Some rices, like basmati and jasmine, are known for their fragrance, while other species, like Arborio and sushi rice, have a high starch content. For this soup, you want the rice to fall apart and thicken the broth, and sushi rice is perfect for that task.

Thinly slice the white parts of the scallions. Slice 4 inches of the green tops into ¼-inch slices. Set aside the white rings and green tops separately.

Combine the stock, white scallion rings, and ginger in a saucepan, and bring to a boil over high heat, stirring occasionally.

While the stock heats, rinse the rice in a sieve until the water coming from the rice is clear. Add the rice to the boiling stock, and reduce the heat to very low. Simmer the soup, covered, stirring occasionally, for 25 to 30 minutes, or until the rice is falling apart.

While the soup simmers, combine the pork, fish sauce, and sugar in a small bowl, and mix well. Heat 2 teaspoons of the oil in a skillet over medium-high heat. Cook the shallot, stirring occasionally, for 3 to 5 minutes, or until the shallot is lightly browned. Scrape the shallot out of the skillet, and set aside.

Add the remaining oil to the skillet. Crumble the pork into the skillet, and stir-fry until no pink remains. Remove the pork from the skillet with a slotted spoon, and set aside.

Add the pork and fried shallot to the soup, and simmer for 3 to 5 minutes, or until the pork is cooked through. Add the green scallion tops and cilantro, and simmer 1 minute. Season the soup to taste with salt and pepper, and serve immediately.

NOTE: The soup can be prepared up to 2 days in advance and refrigerated, tightly covered. Reheat over low heat, stirring occasionally. Add stock or water if the soup needs thinning after reheating.

Variation

Substitute ground turkey for the pork.

Hot and Sour Soup

ADAPTED FROM SUSANNA FOO'S GOURMET KITCHEN, RADNOR, PENNSYLVANIA

Back in the late 1960s, I was introduced to hot and sour soup at a small hole-in-the-wall Chinese restaurant in Harlem. It was my first venture into the wonders of spicy Chinese food and remains one of my favorites. This is truly warming on a chilly day.

Serves 6 to 8

⅓ pound lean boneless pork

1 tablespoon brandy

¼ cup cornstarch, divided

¼ cup soy sauce, divided

2 quarts Chicken Stock (page 14) or purchased stock, divided

12 dried tree ear mushrooms

12 dried lily bud mushrooms

3 tablespoons white wine vinegar, or to taste

1½ teaspoons freshly ground white pepper, or to taste

¼ teaspoon cayenne, or to taste

1 ounce fresh shiitake mushrooms, stemmed and cut into ¼-inch slivers

6 ounces firm tofu, drained and cut into ½-inch dice

2 large eggs, lightly beaten

2 teaspoons Asian sesame oil

Salt to taste

½ cup thinly sliced scallion greens for garnish

2 tablespoons chopped fresh cilantro for garnish

....

Unlike dried shiitake mushrooms, which are the most common ones used in Chinese cooking, tree ear mushrooms, sometimes called cloud ear, expand greatly when rehydrated. They've been used in Chinese cooking since the sixth century. After rehydrating, examine them carefully and discard any stems you see. Then slice them into shreds.

Place the pork on a sheet of plastic wrap in the freezer for 15 minutes or until firm. Slice the pork into ½-inch-thick slices, and then stack the slices and cut them into thin shreds. Combine the pork, brandy, 1 tablespoon cornstarch, and 1 tablespoon of the soy sauce in a bowl, and mix well.

Bring 2 cups of the stock to a boil in a small saucepan or in the microwave oven. Add the tree ear mushrooms and lily bud mushrooms. Soak the mushrooms in the boiling stock, pushing them down into the liquid with the back of a spoon, for 10 minutes. Drain the mushrooms, reserving the stock. Slice the tree ear mushrooms into shreds. Strain the stock through a sieve lined with a paper coffee filter or paper towel. Set aside.

Place the mushroom stock, remaining stock, remaining soy sauce, vinegar, pepper, and cayenne in a 4-quart soup pot. Bring to a boil over medium-high heat, stirring occasionally. Mix the remaining cornstarch with ¼ cup cold water, and stir well to dissolve the cornstarch. Add the mixture to the boiling soup along with the pork. Simmer, uncovered, for 20 minutes. Add the rehydrated mushrooms, fresh mushrooms, and tofu, and simmer for another 10 minutes.

Slowly add the eggs to the simmering soup, stirring gently in one direction. When the eggs are added, stir in the sesame oil, and season to taste with salt and additional pepper. To serve, ladle into bowls, sprinkling each serving with scallion greens and cilantro.

NOTE: The soup can be prepared up to 2 days in advance and refrigerated, tightly covered. Reheat over low heat, stirring occasionally. Do not prepare the garnish until just prior to serving.

Variation

Substitute chicken or beef for the pork.

Italian Wedding Soup

Tasty greens, swirls of egg, lots of heady Parmesan, and flavorful meatballs are the hallmarks of this soup. Wedding soup is actually Italian-American rather than tied to any Italian region. The name is a mistranslation of *minestra maritata* which has nothing to do with nuptials, but is a reference to the fact that green vegetables and meats go well together. While traditionally the meatballs are dropped into the simmering soup to cook, I find it more visually appealing to brown them first in the oven.

Serves 6 to 8

3 large eggs, divided

½ cup seasoned Italian breadcrumbs

¼ cup whole milk

1 small onion, grated

2 garlic cloves, minced

1/4 cup chopped fresh Italian parsley

1 cup freshly grated Parmesan cheese, divided

3/4 pound ground veal

1/2 pound ground pork

Salt and freshly ground black pepper to taste

2 quarts Chicken Stock (page 14) or purchased stock

1 (1-pound) head of escarole, cored, and coarsely chopped

Nonstick cooking spray

....

If you're not sure how fresh your eggs are, place them in a mixing bowl filled with cold water. As eggs age, they develop air pockets, so older eggs float while fresher ones sink. If the eggs are floating high on the surface of the water, it's best to get a fresh dozen.

Preheat the oven to 425°F, line a baking sheet with heavy-duty aluminum foil, and grease the foil with nonstick cooking spray.

Combine 1 egg with the breadcrumbs, milk, onion, garlic, parsley, and ½ cup Parmesan, and mix well. Add the veal and pork, season to taste with salt and pepper, and mix well. Form the mixture into 1-inch meatballs, and arrange them on the prepared baking sheet. Bake the meatballs for 10 to 12 minutes, or until lightly browned.

Combine the chicken stock and escarole in a 4-quart soup pot, and bring to a boil over medium-high heat. Reduce the heat to low, and simmer the soup, uncovered, for 10 minutes. Add the meatballs, and simmer for an additional 5 minutes, or until the escarole is tender.

Whisk the remaining 2 eggs with 2 tablespoons of the remaining cheese. Stir the soup and gradually add the egg mixture to form thin strands. Season to taste with salt and pepper, and serve immediately, passing the remaining cheese separately.

NOTE: The soup can be prepared up to 2 days in advance and refrigerated, tightly covered. Reheat over low heat, stirring occasionally.

Variations

- Substitute ground turkey for the ground veal and pork.

- Add ½ to ¾ cup ditalini or orzo to the soup along with the meatballs, and cook until the pasta is al dente.

Sweet Potato and Ham Chowder

Here's another soup coming straight out of the South, and Buttermilk Biscuits (page 227) are the best to serve with it. Herbs balance the innate sweetness of the potato, and the addition of hearty ham elevates it to meal-in-a-bowl status. Crunchy cole slaw goes nicely with it, too.

Serves 6

4 tablespoons (½ stick) unsalted butter, divided

2 tablespoons olive oil

1 medium onion, diced

2 celery ribs, diced

1 large carrot, diced

2 garlic cloves, minced

3 tablespoons all-purpose flour

1 quart Ham Stock (page 20), Chicken Stock (page 14), or purchased stock

3 cups light cream

3 medium sweet potatoes (about 6 ounces each), peeled and diced

2 tablespoons chopped fresh parsley

2 teaspoons fresh thyme leaves

2 teaspoons chopped fresh rosemary

1 bay leaf

1½ to 2 cups diced cooked ham

Salt and freshly ground black pepper to taste

½ cup sour cream or crème fraîche, for garnish

3 tablespoons snipped fresh chives, for garnish

Heat 2 tablespoons of the butter and the oil in a 4-quart soup pot over medium-high heat. Add the onion, celery, carrot, and garlic, and cook, stirring frequently, for 3 minutes, or until the onion is translucent.

Reduce the heat to low, add the remaining butter, and stir in the flour. Cook, stirring constantly, for 1 minute, or until the mixture turns slightly beige, is bubbly, and appears to have grown in volume. Increase the heat to medium, and slowly whisk in the stock and cream. Bring to a boil, whisking frequently.

Add the sweet potato cubes, parsley, thyme, rosemary, and bay leaf. Bring to a boil, then reduce the heat to low and simmer the soup, partially covered and stirring it occasionally, for 15 minutes, or until the sweet potatoes are very tender. Add the ham and cook for 3 minutes.

Remove and discard the bay leaf, season the soup to taste with salt and pepper, and serve immediately, garnishing each serving with sour cream and chives.

NOTE: The soup can be prepared up to 2 days in advance and refrigerated, tightly covered. Reheat over low heat, stirring occasionally. Add milk or cream if the soup needs thinning after reheating.

One of the wonderful things about ham stock is the smoky nuance it adds to soups. Another way to achieve that same undertaste is by substituting bacon grease for the butter and vegetable oil specified in the recipe.

Caldo Gallego

Caldo gallego translates literally as "soup from Galicia," which is the birthplace of this popular Spanish soup that blends beans and greens with different types of sausage. Jose Garces, who opened Amada in 2005 and was awarded the James Beard Award for Outstanding Chef in the Mid-Atlantic Region in 2009, developed this version.

Serves 6 to 8

2 cups small white navy beans

1 tablespoon olive oil

½ pound bacon, cut into ½-inch pieces

1 large onion, diced

3 garlic cloves, minced

1 teaspoon Spanish paprika

½ pound chorizo de Bilbao, diced

1 (½-pound) smoked pork hock, skin scored

9 cups Ham Stock (page 201), Chicken Stock (page 14), or purchased stock

2 Yukon Gold potatoes, peeled and diced

2 cups firmly packed shredded escarole

3 cups firmly packed shredded turnip greens

Salt and freshly ground black pepper to taste

....

Chorizo de Bilbao is a semi-cured sausage and one of Spain's most popular cooking chorizos. It originated in the Basque provinces around Pamplona. The pungent, slightly firm meat is seasoned with the usual Spanish trinity of garlic, pimento, and pepper, but it's also laced with cumin and oregano. It's fairly easy to find, especially in Hispanic markets.

Rinse the beans in a colander and place them in a mixing bowl covered with cold, salted water. Allow the beans to soak overnight. Alternatively, place the beans into a saucepan of salted water and bring to a boil over high heat. Boil 1 minute. Turn off the heat, cover the pan, and soak the beans for 1 hour. With either soaking method, drain the beans, discard the soaking water, and cook or refrigerate immediately.

Heat the oil in a 4-quart soup pot over medium-high heat. Add the bacon and cook for 5 to 7 minutes, or until crisp. Remove the bacon from the pot with a slotted spoon, and drain on paper towels. Set aside.

Add the onion and garlic, and cook, stirring frequently, for 3 minutes, or until the onion is translucent. Stir in the paprika and cook for 1 minute, stirring constantly. Add the beans, chorizo, pork hock, and stock, and bring to a boil over high heat, stirring occasionally.

Reduce the heat to low, and simmer, partially covered, for 1¼ hours. Remove the pork hock, and when cool enough to handle, shred the meat and discard the skin and bones. Set aside.

Add the potatoes, escarole, and turnip greens to the soup, and cook for 45 minutes to 1 hour, or until the beans are very soft. Season the soup to taste with salt and pepper, and serve immediately, garnishing each serving with bacon and some of the shredded pork meat.

NOTE: The soup can be prepared up to 2 days in advance and refrigerated, tightly covered. Reheat over low heat, stirring occasionally.

Cheddar Soup with Bacon

ADAPTED FROM THE SOUPBOX, CHICAGO, ILLINOIS

Here's a soup that takes the chill out of the most frosty day in the Windy City. The stock and beer base is joined with a béchamel sauce into which lots of sharp cheddar is added. This thick and rich soup is a great one to serve in Bread Bowls (page 216).

Serves 6 to 8

¾ pound bacon, diced

1 medium onion, chopped

1 medium carrot, chopped

2 celery ribs, chopped

2 garlic cloves, minced

3 cups Chicken Stock (page 14) or purchased stock

1 (12-ounce) can or bottle lager beer

4 tablespoons (½ stick) unsalted butter

¼ cup all-purpose flour

3 cups whole milk

5 cups firmly packed grated sharp cheddar cheese

1 tablespoon whole grain mustard

2 teaspoons hot red pepper sauce or to taste

Salt and freshly ground black pepper to taste

....

It can sometimes be difficult to separate slices of bacon when they're chilled because they're right out of the refrigerator. Throw the whole amount into your pan and within one minute the slices will warm up and you can separate them from each other with tongs.

Cook the bacon in a 4-quart soup pot over medium-high heat for 5 to 7 minutes, or until crisp. Remove the bacon from the pot with a slotted spoon, and drain on paper towels. Set aside.

Discard all but 3 tablespoons of bacon grease from the pot. Add the onion, carrot, celery, and garlic. Cook, stirring frequently, for 3 minutes, or until the onion is translucent. Add the stock and beer and bring to a boil. Reduce the heat to low and simmer the soup, uncovered, for 15 minutes, or until the vegetables are tender.

While the soup simmers, heat the butter in a saucepan over medium-low heat. Stir in the flour and cook, stirring constantly, for 1 minute, or until the mixture turns slightly beige, is bubbly, and appears to have grown in volume. Increase the heat to medium, and slowly whisk in the milk. Bring to a boil, whisking frequently. Reduce the heat to low, and simmer the sauce for 1 minute.

Add the sauce to the soup mixture, and bring back to a simmer. Add the cheese to the soup by ½-cup measures, stirring until the cheese melts before making another addition. Return half of the bacon to the pot, and stir in the mustard and hot red pepper sauce. Season to taste with salt and pepper and serve immediately, garnishing each serving with some of the remaining bacon.

NOTE: The soup can be prepared up to 2 days in advance and refrigerated, tightly covered. Reheat over low heat, stirring occasionally. Add milk or cream if the soup needs thinning after reheating.

Variation

Substitute Gruyère or Swiss cheese for the cheddar.

Kale Soup with Linguiça (Caldo Verde)

There is a strong Portuguese influence in the cooking of southern New England, dating back to the early-nineteenth-century whaling era. I encountered this soup first while living on Nantucket, and there are versions of it on the menus of every Portuguese restaurant in Providence, too. The combination of spicy sausage with hearty greens is both delicious and visually pleasing. Serve it with Crispy Herbed Breadsticks (page 220).

Makes 4 to 6 servings

1 tablespoon olive oil

½ pound linguiça, chouriço, or smoked kielbasa, diced

1 large onion, diced

2 garlic cloves, minced

1½ pounds boiling potatoes, peeled and diced

5 cups Chicken Stock (page 14) or purchased stock

1 pound fresh kale

Salt and freshly ground black pepper to taste

....

Kale is a member of the cabbage family, now seen as superfoods because of their high levels of phytonutrients, especially a group called the glucosinolates. These sulfur-containing compounds have a proven track record of lowering the risk of certain cancers, including colorectal cancer, breast cancer, and prostate cancer. In addition, the glucosinolates have antiviral and antibacterial properties, as well as anti-inflammatory effects.

Heat the oil in a 4-quart soup pot over medium-high heat. Add the sausage and cook, stirring frequently, for 3 to 5 minutes, or until browned. Remove from the pot with a slotted spoon, and set aside. Discard all but 2 tablespoons of grease from the pot.

Add the onion and garlic, and cook, stirring frequently, for 3 minutes, or until the onion is translucent. Add the potatoes and stock to the pot, and bring to a boil over medium-high heat. Simmer, partially covered, for 20 to 25 minutes, or until the potatoes are tender.

While the soup simmers, prepare the kale. Rinse the kale and discard the stems and center of the ribs. Cut the leaves crosswise into thin slices.

Allow the soup to cool for 10 minutes. Purée with an immersion blender, or in a food processor fitted with the steel blade. If using a food processor, you may have to work in batches.

Bring the soup to a boil over medium heat, stirring occasionally. Return the sausage to the pot and stir in the kale. Reduce the heat to low, and simmer, covered, for 20 to 30 minutes, or until the kale is cooked and tender. Season the soup to taste with salt and pepper, and serve immediately.

NOTE: The soup can be prepared up to 2 days in advance and refrigerated, tightly covered. Reheat over low heat, stirring occasionally. Add stock or water if the soup needs thinning after reheating.

Variation

Substitute escarole or Swiss chard for the kale.

Pepperoni Soup

This recipe comes from the kitchen of executive chef David Bull's grandmother, and it is like a liquid version of the flavors you get when you take a bite of gooey pepperoni pizza. Serve it with a raw fennel salad or a tossed salad with balsamic vinaigrette.

Serves 6 to 8

3 tablespoons unsalted butter

3 tablespoons olive oil

½ pound pepperoni, cut into small dice

2 large onions, diced

3 celery ribs, diced

6 garlic cloves, minced

⅓ teaspoon celery seeds

1 teaspoon crushed red pepper flakes or to taste

3 tablespoons chopped fresh basil

3 tablespoons chopped fresh parsley

2 tablespoons chopped fresh oregano

1 cup tomato purée

⅓ cup Sauternes or other late-harvest sweet wine

2½ cups tomato juice

1½ cups tomato sauce

Salt and freshly ground black pepper to taste

2 to 3 cups grated whole-milk mozzarella cheese, for garnish

2 cups Croutons (page 24), for garnish

Heat the butter and oil in a 4-quart soup pot over medium-high heat. Add the pepperoni and cook, stirring frequently, for 8 minutes, or until the pepperoni is browned. Add the onions, celery, garlic, celery seeds, and red pepper flakes. Cook, stirring frequently, for 3 minutes, or until the onions are translucent. Add the basil, parsley, and oregano. Cover the pot, reduce the heat to low, and cook, stirring occasionally, for 10 minutes, or until the vegetables soften.

Add the tomato purée, and cook for 2 minutes over medium-high heat, stirring constantly. Add the Sauternes and cook for 1 minute. Add the tomato juice, tomato sauce, and 1½ cups water to the pot. Bring to a boil over high heat. Reduce the heat to low and simmer, uncovered, for 20 minutes. Season to taste with salt and pepper, and serve immediately, garnishing each serving with grated mozzarella and croutons.

NOTE: The soup can be prepared up to 2 days in advance and refrigerated, tightly covered. Reheat over low heat, stirring occasionally.

Cooking vegetables covered is referred to by chefs as "sweating" them. It's a good term to know because you frequently see it in chefs' recipes. The "sweating" can be done at the onset of cooking, which is a way to caramelize onions, or it can occur later in the process to soften vegetables, as is the case in this recipe. What's important to remember is to have the heat very low and to stir the vegetables from time to time.

German Sausage and Sauerkraut Soup

I entered journalism as a reporter at the *Cincinnati Enquirer*, and the city had a rich German heritage from waves of nineteenth-century immigration. A restaurant named Grammer's in a neighborhood dubbed Over-the-Rhine opened in 1872 and was still going strong a century later. I always ordered the sauerkraut soup there, and when I moved from the city I worked on replicating it. This is hearty, and like a more liquid version of *choucroute garnie*.

Serves 6 to 8

1 (1-pound) package sauerkraut

1 tablespoon olive oil

1 pound smoked sausage, such as fresh kielbasa, removed from the casing and diced

1 large onion, diced

1 large carrot, sliced

1 celery rib, sliced

2 garlic cloves, minced

1 cup dry white wine

3 tablespoons gin

7 cups Ham Stock (page 20), Chicken Stock (page 14), or purchased stock

2 russet potatoes, peeled and diced

1 tablespoon fresh thyme leaves

1 teaspoon caraway seeds

1 bay leaf

Salt and freshly ground black pepper to taste

Place the sauerkraut in a colander and run cold water over it for 3 minutes. Wring it out in your hands, and set aside.

Heat the oil in a 4-quart soup pot over medium-high heat. Add the sausage and cook, stirring frequently, for 3 to 5 minutes, or until the sausage is browned. Add the onion, carrot, celery, and garlic. Cook, stirring frequently, for 3 minutes, or until the onion is translucent.

Add the wine and gin, and cook until the liquid is almost totally evaporated. Add the sauerkraut, stock, potatoes, thyme, caraway seeds, and bay leaf. Bring to a boil, then reduce the heat to low and simmer, stirring occasionally, for 30 to 40 minutes, or until the potatoes and sauerkraut are tender.

Remove and discard the bay leaf, season the soup to taste with salt and pepper, and serve immediately.

NOTE: The soup can be prepared up to 2 days in advance and refrigerated, tightly covered. Reheat over low heat, stirring occasionally.

....

It's important to rinse sauerkraut very well when cooking with it rather than putting it on a hot dog. The brine that ferments shreds of cabbage into sauerkraut is very salty and pungent, and it would take over the soup if not handled carefully.

Garlic Soup with Pancetta

ADAPTED FROM PIPERADE, SAN FRANCISCO, CALIFORNIA

Chef Gerald Hirigoyen says this soup is a famous breakfast in his native Basque country for shepherds to warm themselves before going out to tend their flocks. The garlic becomes sweet and nutty when poached this way, and while I'm not sure I'd really eat this for breakfast, I adore it as a casual supper with a salad.

Serves 4 to 6

10 ounces pancetta

¼ cup rendered duck fat or olive oil

1 large onion, diced

20 garlic cloves, thinly sliced

2 quarts Chicken Stock (page 14) or purchased stock

1 baguette, preferably stale

3 large eggs, beaten

Salt and freshly ground black pepper to taste

Cut the pancetta into ¾-inch slices and then cut the slices into ¾-inch cubes.

Heat the duck fat in a 4-quart soup pot over medium-high heat. Add the pancetta and cook, stirring frequently, for 5 to 7 minutes, or until it crisps and renders its fat. Remove from the pot with a slotted spoon and set aside.

Add the onion and garlic to the pot and cook, stirring frequently, for 3 minutes, or until the onion is translucent. Return the pancetta to the pot and add the stock. Bring to a boil over high heat, then reduce the heat to low and simmer, partially covered, for 20 minutes.

While the soup simmers, preheat the oven to 400°F. Slice the baguette into ½-inch-thick slices and arrange them on a baking sheet. Toast the bread for 15 to 18 minutes, or until browned and crisp. Remove the bread from the oven and set aside.

Slowly pour the eggs into the soup in a thin stream, whisking constantly. Season the soup to taste with salt and pepper.

To serve, place 2 baguette slices on the bottom of each soup bowl and ladle the soup over the bread. Serve immediately.

NOTE: The soup can be prepared up to 2 days in advance and refrigerated, tightly covered. Reheat over low heat, stirring occasionally. The toast can also be prepared up to 2 days in advance and kept at room temperature in an airtight container.

Pancetta, like American bacon, is made from pork belly, but the Italian meat is cured with salt and other spices rather than smoked and it's sold in a roll rather than sliced. It adds a richness and great flavor to a variety of dishes. Like bacon, it should be cooked until crispy.

Italian Sausage and Chestnut Soup

I first had this soup at Lidia Bastianich's fabulous Felidia restaurant in New York, and the creamy, earthy chestnuts laced with a bit of heady Marsala are a wonderful base for the bits of sausage. Serve it with a tossed salad and Focaccia (page 219).

Serves 4 to 6

3 tablespoons unsalted butter

1 small onion, chopped

1 celery rib, chopped

1 small carrot, chopped

1 garlic clove, minced

6 cups Chicken Stock (page 14) or purchased stock

2 tablespoons chopped fresh parsley

1 tablespoon chopped fresh rosemary

1 bay leaf

1 (15-ounce) jar cooked chestnuts, chopped

⅓ cup dry Marsala

1 tablespoon olive oil

½ pound sweet Italian sausage

½ cup heavy cream

Salt and freshly ground black pepper to taste

Heat the butter in a 4-quart soup pot over medium-high heat. Add the onion, celery, carrot, and garlic. Cook, stirring frequently, for 3 minutes, or until the onion is translucent.

Add the stock, parsley, rosemary, bay leaf, chestnuts, and Marsala to the pot, and bring to a boil over medium-high heat, stirring occasionally. Cover the pot, reduce the heat to low, and simmer for 20 minutes, or until the vegetables are soft.

While the soup simmers, heat the oil in a skillet over medium-high heat. Crumble the sausage into the skillet and cook, breaking up lumps with a fork, for 3 to 5 minutes, or until browned. Set aside.

Remove and discard the bay leaf from the soup. Allow to cool for 10 minutes. Purée with an immersion blender, or in a food processor fitted with the steel blade. If using a food processor, you may have to work in batches.

Add the sausage and cream to the soup, and bring to a boil over medium heat. Simmer the soup for 10 minutes, uncovered, over low heat. Season to taste with salt and pepper, and serve immediately.

NOTE: The soup can be prepared up to 2 days in advance and refrigerated, tightly covered. Reheat over low heat, stirring occasionally. Add milk or cream if the soup needs thinning after reheating.

Variation

Substitute golden sherry for Marsala.

....

Marsala is a fortified wine, similar to Madeira and sherry, made in Sicily from a variety of grapes grown around the town of Marsala. It was very popular in the English market in the early nineteenth century after Lord Nelson made it his choice as an onboard drink.

9 Breads, Quick Breads, and Rolls

Breads are the immediate go-to food to accompany a bowl of soup, and the emphasis in this chapter is on breads with a crunchy exterior to serve as a foil against the inherent softness of the soup. Just as there are soups from around the world in the previous chapters of this book, the breads are also international in scope.

Many of the soup recipes refer to these breads because they complement each other so well. You'll find long, crisp Parmesan Breadsticks (grissini; page 228) and flavorful Focaccia (page 214) to accompany Italian and other Mediterranean recipes. And there's nothing like a wedge of Skillet Cornbread (page 223) to perch on the edge of a bowl of chowder or gumbo.

Yeast Breads

If you number yourself in the group of cooks who are afraid of working with yeast, now is the time to take the plunge. The whole process could not be easier, and here's a primer on how to work with this live leavening agent.

Yeast is a single-celled fungus, of which hundreds of species have been identified. Those of the genera *Saccharomyces* and *Candida* are the most useful for breads and beer. The single cells are very small: hundreds of millions of them would fit into a teaspoon. While green plants feed via photosynthesis, yeast feeds on carbohydrates and excretes alcohol while producing carbon dioxide. That's why yeast is as good a friend of the brewer as it is of the baker. Given plenty of air and some food, yeast grows fast and produces a lot of carbon dioxide. It is the pressure of this gas that makes the bread rise.

There are two types of yeast on the market. Active dry yeast is a dormant form of yeast and needs to be rehydrated (or "proofed") prior to being used in a recipe. This means that the yeast needs to be dissolved in warm water, as explained below. Instant yeast is different than active dry yeast in that it does not need to be proofed prior to using in a recipe. The granules of instant yeast are smaller than those of active dry yeast and you can add the yeast directly in with all the other dough ingredients without letting it activate in warm water first.

It's best to use the type of yeast specified in a recipe, but if you want to save the ten minutes of proofing time, you can substitute instant yeast for dry active yeast.

All bread depends on the interaction of some sort of flour, liquid, and leavening agent. When the proteins in wheat flour combine with water, they form gluten. Gluten is both plastic and elastic. This quality means that it will hold the carbon dioxide produced by the yeast, and will not allow it to escape or break. It is this plasticity that allows bread to rise before it is baked, at which time the structure of the dough solidifies from the heat of the oven.

Commercially produced yeast first appeared in the United States in the 1860s. Charles and Maximilian Fleischmann, immigrants from Austria-Hungary who settled in Cincinnati, patented and sold standardized cakes of compressed yeast. By the early twentieth century, factory-produced yeast was widely available. Cookbook recipes began specifying that commercial yeast be added directly to bread dough in sufficient quantities to leaven it in less than two hours.

PROOFING IS THE FIRST STEP

Yeast, unlike baking soda and baking powder, is an organic leavening agent, which means that it must be "alive" in order to be effective. Overly high temperatures can kill yeast and, conversely, cold temperatures can inhibit the yeast's action. That is why dry yeast should be refrigerated. It will keep for several months.

To make sure your dry yeast is alive, you should start with a step called "proofing." Combine the yeast with warm liquid (110°F to 115°F) and a small amount of flour or sugar. If the water is any hotter, it might kill the yeast. Use a meat thermometer to take the temperature, or check to make sure it feels warm but not hot on the underside of your wrist.

Let the mixture rest at room temperature until a thick surface foam forms, which indicates that the yeast is alive and can be used. If there is no foam, the yeast is dead and should be discarded. After your proofing is successful, you are ready to make the dough.

THE NEED FOR KNEADING

To have the network of strands of gluten form properly, the proteins in the flour need to be physically coaxed. That is the process known as kneading. The same holds true for pasta dough.

I must admit that it has been many years since I kneaded dough by hand, because my stand mixer has a dough hook attachment. But I did knead a few of these recipes to calculate how much time it takes and also to observe the dough more closely.

When you start kneading dough, it's a shaggy and sticky mass. When the gluten formation is complete and the dough is properly kneaded, it will be shiny to look at, springy to the touch, and no longer sticky. Those are the clues that your dough is ready to rise.

The right temperature is necessary for dough to rise. There are some tricks to creating a warm-enough temperature in a cold kitchen. Set a foil-covered electric heating pad on low, and put the bowl of dough on the foil; put the bowl in the dishwasher and set it for just the drying cycle; put the bowl in your gas oven to benefit from the warmth of the pilot light; put the bowl in any cold oven over a large pan of boiling-hot water.

Chemical Leavening Agents

The breads not given a rise by yeast in this chapter rely on chemical leavening agents—baking soda and baking powder.

Baking soda is also known by its official name, sodium bicarbonate. When heated, this chemical compound forms carbon dioxide gas to make quick breads rise. But here's the problem. That's not all it produces.

When heated, sodium bicarbonate also produces sodium carbonate, which has a nasty and unpleasant alkaline flavor. But if you mix baking soda with an acid like lemon juice or buttermilk, the sodium carbonate is partially neutralized and leaves behind less aftertaste. This acid also helps the carbon dioxide gas release more quickly.

Baking powder is basically just baking soda with an acid already added in, so there doesn't have to be one elsewhere in the recipe. Each teaspoon of baking powder contains ¼ teaspoon baking soda; the remainder is acid and cornstarch. Baking soda is, as a result, four times as powerful as baking powder, so use only ¼ teaspoon baking soda for each teaspoon of baking powder in a recipe.

....

Chemical leavening is nothing new; Amelia Simmons used pearl ash in her book *American Cookery*, published in 1796. Because carbon dioxide is released at a faster rate through the acid-base reaction than through the fermentation process provided by living yeast, breads made with chemical leavening became known as "quick breads" more than a century ago.

TRANSFORMING QUICK BREADS INTO MUFFINS

....

The batter to make quick breads is identical to muffin batter, so they're interchangeable; the only difference is the amount of time and at what temperature they are baked; it's a logical progression. The smaller the item is, like a standard muffin, the hotter the oven.

A standard tray of a dozen muffins should be baked for 18 to 22 minutes at 400°F, oversized muffins bake for 20 to 25 minutes at 375°F, and quick breads bake for 45 minutes to 1 hour at 350°F.

Focaccia

Focaccia (pronounced foe-KAH-cha), that wonderful Italian bread, is one of the world's great nibble foods and it pairs wonderfully with just about all soups. It contains a fair amount of oil, so additional oil or butter isn't necessary to enjoy it, and it's flat, so it's perfect for splitting to encase the filling for a sandwich.

Serves 12 to 16

3 (¼-ounce) packages active dry yeast

2¼ cups warm water (110°F to 115°F), divided

1 tablespoon granulated sugar

7 cups all-purpose flour, divided, plus additional if necessary

½ cup olive oil, divided, plus more for greasing

1 teaspoon salt

Coarse salt and freshly ground black pepper for sprinkling

Combine the yeast, ¾ cup warm water, sugar, and ½ cup flour in the bowl of a stand mixer fitted with the paddle attachment, and mix well. Set aside for about 10 minutes while the yeast proofs.

When the yeast looks frothy, add the remaining water, ⅓ cup of the oil, the remaining flour, and the salt, and beat at low speed until flour is incorporated to form a soft dough.

Place the dough hook on the mixer, and knead the dough at medium speed for 2 minutes. Raise the speed to high, and knead for an additional 3 to 4 minutes, or until the dough forms a soft ball and is springy. (If kneading by hand, it will take about 10 to 12 minutes.)

Lightly grease the inside of a large mixing bowl with olive oil. Add the dough, turning it so it is lightly greased all over. Cover the bowl loosely with a sheet of oiled plastic wrap or a damp tea towel, and place it in a warm, draft-free spot. Allow the dough to rise for 1 to 2 hours, or until it has doubled in bulk.

Place the oven racks in the middle and lowest positions. Place a lipped baking sheet on the lower rack. Preheat the oven to 450°F and generously oil a lipped 17 x 11-inch baking sheet. Bring a kettle of water to a boil, and have a spray bottle of water handy.

Punch the dough down, and gently press it into the oiled baking sheet. Allow the dough to rest for 5 minutes if it is difficult to work with. Cover the baking sheet with oiled plastic wrap, and let the dough rise in a warm place until doubled in bulk, about 30 minutes.

Make indentations in the dough at 1-inch intervals with oiled fingertips. Drizzle the top of the dough with the remaining oil, and sprinkle with coarse salt and pepper.

Pour 1 cup of boiling water into the heated baking pan and place the bread above it on the upper rack. Spray the walls of the oven with the spray bottle, close the oven door and wait 30 seconds, and then spray the oven walls again.

Bake the bread for 25 to 30 minutes, or until deep golden on top and pale golden on bottom. Transfer to a wire cooling rack and serve warm or at room temperature.

NOTE: The bread, covered tightly in plastic wrap, can be kept at room temperature for up to 1 day, or refrigerated for up to 5 days.

Variations

- Onion Focaccia: Heat 3 tablespoons of olive oil in a skillet over medium heat. Add 2 large sweet onions, thinly sliced, and toss to coat the onions with the oil. Cook over low heat, covered, for 10 minutes. Uncover the pan, raise the heat to medium-high, and sprinkle the onions with granulated sugar, salt, and pepper. Cook the onions, stirring frequently, for 12 to 15 minutes, or until medium brown. Spread the onions on top of the unbaked dough.

- Parmesan Olive Focaccia: Sprinkle the top of the unbaked dough with ¾ cup freshly grated Parmesan cheese, and dot it with chopped olives.

- Herb Focaccia: Sprinkle the top of the unbaked dough with ¾ cup chopped fresh herbs such as rosemary, basil, oregano, or some combination.

- Meaty Focaccia: Sprinkle the top of the unbaked dough with ¾ cup chopped pepperoni, salami, or prosciutto and ½ cup shredded whole-milk mozzarella cheese.

- Garlic Focaccia: Soak 6 garlic cloves, peeled and minced, in the olive oil for 2 hours before making the dough. Either strain and discard the garlic, or include it on the unbaked dough if you really like things garlicky.

- Sun-Dried Tomato Focaccia: Sprinkle the top of the unbaked dough with ¾ cup chopped sun-dried tomatoes packed in olive oil.

Bread Bowls

The popularity of bread bowls today validates that "everything old is new again." After all, during the Middle Ages, stews were always served on slices of stale bread. Even if a soup is very thick, the bread bowls should only be filled just before being presented at the table. I have had better luck with bread bowls since I started crisping them in the oven before filling them.

Makes 6 to 8 bread bowls

2 (¼-ounce) packages active dry yeast

2 ½ cups warm water (110°F to 115°F), divided

1 tablespoon granulated sugar

7 cups all-purpose flour, divided, plus additional if necessary

3 tablespoons nonfat dry milk powder

½ cup olive oil, divided

1 teaspoon salt

....

I started using nonfat dry milk powder in breads a few years ago when writing the book *Gluten-Free Breads* (Running Press, 2013). In addition to augmenting the nutritional profile of the breads with a healthy dose of calcium, the powder is high in protein, which helps the breads to rise, and keeps them moist once baked.

Combine the yeast, ¾ cup warm water, sugar, and ½ cup flour in the bowl of a stand mixer fitted with the paddle attachment, and mix well. Set aside for about 10 minutes while the yeast proofs.

When the yeast looks frothy, add the remaining water, dried milk powder, 2 tablespoons of the oil, remaining flour, and salt, and beat at low speed until the flour is incorporated to form a soft dough.

Place the dough hook on the mixer, and knead the dough at medium speed for 2 minutes. Raise the speed to high, and knead for an additional 3 to 4 minutes, or until the dough forms a soft ball and is springy. (If kneading by hand, it will take about 10 to 12 minutes.)

Lightly grease the inside of a large mixing bowl with olive oil. Add the dough, turning it so it is lightly greased all over. Cover the bowl loosely with a sheet of oiled plastic wrap or a damp tea towel, and place it in a warm, draft-free spot. Allow the dough to rise for 1 to 2 hours, or until it has doubled in bulk.

Line a baking sheet with parchment paper or a silicone baking mat. Punch down the dough and divide it into 6 to 8 pieces. Form each piece into a ball with greased hands and arrange them on the prepared baking sheet. Cover the baking sheet with oiled plastic wrap, and let rise in a warm place until doubled in bulk, about 30 minutes.

Place the oven racks in the middle and lowest positions. Place a lipped baking sheet on the lower rack. Preheat the oven to 425°F toward the end of the rising time. Bring a kettle of water to a boil, and have a spray bottle of water handy.

Pour 1 cup of boiling water into the heated baking pan and place the bread on the upper rack. Spray the walls of the oven with the spray bottle, close the oven door and wait 30 seconds, and then spray the oven walls again.

Bake the breads for 25 to 30 minutes, or until brown and sound hollow when tapped on the bottom. Cool the breads for 5 minutes, and then transfer them to a wire rack to cool completely.

Slice ¾ inch off the top of each bread with a serrated bread knife. Use your fingers to pull out the interior of the bread, leaving a ⅓-inch shell. (Save all the bread and tops for breadcrumbs.) Allow the bread to sit for at least 4 hours, or preferably overnight.

Preheat the oven to 350°F. Brush the interiors of the bread bowls with the remaining olive oil and arrange them on a baking sheet. Bake them for 12 to 15 minutes, or until browned and crisp. Remove from the oven, fill with soup, and serve immediately.

NOTE: The breads can be baked, hollowed, and crisped up to 2 days in advance and kept at room temperature, tightly covered. Warm them in a 300°F oven for 5 minutes before filling them with soup.

Limpa

This Swedish version of rye bread, also known as Vörtlimpa, has a combination of aromatic spices and some orange zest too. The bread is wonderful with hearty bean soups and also with vegetable soups.

Serves 8

1 (¼-ounce) package active dry yeast

2 tablespoons firmly packed light brown sugar

¾ cup whole milk, heated to 110°F to 115°F

1½ to 1¾ cups all-purpose flour, divided

½ cup freshly squeezed orange juice

3 tablespoons molasses

2 tablespoons unsalted butter, melted and cooled

2 teaspoons grated orange zest

2 tablespoons caraway seeds, divided

1 teaspoon anise seed

½ teaspoon salt

1 cup rye flour

½ cup quick oats (not instant or old-fashioned)

Olive oil or softened butter, for greasing

1 large egg white, beaten

....

It's always easier to grate the zest off a citrus fruit before the juice is squeezed out of it. That's yet another reason to read a recipe from top to bottom before beginning it. The juice in this recipe is actually specified before the zest in the ingredient list, but it should be grated first.

NOTE: The bread can be baked up to 1 day in advance. Don't cover it until it is completely cool, and then wrap it airtight with plastic wrap.

Combine the yeast, brown sugar, warm milk, and ⅓ cup all-purpose flour in the bowl of a stand mixer fitted with the paddle attachment and mix well. Set aside for about 10 minutes while the yeast proofs.

When the yeast looks frothy, add the orange juice, molasses, butter, orange zest, 2 teaspoons caraway seeds, anise seed, salt, rye flour, oats, and remaining all-purpose flour, and beat at low speed until the flour is incorporated to form a soft dough.

Place the dough hook on the mixer, and knead the dough at medium speed for 2 minutes. Raise the speed to high, and knead for an additional 3 to 4 minutes, or until the dough forms a soft ball and is springy. (If kneading by hand, it will take about 10 to 12 minutes.)

Lightly grease the inside of a large mixing bowl with olive oil or softened butter. Add the dough, turning it so it is lightly greased all over. Cover the bowl loosely with a sheet of oiled plastic wrap or a damp tea towel, and place it in a warm, draft-free spot. Allow the dough to rise for 1 to 2 hours, or until it has doubled in bulk.

Grease a baking sheet. Punch down the dough, turn it out onto a floured surface, and knead it a few times. Form the dough into a 7-inch mound on the baking sheet. Cover it with a sheet of greased plastic wrap or a damp tea towel and allow it to rise for 45 minutes to 1 hour, or until almost doubled in bulk.

Preheat the oven to 375°F toward the end of the rising time. Brush the top of the bread with the egg white and sprinkle with the remaining caraway seeds.

Bake the bread for 30 to 40 minutes, or until it is browned and sounds hollow when the bottom is tapped. Cool for 5 minutes before serving.

Pretzel Rolls

These very easy rolls have a tantalizing texture that is like a cross between a light roll and a dense bagel because they're boiled briefly before they're baked. They really do taste like soft pretzels, and they pair beautifully with any thick and hearty soup.

Serves 8

1 (¼-ounce) envelope active dry yeast

1⅛ cups warm water (110°F to 115°F), divided

3 tablespoons granulated sugar, divided

2¾ cups bread flour, divided

¾ teaspoon salt

Cornmeal for dusting

Olive oil, for greasing

¼ cup baking soda

1 large egg white, beaten

Kosher salt or coarse sea salt for sprinkling

Combine the yeast, ¾ cup warm water, 1 tablespoon sugar, and ½ cup flour in the bowl of a stand mixer fitted with the paddle attachment, and mix well. Set aside for about 10 minutes while the yeast proofs.

When the yeast looks frothy, add the remaining water, remaining flour, and salt, and beat at low speed until the flour is incorporated to form a soft dough.

Place the dough hook on the mixer, and knead the dough at medium speed for 2 minutes. Raise the speed to high, and knead for an additional 3 to 4 minutes, or until the dough forms a soft ball and is springy. (If kneading by hand, it will take about 10 to 12 minutes.)

Lightly grease the inside of a large mixing bowl with olive oil. Add the dough, turning it so it is lightly greased all over. Cover the bowl loosely with a sheet of oiled plastic wrap or a damp tea towel, and place it in a warm, draft-free spot. Allow the dough to rise for 1 to 2 hours, or until it has doubled in bulk.

Grease a baking sheet. Punch the dough down and divide it into 8 pieces. Form each piece into a ball, and place the balls on the prepared baking sheet, flattening the tops of the balls lightly. Cover the baking sheet with oiled plastic wrap, and let rise in a warm place until doubled in bulk, about 30 minutes.

Preheat the oven to 425°F. Grease another baking sheet and sprinkle it with cornmeal. Bring 8 cups of water to a boil in large saucepan over high heat. Add the baking soda and the remaining 2 tablespoons sugar. Add as many rolls as will fit comfortably in the pan and boil for 1 minute per side, turning gently with a slotted spatula. Allow the water to drain off, and arrange the rolls on the cornmeal-dusted baking sheet. Repeat until all are blanched.

Brush the tops of the rolls with the egg white, and then sprinkle with coarse salt. Use a razor blade and cut diagonal lines on the tops of the rolls.

Place the rolls in the center of the oven and reduce the oven temperature to 375°F. Bake for 20 to 25 minutes, or until brown and crusty. Cool for 5 minutes before serving.

NOTE: The rolls can be baked up to 1 day in advance and kept at room temperature, tightly covered with plastic wrap once cooled. You can reheat them in a 350°F oven for 5 minutes before serving.

....

When making slashes in yeast dough, it's really important to use a razor blade or a very sharp serrated knife. If the cutting object isn't incredibly sharp the dough will deflate.

Crispy Herbed Breadsticks

What I'm after when serving bread with soup is a lot of crunch to contrast the soft texture of the foods swimming in the broth. That's why I adore these flavorful strips with herbs and cheese in the dough and a mixture of healthful and attractive seeds as a coating.

Serves 8

BREAD

1 (¼-ounce) package active dry yeast

1½ cups warm water (110°F to 115°F), divided

1 tablespoon granulated sugar

4¼ cups bread flour, divided

¼ cup freshly grated Parmesan

2 tablespoons *herbes de Provence*

1 teaspoon salt

3 garlic cloves, minced (optional)

Olive oil, for greasing

TOPPING

1 large egg

2 tablespoons poppy seeds

2 tablespoons toasted sesame seeds

2 tablespoons flaxseed

1 tablespoon caraway seeds

Combine the yeast, ¾ cup warm water, sugar, and ½ cup flour in the bowl of a stand mixer fitted with the paddle attachment, and mix well. Set aside for about 10 minutes while the yeast proofs.

When the yeast looks frothy, add the remaining water, remaining flour, Parmesan, *herbes de Provence*, salt, and garlic (if using). Beat at low speed until the flour is incorporated to form a soft dough.

Place the dough hook on the mixer, and knead the dough at medium speed for 2 minutes. Raise the speed to high, and knead for an additional 3 to 4 minutes, or until the dough forms a soft ball and is springy. (If kneading by hand, it will take about 10 to 12 minutes.)

Lightly grease the inside of a large mixing bowl with olive oil. Add the dough, turning it so it is lightly greased all over. Cover the bowl loosely with a sheet of oiled plastic wrap or a damp tea towel, and place it in a warm, draft-free spot. Allow the dough to rise for 1 to 2 hours, or until it has doubled in bulk.

Preheat the oven to 400°F and generously oil a lipped 17 x 11-inch baking sheet. Punch the dough down, and gently press it into the prepared baking sheet. Allow the dough to rest for 5 to 10 minutes if it is difficult to work with. Cut the dough into 1-inch strips horizontally and then cut the strips down the middle vertically using a pizza wheel or a sharp serrated knife. Cover the baking sheet with oiled plastic wrap, and let rise in a warm place until doubled in bulk, about 30 minutes.

For the topping, beat the egg with 1 tablespoon cold water. Combine the poppy seeds, sesame seeds, flaxseed, and caraway seeds in a small bowl. Brush the top of the dough with the egg wash and sprinkle the seeds evenly over the surface.

Bake the breadsticks for 20 to 30 minutes, or until deep golden on top and pale golden on bottom. Remove the pan from the oven and allow the bread to cool for 5 minutes. Cut along the score lines with a sharp serrated knife and serve immediately.

NOTE: The breadsticks, covered tightly in plastic wrap, can be kept at room temperature for up to 1 day, or refrigerated for up to 5 days.

Variation

Omit the *herbes de Provence* and garlic from the dough, and substitute an additional ½ cup of Parmesan for the seeds in the topping.

....

Sesame seeds add more than delicious flavor to foods. These tiny seeds grown in almost all tropical regions are a very good source of copper and magnesium. Copper is known for its use in reducing some of the pain and swelling of rheumatoid arthritis. Magnesium is important in the functioning of both our respiratory and vascular systems.

Skillet Cornbread

Iron skillets make the best cornbread. It's that simple. By preheating the pan the sugar caramelizes and gives you a slightly crisp crust that forms a contrast to the buttery interior of the bread. This is wonderful served with any cream-based soup, and certainly with Southern soups like gumbo.

Serves 8

1½ cups finely ground yellow cornmeal

⅔ cup all-purpose flour

¼ cup granulated sugar

2 teaspoons baking powder

½ teaspoon baking soda

¼ teaspoon salt

¾ cup buttermilk, shaken

4 tablespoons (½ stick) unsalted butter, melted and cooled

2 large eggs, at room temperature

1 cup canned cream-style corn

2 tablespoons vegetable oil

Preheat the oven to 400°F and place a 10-inch ovenproof skillet in the oven as it preheats.

Combine the cornmeal, flour, sugar, baking powder, baking soda, and salt in a mixing bowl and whisk well. In another mixing bowl, combine the buttermilk, butter, eggs, and corn. Whisk well. Add the dry ingredients to the wet ingredients and stir well to combine.

Remove the skillet from the oven, add the oil, and tilt the pan around to coat evenly. Scrape the batter into the skillet and spread evenly. Bake the cornbread for 25 to 30 minutes, or until a toothpick inserted into the center comes out clean. Allow to cool for 5 minutes before slicing. Serve hot or at room temperature.

NOTE: The cornbread can be baked up to 1 day in advance and kept at room temperature, loosely covered with plastic wrap.

Variations

• Substitute honey or maple syrup for the sugar.

• Add 2 tablespoons chopped fresh sage to the batter.

• Add ¼ cup chopped pimiento to the batter and substitute ½ cup grated cheddar for ¼ cup of the cream-style corn.

Corn is a good source of vitamin C and also contains lycopene, the chemical that gives tomatoes their red color. According to the American Dietetic Association, your body absorbs more healthful lycopene from canned corn—both whole-kernel and creamed—than it does from fresh corn.

Garlic and Cheese Bread

There are tons of occasions when time doesn't permit making your own bread from scratch, but slathering an artisan baguette from a good bakery with a mixture of butter, garlic, and herbs is a close second. This aromatic version is a hit every time I serve it.

Serves 6 to 8

½ cup (1 stick) unsalted butter, at room temperature

2 tablespoons extra-virgin olive oil

4 to 6 garlic cloves, peeled

3 tablespoons fresh parsley

2 scallions, white parts and 4 inches of green tops, sliced

⅔ cup freshly grated Parmesan cheese, divided

Salt and freshly ground black pepper to taste

1 (14-inch) French baguette

Preheat the oven to 375°F and line a baking sheet with heavy-duty aluminum foil.

Combine the butter, oil, garlic, parsley, scallions, ⅓ cup of the Parmesan, salt, and pepper in a food processor fitted with the steel blade. Chop very finely using on-and-off pulsing.

Cut the bread in half lengthwise and spread the butter mixture evenly on both halves. Sprinkle the remaining Parmesan on top.

Bake the bread for 10 to 12 minutes, or until browned and hot. Allow to cool for 2 minutes, then slice and serve immediately.

NOTE: The bread can be prepared for baking up to 2 days in advance and refrigerated, tightly covered with plastic wrap.

Variation

Omit the garlic, substitute Gruyère or cheddar for the Parmesan, and use 4 tablespoons of some combination of parsley, thyme, oregano, and tarragon in the butter mixture.

....

I do not suggest making garlic bread on the grill, but it can be made in the oven broiler. Set the rack so that the baking sheet will be 8 inches from the heat source. Brush the bottom halves of the cut surfaces with olive oil and broil for 1 to 1½ minutes, or until lightly browned and crisp. Turn the bread over, slather the butter on the cut sides, sprinkle with the cheese, and broil for 2 to 3 minutes, or until bubbly and brown.

Irish Soda Bread

Soda bread is easy to make, and the contrast of the sweet raisins and zesty caraway seeds dotting the dough enlivens its flavor. This is a wonderful chewy bread to serve with bean soups, regardless of the cuisine from which they come.

Serves 8

1½ cups all-purpose flour

1 cup whole-wheat flour

¼ cup granulated sugar

1½ teaspoons baking powder

½ teaspoon baking soda

½ teaspoon salt

4 tablespoons (½ stick) unsalted butter, melted and cooled

1 cup buttermilk, shaken

1 large egg

¾ cup raisins, preferably a blend of colors

2 tablespoons caraway seeds, divided

1 tablespoon cornstarch

· ·

The purpose of the cornstarch slurry is to act as "glue" for the remaining caraway seeds. It will also give the top of the bread a lovely patina. An alternative to cornstarch is an egg wash, but I prefer the cornstarch for rustic breads that are baked for a long time.

Preheat the oven to 375°F. Generously grease a baking sheet.

Combine the all-purpose flour, whole-wheat flour, sugar, baking powder, baking soda, and salt in a large mixing bowl, and whisk well. Combine the butter, buttermilk, and egg in another mixing bowl, and whisk well.

Add the wet ingredients to the dry ingredients, and stir to combine; the dough will be sticky. Stir in the raisins and 1 tablespoon of the caraway seeds.

Scrape the dough onto a heavily floured surface and knead it a few times to form it into a round loaf. Transfer the dough to the prepared baking sheet.

Combine the cornstarch and 2 tablespoons cold water in a small bowl, and stir well. Brush the mixture on top of the dough, and sprinkle with the remaining caraway seeds. Cut a large X about ¾ inch deep in the center of the dough.

Bake the bread in the center of the oven for 45 to 55 minutes, or until the crust is brown and a toothpick inserted in the center comes out clean. Cool on the baking sheet for 10 minutes, then transfer it to a cooling rack. The bread can be served warm or at room temperature.

NOTE: The bread, covered tightly in plastic wrap, can be kept at room temperature for up to 1 day, or refrigerated for up to 5 days.

Variations

- Substitute dried currants for the raisins.
- Omit the raisins and caraway seeds and add 6 chopped scallions, white parts and 4 inches of green tops, to the dough.

Cheddar Beer Bread

Beer bread is the best of all worlds; it's a quick bread but it still delivers a yeasty flavor and aroma. Beer and bread share a common fermenting process: Yeast is used to turn sugar into alcohol. While you could make beer bread without baking soda or baking powder, the resulting bread is really dense, which is why I add additional leavening. This bread is a natural with hearty vegetable or bean soups.

Serves 8

Vegetable oil spray

1 large egg

1 (12-ounce) can or bottle of ale or other hearty dark beer

3 tablespoons unsalted butter, melted and cooled

1 cup grated sharp cheddar cheese, divided

1 teaspoon baking powder

½ teaspoon salt

½ teaspoon baking soda

3½ cups all-purpose flour

Preheat the oven to 375°F and liberally grease a 9 x 5-inch loaf pan with vegetable oil spray.

Combine the egg, beer, and melted butter in a mixing bowl, and whisk well. Add ¾ cup of the cheese, baking powder, salt, and baking soda, and whisk well again. Add the flour, and mix gently until just combined.

Scrape the batter into the prepared pan, and level the top with a rubber spatula dipped in cold water. Sprinkle with the remaining cheese.

Bake the bread in the center of the oven for 45 to 55 minutes, or until it registers 210°F on an instant-read thermometer inserted into the center. Remove the bread from the oven and place the pan on a wire cooling rack for 5 minutes. Turn the bread out onto the rack, and allow it to cool to room temperature before slicing.

NOTE: The bread can be prepared up to 2 days in advance. Wrap it tightly with plastic wrap and store at room temperature.

Variations

- Substitute olive oil for the melted butter and substitute ½ cup chopped sun-dried tomato and ¼ cup chopped black olives for the cheese.

- Substitute jalapeño Jack for the cheddar cheese and add 1 tablespoon ground cumin to the batter.

- Add 1 tablespoon *herbes de Provence* to the batter.

Unlike making yeast bread, the very character of beer bread changes with which beer is selected. Lager gives you an aromatic loaf in which other ingredients emerge with stronger flavors, while an ale or stout really dominates the taste.

Buttermilk Biscuits

The secret to tender and flaky biscuits, the kind they always serve south of the Mason-Dixon Line, is using flour made from soft winter wheat that is low in protein so it doesn't form too much tough gluten. White Lily flour is the standard, although it's difficult to find outside its home region. That's why I developed this recipe using cake flour. It replicates that heavenly texture nicely. There are a lot of Southern recipes in this book, and biscuits are the perfect bread to make with them.

Makes 12 to 14 biscuits

1¼ cups all-purpose flour, plus more for the counter

¾ cup cake flour

2½ teaspoons baking powder

½ teaspoon salt

½ teaspoon baking soda

¾ cup (1½ sticks) unsalted butter, chilled and cut into ½-inch pieces, divided

¾ cup buttermilk, shaken

....

Biscuits—moist, tender, and rich—can be baked as an alternative to a yeast-leavened bread, and they are made far more quickly than even baking powder–leavened quick breads. And there is an entire family of baked goods created with the same simple technique—English tea scones are biscuits with eggs, shortcakes are biscuits with a higher percentage of fat, cobblers are biscuits baked on top of fresh fruit, and dumplings are biscuits steamed on top of a stew.

Preheat the oven to 450°F, place a rack in the lower third, and grease a baking sheet.

Combine the all-purpose flour, cake flour, baking powder, salt, and baking soda in a food processor fitted with the steel blade. Pulse a few times to blend. Reserve 2 tablespoons of the butter. Add the remaining butter to the food processor and cut it in using on-and-off pulsing until the mixture resembles coarse crumbs. Alternately, cut in the butter in a mixing bowl using a pastry blender or your fingertips.

Scrape the mixture into a mixing bowl, and make a well in the center. Add the buttermilk, and stir together quickly until a sticky dough forms.

Turn the dough out onto a well-floured surface, such as a counter or a pastry board, and knead it 10 times to create a bit more gluten. Pat the dough into a circle 1 inch thick. Cut out circles with a 2-inch cutter, and arrange them close together on the prepared baking sheet. Gather up the scraps of dough and form them into additional biscuits. Melt the reserved butter and brush it over the tops of the biscuits.

Bake the biscuits for 15 to 18 minutes, or until golden brown. Serve immediately.

NOTE: The biscuits can be formed and then frozen on a baking sheet. Allow them to sit at room temperature for 20 minutes before baking.

Variations

- Add ½ cup grated sharp cheddar and 1 (4-ounce) can chopped mild green chiles, drained well, to the dough.

- Add 1 teaspoon coarsely ground black pepper to the dough.

- Add ¼ cup finely chopped scallions to the dough.

Parmesan Breadsticks

To me, crispy breadsticks, called *grissini* in Italian, are the ultimate carbohydrate to serve with soup; they're all crunch. This recipe is easy and fast to make because it calls for chemical leavening agents rather than yeast. What's also nice is that the breadsticks can double as a centerpiece if you place them in a drinking glass in the middle of the table.

Makes 20 breadsticks

⅓ cup all-purpose flour, plus more for dusting

¼ cup rye flour

½ teaspoon baking powder

¼ teaspoon baking soda

½ teaspoon granulated sugar

2 teaspoons kosher salt, divided

¼ cup buttermilk, shaken

1 tablespoon unsalted butter, melted and cooled

1 large egg

½ cup freshly grated Parmesan cheese

1 tablespoon caraway seeds

1 tablespoon fennel seeds, crushed

....

Once you've made these a few times and see how easy they are, you'll probably add them to your repertoire. You can spread half of a stick with a cheese like herbed Boursin and then wrap it in prosciutto or salami as a hors d'oeuvre.

Preheat the oven to 350°F, positioning the racks in the upper and lower thirds. Line two baking sheets with parchment paper or silicone baking mats.

Combine the all-purpose flour, rye flour, baking powder, baking soda, sugar, and ½ teaspoon kosher salt in a mixing bowl and whisk well. Combine the buttermilk and butter in a small cup and beat well.

Add the buttermilk mixture to the dry ingredients and stir to combine. Turn the dough onto a floured surface and knead for 1 minute. Form the dough into a log, and cut it into 20 pieces. Roll each piece with your hands into an 8-inch rope, and arrange the ropes on the prepared baking sheets.

Beat the egg with 1 teaspoon water, and brush the egg wash onto the ropes, rolling them around to coat them completely. Sprinkle the ropes with the remaining salt, Parmesan, caraway seeds, and fennel seeds.

Bake the ropes in the upper and lower thirds of the oven for 20 to 22 minutes, or until brown and crisp. Switch the position of the sheets after 10 minutes. Transfer the *grissini* to wire racks to cool completely.

NOTE: The *grissini* can be prepared up to 3 days in advance and kept at room temperature in an airtight container.

Variations

• Substitute ¼ cup of sesame seeds for the Parmesan, caraway seeds, and fennel seeds.

• Add 1 tablespoon *herbes de Provence* to the dough and omit the caraway seeds and fennel seeds.

Popovers

Popovers are testimony to the power of eggs alone; they rise high with no yeast, baking powder, or other leavening agent. After experimenting for many years, I've concluded that baking them in Pyrex cups rather than muffin tins is best because the glass conducts heat so well. Everyone loves popovers, and they go with all soups, too.

Makes 8 popovers

3 large eggs, at room temperature

1 cup whole milk, at room temperature

2 tablespoons unsalted butter, melted and cooled

½ teaspoon salt

1 cup all-purpose flour

....

The key to perfect popovers is self-restraint. If the door is opened and a draft enters the oven, the chemistry of the popovers is ruined and you'll end up with thick crêpes because the batters are almost identical. Here's how the popover works: The high proportion of liquid in the batter creates steam that causes the popovers to puff up. The conversion of the liquid in the batter to steam is dramatic because 1 part liquid converts to 1600 parts steam. The proteins in the eggs cause the popover batter to stretch, hold the steam, and eventually solidify to form crusty walls. If you open the oven door, none of this happens.

Preheat the oven to 400°F and grease 8 (5-ounce) Pyrex cups heavily with softened butter.

Combine the eggs, milk, melted butter, and salt in a blender or food processor fitted with the steel blade. Blend until thoroughly mixed. Add the flour, and mix again, scraping down the sides of the bowl if flour is stuck to them.

Fill each greased cup halfway with the batter, and arrange the cups on a baking sheet. Bake the popovers in the center of the oven *without opening the oven door* for 35 to 40 minutes, or until brown and puffed.

Insert a paring knife into the side of each popover to allow steam to escape. Release the popovers from the cups with the tip of a knife, and serve immediately.

NOTE: The batter can be prepared up to 4 hours in advance and kept at room temperature. Mix it well again before filling the cups.

Variations

- Dust the greased cups with freshly grated Parmesan cheese and add 2 teaspoons *herbes de Provence* or Italian seasoning and 1 garlic clove pressed through a garlic press to the batter.

- Add 1 teaspoon grated lemon or orange zest to the batter.

Gougères

While these classic cheese puffs from Burgundy are served as a hors d'oeuvre, I really like them as an accompaniment to soups, too. Their crispy texture serves as a wonderful foil to all soups and I'm especially fond of serving them with puréed cream soups.

Makes about 4 dozen gougères

1 cup Chicken Stock (page 14) or purchased stock

6 tablespoons (¾ stick) unsalted butter, cut into thin slices

½ teaspoon salt

Pinch of freshly grated nutmeg

Pinch of freshly grated white pepper

1 cup all-purpose flour

4 large eggs

1 cup grated Gruyère

....

Using stock rather than water in the dough creates a richer flavor. This is a trick taught to me by Bruce Tillinghast, a wonderful chef in Providence, who studied with the legendary Madeleine Kamman.

Preheat the oven to 400° F, and line 2 baking sheets with parchment paper or silicone baking mats.

Combine the stock, butter, salt, nutmeg, and pepper in a small saucepan, and bring to a boil over medium-high heat, stirring occasionally. Remove the pan from the heat, and add the flour all at once. Using a wooden paddle or wide wooden spoon, beat flour into the liquid until it is smooth. Then place the saucepan over high heat and beat the mixture constantly for 1 to 2 minutes, until it forms a mass that leaves the sides of the pan and begins to film the bottom of the pot.

Transfer the mixture to a food processor fitted with the steel blade. Add the eggs, 1 at a time, beating well between each addition and scraping the sides of the work bowl between each addition. Then add the cheese, and mix well again.

Using a spoon dipped in cold water, form the dough into mounds 1 inch in diameter and ½ inch high onto the baking sheets, allowing 2 inches between puffs.

Bake the puffs for 20 to 22 minutes, or until golden brown and crusty to the touch. Remove the pans from the oven, and using the tip of a paring knife, cut a slit in the side of each puff to allow the steam to escape. Turn off the oven, and place the baked puffs back into the oven with the oven door ajar for 10 minutes to finish crisping. Remove from the oven, and serve immediately.

NOTE: The puffs can be made up to 2 days in advance and refrigerated, tightly covered; they can also be frozen for up to 2 months. Reheat chilled puffs in a 350°F oven for 5 to 7 minutes and frozen puffs for 10 to 12 minutes.

Variation

Substitute cheddar or jalapeño Jack for the Gruyère.

Socca

Socca, made with garbanzo bean flour, is a street food unique to Nice and other parts of France's sun-drenched Côte d'Azur. This delicious flatbread shows the influence of North Africa on the northern coast of the Mediterranean, and it's scented with garlic and rosemary. Serve it with any French, Italian, or Spanish soup.

Serves 6

1 cup garbanzo bean flour

½ teaspoon salt

¾ teaspoon freshly ground black pepper

2 tablespoons chopped fresh rosemary, divided

5 tablespoons olive oil, divided

2 shallots, finely chopped

2 garlic cloves, minced

Combine the garbanzo bean flour, salt, and pepper in a mixing bowl. Slowly whisk in 1 cup of lukewarm water until smooth. Whisk in 1 tablespoon of the rosemary, 2 tablespoons of the olive oil, the shallots, and the garlic. Allow the batter to sit for at least 2 hours.

Place one oven rack in the broiler position and the other in the center of the oven. Preheat the oven to 450°F with a 12-inch skillet in it, heating the skillet for 10 minutes. Add 2 tablespoons of oil to the skillet and tilt the pan around to coat evenly. Add the batter and bake for 12 to 15 minutes, or until the edges of the pancake are set.

Remove the skillet from the oven and preheat the oven broiler. Broil the bread 6 inches from the broiler element for 2 to 3 minutes, or until firm brown spots appear. Brush the bread with the remaining oil, sprinkle with the remaining rosemary, and serve hot.

NOTE: The batter can sit at room temperature for up to 12 hours.

Garbanzo bean is one of the legumes ground into flour that is used frequently in gluten-free baking, so you will find it with those ingredients at supermarkets or it can be ordered online. Most gluten-free protein flours have far more nutritional value than all-purpose wheat flour, too.

Acknowledgments

While testing recipes and writing them are solitary ventures, transforming those recipes into an exciting book to hold in your hands is always a group effort. My thanks go:

To Kristen Green Wiewora, my visionary editor at Running Press who shared my enthusiasm for the concept of a soup book, and to Zachary Leibman of Running Press with whom I worked on the book's production.

To all of the talented chefs around the country who cook and serve their soups of the day in diverse settings, and were willing to share their recipes.

To the many members of my vintage grapevine of food professionals who tipped me off to some of these chefs whose dishes I didn't know, with a special thanks to John Mariani, my dear friend and the best restaurant resource in the country.

To Joshua McDonnell, the talented designer at Running Press who made these photos so dramatic and enticing, and whose design makes this book a delight to hold.

To Felicia Perretti, a truly talented food photographer.

To Brian Croney, the food stylist who made all these soups look truly good enough to eat, and to Lisa Russell, for finding such inventive and enticing props to show the soups.

To Ed Claflin, my agent, for his constant support, encouragement, and humor.

To my dear family for their love and support, especially to Nancy and Walter Dubler; Ariela Dubler; Jesse Furman; Ilan, Mira, and Lev Dubler-Furman; Joshua Dubler; Lisa Cerami; Zahir and Charlie Cerami; David Krimm, and Peter Bradley.

To my many friends who shared bowls of soup with me and critiqued my work, including Constance Brown, Kenn Speiser, Fox Wetle, Richard Besdine, Vicki Veh, Joe Chazan, Kim Montour, Nick Brown, Karen Davidson, Bruce Tillinghast, Beth Kinder, Ralph Kinder, Sylvia Brown, Christine Chronis, Kathleen Hittner, and Barry Hittner.

And to Patches and Rufous, my wonderful feline companions, who kept me company from their perches in the office and endorsed all the cream soups when permitted.

Index

C